CHINA TRADE AGREEMENTS

Second Edition, Revised

Thomas C.W. Chiu

Taylor & Francis

Philadelphia • New York • London

USA	Publishing Office:	Taylor & Francis • New York 3 East 44th St., New York, NY 10017
	Sales Office:	Taylor & Francis • Philadelphia 242 Cherry St., Philadelphia, PA 19106-1906
UK		Taylor & Francis Ltd. 4 John St., London WC1N 2ET

China Trade Agreements Second edition, revised

Copyright © 1988 Taylor & Francis Inc.

First Edition published 1985. Second Edition 1988
Typeset by Four Way Phototypesetting Co., Hong Kong
Printed in the United States of America

Library of Congress Cataloging in Publication Data

Chiu, C. W. (Chor-wing)
  China trade agreements.

  Rev. ed. of: China trade agreement / C. W. Chiu.
c1985
  1. Commercial law—China—Forms. 2. Investments,
Foreign—Law and legislation—China—Forms. 3. Foreign
trade regulation—China—Forms. I. Chiu, C. W.
(Chor-wing). China trade agreement. II. Title.
LAW   346.51′07′0269   87-30170
ISBN 0-8002-8000-8   345.10670269

To S.K.

CONTENTS

PART II: STANDARD CONTRACTS PREPARED BY THE PRC GOVERNMENT

PART III: CONTRACTS AND RELATED DOCUMENTS EXECUTED IN 1987

APPENDICES

PREFACE

This book is divided into three parts which are arranged in accordance with the stages of development, from a trade talk to the final stage of an agreement or a contract. Thus the following arrangement:

Part I   Memorandum of Discussion
Part II   Letter of Intent
Part III Agreement/Content

China trade is mainly a kind of trade involving China traders and respective Chinese authorities, as Chinese businessmen are government officials; they are more apt to put everything on paper. For this reason, they will make a lot of written metaphors, like the Memorandum of Discussion and Letter of Intent which will be signed long before the signing a formal agreement.

Although these Memoranda or Letters are of no legal binding effect, they are of utmost importance to meet the requirements of your Chinese trading counterparts.

In recent years, licensing and technology transfer have become popular investment items in China trade. Therefore, the majority of contents has been emphasised on this aspect.

The official name of the country is The People's Republic of China (PRC). It is referred to throughout this book either as the PRC or as China.

The agreement precedents presented in this book cannot be and are not intended to be exhaustive and, while every effort has been made to ensure the accuracy of the agreement precedents in this book, the author and published accept no responsibility for any errors or omissions.

Summer 1987

T.C.W.C.

ACKNOWLEDGEMENTS

Preparation of a broad treatment of agreement precedants of P.R.C. like this book requires the moral support and technical assistance from experts and friends in the China Trade circle.

Special thanks are given to Professor Xiujin Luo of China Association for International Exchange of Personnel, Professor Yuwen Yu of Materia Medicia, China, and Professor Ling Li of Academy of Social Sciences, China for their encouragement.

I personally wish to thank Mr. Anthony Selvey, Managing Director of the Taylor & Francis Group, Ms. Kate McKay, President of Taylor & Francis Inc., Mr. Jung Ra, Book Publishing Manager of Taylor & Francis Inc., and the publisher for publication of this book.

I wish to thank Mr. Colin Walsh and Mr. Tony Littlechild of Book Productions Consultants, Cambridge England for introducing my books to the publisher. I wish to thank my friend Burkhard Finke, a practising lawyer in the Federal Republic of Germany, for his advice on the attitudes of China traders in Europe.

I am grateful to Mr. and Mrs. Frankie Ho of Four Way Photo Typesetting Company who have rendered superb typesetting and artwork services for this book.

Finally, I would like to thank Miss Joyce Chan who typed the manuscript.

Summer 1987

T.C.W.C.

INTRODUCTION

China, under the leadership of Deng, is approaching an era of multi-national business transactions. China trader is no longer a terminology that appears to be alien in the business world. Since 1979, many China trade agreements have been signed to mark the milestone of China's Open Door Policy.

Unlike those of the outside world or her trading counterparts, China's legal system, as lots of China traders have complained, is incomplete and cannot adapt to the international trading system. The worst thing is the 1981 promulgation of Provisional Regulations of Lawyers that hampered foreign lawyers (including lawyers of Chinese origin but not being a Chinese national) from practising in China and giving advice to their clients engaged in China trade. However, this does not necessarily mean that nothing can be done about this. An experienced businessman will try various methods to get around this hurdle and prevents oneself from trading with China without legal protection. This feeling or trend is more or less shared by those international lawyers, in fact, I would rather call them flying lawyers. Legal advice and support are indoubtedly valuable but not every China trader will need a lawyer from a stage as early as a simple trade talk or to enter into Letter of Intent with trading counterparts. For this reason, this book is compiled to suit this need.

Lawyers and anyone who render professional services to clients engaging in China trade will also find this book a must for their reference.

The agreements or their preliminary forms (e.g. Memorandum of Discussion, Letter of Intent) in this book were compiled and rewritten with reference to those agreements signed since 1979. Although these agreements do not cover every area of China trade, readers and/or China traders may modify some of the wordings in an individual agreement which they are going to sign and is of similar nature to the sample agreements lister in this book.

In order to provide background knowledge about Commercial Contract practice in China, I have listed have under full tent of ''Foreign Economic Contract Law of the PRC'' which was adopted at the Tenth Session of the Standing Committee of the National People's Congress on March 21, 1985.

The Law
=====

Chapter I :   General Provisions

Article 1:   The Law is enacted with a view to protecting the lawful rights and interests of the concerned parties to foreign economic contracts and promoting the development of China's foreign economic relations.

Article 2:   This Law applies to economic or trade contracts (hereinafter referred to as Contracts), but exclusive of international transport contracts, concluded between enterprises or other economic organizations of the People's Republic of China and foreign enterprises and other economic organizations or individuals.

Article 3:   Contracts should be made in conformity with the principles of equality and mutual benefit, and of achieving unanimity through consultations.

Article 4:   Contracts must be made in accordance with the law of the People's Republic of China and should not be prejudicial to the public interests of society of the People's Republic of China.

Article 5:   The parties to a foreign trade contract may choose the law applicable to the settlement of disputes arising over the contract. In the absence of such a choice by the parties concerned, the law of the country which has the closest connection with the contract applies.

The equity of contractual joint venture contracts and the contracts of cooperative exploration and development of natural resources which are performed within the territory of the People's Republic of China must be governed by the law of the People's Republic of China.

In case no relevant provision is stipulated in the law of the People's Republic of China, international practice may apply.

Article 6:   When a provision in a certain international treaty, which the People's Republic of China has concluded or participated in, concerning contracts, is different from those stipulated in the law of the People's Republic of China, the provision of the international treaty applies, with the exception of clauses that the People's Republic of China has publicly stated its reservation.

Chapter II :   Formation of Contract

Article 7:   A contract is established when the terms of the contract are aggreed upon in writing and signed by the parties to it. However, where an agreement is reached through correspondence by mail, cable or telex and one party requests that a confirmation letter be signed, the contract is established when the confirmation letter is signed.

Contracts subject to approval by the state as stipulated by the law or administrative regulations of the People's Republic of China shall be established only when the approval is granted.

Article 8:   All appendices stipulated in a contract are an integral part of that contract.

Article 9:   Contracts that violate the law or the public interests of the People's Republic of China are invalid.

In case where provisions of a contract are found to be inconsistent with the law or the public interests of the People's Republic of China, the validity of the contract is not derogated after the said provisions are nullified or revised through consultations by the parties to the contract.

Article 10: Contracts concluded by means of fraud or under duress are invalid.

Article 11: The payty who is responsible for the invalidity of the contract is obligated to pay the other party concerned a sum equal to the loss arising from the invalidation of the contract.

Article 12: In general, the following terms should be included in a contract:

(1) name and address, nationality, place of business or domicile of the parties;

(2) date and place where the contract is signed;

(3) type of contract, and the kind and scope of the subject matter of the contract;

(4) technical conditions, quality, standard, specifications and quality of the subject matter of the contract;

(5) time limit, place and method of performance;

(6) terms on price, amount and way of payment and various incidental expenses;

(7) whether the contract can be assigned of the terms and conditions for assignment;

(8) damages and other liabilities for breach of contract;

(9) ways for settlement of disputes when disputes arise over contract;

(10) language to be used in the contract and its effectiveness.

Article 13: The limits of risks borne by each party for the subject matter to be performed should be specified in the contract depending on the situation, and the range of insurance for the subject matter should also be specified when necessary.

Article 14: With regard to a contract that needs to be performed continuously over a rather long period, the parties shall set the time limit for the contract, and conditions for extending or terminating the contract before expiration.

Article 15: A guarantee clause may be agreed upon by the parties in the contract. The guarantor assumes the liability within the agreed scope of guarantee.

Chapter III : Performance of Contract and Liabilities
for Breach of Contract

Article 16: Once established in accordance with law, a contract is legally binding. The parties should fulfill all obligations stipulated in the contract. No party should arbitrarily alter or terminate the contract.

Article 17: A party may suspend performance of his obligations when it is proved by conclusive evidence that the other party cannot perform his obligations accordingly, but in so doing the other party must be promptly notified. When the other party provides full guarantee for performing his obligations, contract performance shall be resumed. A party who suspends his performance without furnishing conclusive evidence should assume the liability for breach of contract.

Article 18: When a party fails to perform, or his performance does not conform to the agreed contractual obligations, namely, the contract is breached, the other party is entitled to ask the party in default to adopt reasonable remedial measures or claim for damages. If the losses suffered by the other party are not paid in full after the remedial measures are taken, that other party retains the right to claim for damages.

Article 19: Damages for breach of contract by a party consist of a sum equal to the loss suffered by the other party as a consequence of the breach. However, the damages may not exceed the loss which the party in breach ought to have foreseen at the time of the conclusion of the contract as a possible consequence of breach of the contract.

Article 20: The parties may agree upon in a contract that a certain amount of liquidated damages shall be paid to the other party if one party violates the contractual obligations, and may also agree upon a method for calculating the damages arising over such a breach of contract.

The liquidated damages shall be regarded as damages caused by a breach of contract. However, if the fixed amount of the liquidated damages is substantially more or substantially less than the resultant loss, the parties may request a court or arbitration agency to have it appropriately lowered or increased.

Article 21: In case both parties are in breach of the contract, both parties shall bear the relevant losses in accordance with the responsibilities due to them.

Article 22: A party who suffers a loss arising from a breach of contract by the other party should take appropriate measures in time to prevent the loss from aggravating. If he fails to take such measures and consequently aggravation of the loss results, he shall lose the right to claim damages for the aggravated part of the loss.

Article 23: If a party fails to pay at the appointed time the amount agreed upon in the contract or any other amount related to the contract that should have been paid, the other party is entitled to payment of principal plus interest for the delay. The rate of interest and how it should be calculated may be specified in the contract.

Article 24: A party should be exempted from his obligations in whole or in part in case he fails to implement all or part of his obligations as a result of force majeure.

In case a party cannot perform his obligations within the time limit set in the contract due to force majeure, he should be relieved of the liability for late performance for the period during which the consequence of the force majeure is being felt.

Force majeure means an event which the parties cannot foresee at the time of conclusion of the contract and whose occurrence or consequences the parties can neither avoid nor overcome. The range of force majeure may be specified in the contract by the parties.

Article 25: The party who fails to perform, in whole or in part, the contract due to force majeure should inform the other party promptly so as to mitigate the loss which might possibly arise. The former should also furnish the latter, within a reasonable period of time, some documentation issued by the relevant authorities to that effect.

Chapter IV : Assignment of Contract

Article 26: In case a party assigns, in part or in whole, his contractural rights and obligations to a third party, he should obtain the consent of the other party.

Article 27: As for a contract which, as provided by the law or administrative regulations of the People's Republic of China, should be established only after approval has been obtained from the State, the assignment the contractual rights and obligations is also subject to the approval of the original approval authorities, unless otherwise stipulated in the approved contract.

Chapter V : Modification, Cancellation and Termination of Contract

Article 28: A contract may be modified after agreement on its modification has been reached through consultations by the parties concerned.

Article 29: A party is entitled to inform the other party to cancel a contract if any of the following situations occurs:

(1) when the expected economic interests are seriously infringed upon for breach of contract by the other party;

(2) when the other party, who fails to perform the contract within the stipulated time limit, again fails to do so within a reasonable period of time allowed to make up for the delay;

(3) when the contract cannot be performed in its entirety due to the occurrence of force majeure;

(4) when the conditions stipulated in a contract for cancellation have occurred.

Article 30:   Where a contract is made up of several independent parts and part of which may be cancelled, the other parts shall according to the stipulations of the previous article, remain effective.

Article 31:   A contract is terminated if any of the following situations occurs:
(1)   when the contract has been performed in accordance with the conditions stipulated in it;
(2)   when the arbitration tribunal or the court decides to terminate the contract;
(3)   when termination is agreed upon by both parties through consultations.

Article 32:   Notification of or agreement on a contract's modification or termination should be made in writing.

Article 33:   As for a contract which, as stipulated by the law or administrative regulations of the People's Republic of China, should be established only after having been approved by the State, no significant modification can be made unless prior approval is obtained from the original approval authorities; its termination should be filed with the original approval authorities.

Article 34:   A party to a contract is not deprived of his right to claim damages in case of modification, cancellation or termination of the conract.

Article 35:   Any provision for the settlement of disputes stipulated in a contract shall not become invalid because of the termination or cancellation of the contract.

Article 36:   Any provision for settlement of accounts or winding up of operations stipulated in a contract shall remain effective inspite of the cancellation or termaination of the contract.

Chapter VI :   Settlement of Disputes

Article 37:   Disputes arising over a contract ought to be settled, if possible, through consulations or mediation by a third party.
In case the parties concerned are not willing to, or fail to, go through consultations or mediation, they may submit to China's arbitration agency or other arbitration agency in accordance with the arbitration agreement reached afterwards.

Article 38:   In cases where an arbitration clause has not been stipulated in a contract or an arbitration agreement has not been made afterwards, the parties may take their case to a people's court.

Chapter VII :   Supplementary Provisions

Article 39:   The prescription allowed for lodging a lawsuit or submitting to arbitration on disputes arising over a contract on sales of goods is of four years, beginning from the day when the party knows or ought to know that his rights have been infringed upon. The prescription for lodging a lawsuit or submitting to arbitration on disputes arising over other kinds of contracts shall be stipulated separately by law.

Article 40: When new relevant provisions are stipulated by law, the Sino-foreign equity or contractual joint venture contracts and the contract of cooperative exploration and development of natural sources which are approved by the State and performed within the territory of the People's Republic of China may still be performed on the basis of the original contract.

Article 41: This present law may also apply to contracts established before its promulgation, subject to agreement between the parties to the contract concerned through consultations.

Article 42: Rules for the Implementation will be formulated by the State Council in accordance with this Law.

Article 43: This Law shall go into force on July 1, 1985.

Summer 1987   T.C.W.C.

PART I:
MAKING CONTRACTS WITH CHINA
PRELIMINARY STAGE:

MEMORANDUM OF DISCUSSION ON TECHNOLOGY LICENCE

In response to the invitation of the China _____
_____ (hereinafter referred to as SINO),
the _____ ; (hereinafter
referred to as "Investor") visited China from _____ ,
19_____ , travelled to various _____ factories and organizations
in China and conducted many friendly discussions on a proposal for a
technology license with SINO. The parties concerned have reached tentative
understanding and hereby sign this memorandum of discussions.

1. Both parties unanimously agreed that they wish to cooperate on a long
    term basis in conformity with the principles of equality and mutual benefit
    and that such cooperation is feasible.

2. Both parties agree that the major areas for joint cooperation between
    them are the following: _____ , _____ ,
    _____ , _____ and _____ .

3. During the discussions between the parties in , China, during Investor's
    visit the parties agreed upon the following points:

    A. SINO desires to acquire technology which is very advanced by world
        standards and which is adaptable to current conditions in China in the
        area of _____ .

    B. Investor desires to license such technology to SINO.

    C. _____

    D. _____

    E. _____

5. The parties agree that, in order to promote the signing of a license
    agreement between them, they will undertake the following:

    A. Investor will study the information provided to it by SINO during its visit
        and prepare a concrete proposal for a license agreement within the
        next ninety days.

    B. SINO will review the results of its discussions with Investor and
        prepare a draft licensing agreement.

    C. _____

    D. Investor will notify SINO when it has prepared its proposal and the
        parties will conduct further discussions in, China, on such proposal at a
        time mutually agreed upon by the parties.

6. _____

7. This Memorandum of Discussions is signed in both English and Chinese

texts. Both texts are equally authentic.

Dated _____ , 19

(   ) (
              SINO   Investor

By: By:
Name: Name:
Title: Title:
Address: Address:

LETTER/MEMORANDUM OF INTENT

JOINT LETTER OF INTENTION
(JOINT VENTURE ELECTRONIC FACTORY)

Company Limited of   (hereinafter referred to as "Party A") conducted several friendly electronic factory with the Electronic Corporation (hereinafter referred to as "Party B"). Both Party A and Party B have reached mutual understanding and signed this joint venture contract hereunder. Whereas;

1. Both parties unanimously held that in accordance with the Law of the People's Republic of China on Joint Ventures using Chinese and Foreign Investment, and in conformity with the Principle of equality, mutual benefit and co-operation, it may be feasible to build a large, modernized electronic factory in

2. Both parties agree that the contribution of capital investment from each party shall be in equal share. The construction of the electronic factory is to be carried out in phases. In accordance with the needs of business development, it is estimated that the total amount of investment will gradually reach one billion Renminbi yuan.

3. The investment from Party B will include land, factory building, workers' hostel, a part of equipment, necessary public utilities and necessary funds in Renminbi yuan; the investment from Party A may include the provision of equipment and necessary funds in foreign exchange, and will also include the value of Party A's unique Contributions—such as market study, engineering and technical know how—the value of which shall be fairly determined.

4. Both parties agree that:
    (a) the machines and equipment need for the initial stage shall not only represent the level of modern electronic technology in the world, but shall also be adaptable to current conditions in China.
    (b) All expenditures in foreign exchange such as disbursement of profit and importation of necessary materials are to be covered by exporting finished electronic products. Party A will try its best efforts to procure export orders.

5. Both parties agree that the joint venture should proceed in three phases—planning, construction and operation.

6. Both parties agree that during the first-stage construction of the proposed factory, personnel computer can be turned out. To achieve this, adequate machines and equipment should be used. Both parties shall consider using new technology to keep abreast with the constant progress in electronic industry.

7. Party A will within three months by   19   prepare a

market study to determine whether there is a good opportunity to manufacture computer in Chinese and English languages in China for export to other countries.

8. Party B will provide to Party A by _____ 19 ____ detailed specification of products planned to be produced in the joint venture electronic factory for domestic distribution, and will also provide to Party A by 19 ____ detailed information of the costs required to produce computer manufactured for domestic distribution. The above mentioned information is to be used for reference by Party A only. Party B will also provide to Party A before _____ 19 ____ a drawing of the factory site. The drawing will show the dimension of the site, the location of highways (existing and proposed), the location of highways (existing and proposed), the location of railways (existing and proposed) the location of utilities (power, water, gas), and the location of workers' hostels.

9. Both parties agree that after the results and conclusions of the market study are known to both of them, and only if the results of that study show that a good and sufficient export market exist, a delegation from Party B is to be invited to _____ by Party A to conduct detailed discussions with the latter, so as to work out the specific provisions for the joint-venture agreement and enable both parties to sign a formal contract in _____ within 19 ____

10. This joint letter of intention is signed in Chinese and English texts; both texts are equally authentic.

Dated _____ , 19 _____ .

_____   _____
(signed)   (signed)

     Electronic Corporation   Company Limited

MEMORANDUM OF INTENTION
ON
CONSTRUCTION OF A HOLIDAY RESORT

The Mission of The BCD Group of Companies, headed by his Royal Highness of _____ . (hereinafter referred to as "BCD") and the Head Office of The China International Travel Service (hereinafter referred to as "CITS") held preliminary talks between (Date) and (Date) 19 _____ in Peking on the construction of a holiday resort in China.

I. CITS indicated that to develop tourism in China, there was a need to build a holiday resort. BCD expressed its willingness to provide funds, expertise and experience in the construction of such holiday resort. Both sides considered that it is in the interest of both sides to develop cooperation on a mutually beneficial basis.

II. BCD offered to help CITS build _____ , practical comfortable and attractive holiday resort hotels in Chinese scenic spot, with approximately 2500 rooms and would be up to modern international standards, plus one golf field of international standards.

    The two sides exchanged information and indicated their intentions with regard to the construction, financing, operation and management of the holiday resort. They agreed that the discussions had been fruitful and had laid a favourable foundation for future cooperation.

III. The two sides discussed alternative forms of cooperation. The Chinese side indicated that it would be responsible for providing the land, sand, aggregate and labour, regardless of the form of cooperation agreed upon. BCD would finance the holiday resort and assist in the design, construction and purchase of equipment and building materials, etc. from foreign countries.

    All materials and equipment which are available in China should insofar as possible be purchased in China. If these are to be purchased abroad, they should first of all be bought in BCD'S Country, if these are available there and meet international standards.

    The Bank of China shall undertake to guarantee the loans for the holiday resort project. The period for the repayment of the loan will be approximately twenty (20) years. This loan shall consist of a construction period, during which no interest will be paid, followed by a grace period, during which only interest will be paid and followed by a period during which principal and interest will be paid in instalments.

IV. No press release will be made by either party without the prior approval of the other party.

V.   Each side will study the suggestions and requirements of the other side so as to get ready for future discussions.

Done in duplicate in Peking, on _____ 19 _____ , in the English and Chinese languages.

Representatives of The BCD Group of Companies
(SIGNED)

Representatives of the Head Office of China International Travel Service
(SIGNED)

_____

_____

Mr

Mr.

LETTER AGREEMENT/
PROTOCOLS

LETTER AGREEMENT ON CONSIGNMENT
OF
SELLING PHARMACEUTICALS
IN
BEIJING

Through the introduction of the Municipal Import / Export Committee, the ABC BEIJING Friendship Store, (hereinafter referred to as "ABC"), and Medicial Drugs Inc, (hereinafter referred to as "MEDICAL"), start a mutually beneficial business in Beijing. After preliminary discussions, the parties want to put in this letter their preliminary understanding as to the following matters. The parties anticipate that this mutually beneficial understanding will eventually result in a more substantive agreement in the future.

1. ABC will use its best efforts to sell all kinds of health drugs and theraphic medicine (hereinafter referred to as the "DRUGS") for Medical. ABC will not export the DRUGS outside of China.

2. ABC will receive a commission fee which will be negotiated by the parties based upon the retail / consumer price for and the rate of duty charged on the DRUGS. For the term of this letter agreement, the commission fee will be equal to 10% of the retail / consumer price. ABC shall deduct the fee from the gross sales proceeds before ABC remits the gross sales proceeds to Medical.

3. For the first quarter, Medical will supply ABC with the quantity of Drugs. set forth in the attached Schedule. After the first quarter, or sooner if the parties so decide, Medical will supply ABC with additional Drugs either to replace the drugs sold by ABC or to increase the inventory of Drugs available for sale.

4. For the term of this letter agreement, the suggested retail / consumer prices for the Drugs will be those which are set forth in the attached Schedule.

5. Medical will provide for the freight and insurance expenses of the Drugs from Europe to Beijing airport or train station. Medical shall not pay any import, export or customs duties or any industrial or commercial tax or any other duties, taxes or tariffs which are either now or hereafter promulgated.

6. Medical will be liable for any Drugs damaged in transit from Europe to Beijing airport or station, but only if Medical has caused the Drugs to be damaged. Medical will not be liable for any Drugs lost.

7. ABC will provide for the transportation of the Drugs from Beijing airport or train station to the retailing spots and warehouse. ABC will give

Medical any necessary import or customs licenses and governmental approvals. ABC will be liable for any loss or damage to the Drugs while in storage or in transit from Beijing airport or train station.

8. For the term of this letter agreement, Medical will supply any necessary after-sales support in Beijing. After the term of this agreement, the parties will discuss the possibility of rendering such services throughout China by Medical. Medical will also provide for advertising of the Drugs at the retailing spots.

9. Any Drugs which has not been sold by the expiration date stamped on the package will be returned by ABC to Medical within 20 days of the expiration date, and all freight expenses thus incurred will be charged against Medical. Medical will be entitled to replace any film within one month before the expiration date. Medical will pay all freight expenses thus incurred.

10. If Medical so desires, Medical will be entitled to send representatives once a month to Beijing to monitor the sale of the Drugs. ABC will assist Medical in obtaining any necessary visas. While in Beijing the representative will be entitled to review the sales records of ABC which relate to the Drugs and examine the inventory of the Drugs.

11. Within 10 days after the end of each quarter, ABC will clear accounts with Medical and will remit to Medical in United States Dollars, or other currency acceptable to Medical, the gross receipts from the sales made during the quarter, less the commission fee of _____ % or as it may be negotiated in the future. **Medical will also give ABC detailed reports of the quantity, type and price of Drugs sold by ABC during the preceeding quarter.**

12. ABC has obtained all necessary government approvals to enter into and consummate the transactions contemplated by this agreement and, in particular, has obtained any necessary approvals from the appropriate government agencies and officials to remit to Medical the proceeds from the sale of Drugs in United States Dollars, or other currencies acceptable to Medical.

13. This agreement has been prepared in both the Chinese and English languages. Both the Chinese and English versions will have equal control in the event of any disagreement between the parties. The parties will execute two copies of this agreement in both languages.

14. Any disputes which may arise between the parties during the term of this letter agreement will be resolved through friendly discussions. If, as the parties hope, they enter into a more substantive agreement in the future, they will discuss the possibility of using arbitration to settle any future disputes.

15. Amendments to this agreement may be made at any time, provided such amendments are agreed to by both parties.

16. This agreement will be valid and binding when signed and sealed by both parties and will terminate no later than _____ , 19 _____ .

Sealed with the Common)
Seal of the ABC Beijing)
Friendship Store and)
signed by)

Sealed with the Common)
Seal of Medical Drugs Inc)
and signed by)
)
in the presence of :-)

PROTOCOL OF PROCEEDINGS
ON
IRON AND STEEL INDUSTRIAL
CO-OPERATION

At the invitation of the GRAND China Iron & Steel Corporation of China (hereinafter called "SINO"), Easy Steel Mills of   (hereinafter called "INVESTOR"), visited the SINO during the weeks of April, September and September   19____ . A technical seminar on steel refinery was presented by INVESTOR, and technical and commercial discussions were held. Annex 1 to the Protocol contains the names of INVESTOR participants and Annex 2, the principal participants of the SINO.

Both sides expressed satisfaction with the manner in which the meetings were conducted and received, and in the high qualifications of the respective personnel who were present.

Prior to the formal meetings commencing, INVESTOR'S personnel were invited to and had a visit to the SINO'S iron and steel plant. INVESTOR expresses its appreciation to the SINO for its excellent efforts in making the necessary arrangements for the plant visit, which has increased its team's understanding of China's current iron and steel refinery capabilities, requirements, and resources.

The SINO indicated the following areas in which it would be interested to receive specific proposals, if appropriate, from INVESTOR:

1. Technology know how assistance and transfer agreement.

2. The purchase of equipment from INVESTOR which would be necessary for the SINO to install production lines as stipulated in Annex 1. INVESTOR notes that each production line would be capable of producing 100,000 metric tons of steel per annum, or 100,000 metric tons of iron per annum.

3. It was understood that, as a first step, both parties agree to cooperate in the steel refinery area.

    INVESTOR notes that, on the basis of observation and discussion, China already possesses steel refinery capacity sufficient to satisfy the needs of China's current and programmed heavy industrial development. INVESTOR further noted that China should expand its use of automatic sampling system and institute updated steel refinery techniques. Such improved refinery would:

    1. Provide a greater conservation of energy, and

    2. Provide for greater steel throughout from existing steel facilities and offer additional applications.

4. Both INVESTOR and the SINO expressed a desire to establish a long term relationship providing for the continuous development of technology in the Chinese iron and steel refinery industry.

5. INVESTOR expressed its willingness to enter into a long term license arrangement for iron and steel refinery techniques ceramic fibers and / or monolithics with SINO, under which INVESTOR will furnish the following:

   1. Information used by INVESTOR pertaining to mixes and formulations;
   2. Application engineering information, consisting of standards manuals, plant construction design drawings, dry out schedules, and related data;
   3. Operational information, derived from operation and analysis;
   4. Manufacturing information used by INVESTOR in its manufacture and operations.
   5. Quality control procedures used by INVESTOR;
   6. Assembly, erection, installation and start-up information for manufacturing facilities;
   7. Improvements resulting from INVESTOR'S research and development .

6. Consultations and technical assistance from INVESTOR'S technical experts in both the INVESTOR'S own country and China; and

7. Training, in the form of a manpower development program for SINO personnel in INVESTOR'S manufacturing, engineering, and research facilities.

8. INVESTOR is also willing to supply the equipment necessary for the SINO to install a computerized production line.

9. INVESTOR expressed its desire to receive cash payment for both the technology transfer agreements, and the equipment for the production lines. Nevertheless, INVESTOR would consider accepting less cash, the remainder of the payment to be in the form of compensation trade in goods or services acceptable to INVESTOR such as direct products of the SINO.

10. Both parties agreed to cooperate with each other in the interest of establishing a long and friendly relationship, which relationship, it is hoped will lead to further productive relationships between the parties on various subject matters. INVESTOR cordially invited SINO personnel to visit its facilities in its own country.

11. Both parties agreed that, based on their discussions, they will hold further consultations with their personnel in their respective countries.

12. INVESTOR agreed to provide specific proposals to the Bureau on or before _____ , 19 _____ . The SINO agreed to invite INVESTOR personnel to return to China on or before _____ , 19 _____ to carry

forward more detailed discussions and negotiations on the proposals.

13. Both parties agreed that communications between INVESTOR and the SINO with respect to this Protocol are to be addressed as follows:

1. Address of SINO:

_____

_____

2. Address of INVESTOR

_____

_____

Both the SINO and INVESTOR declare their earnest desire to proceed toward concluding mutually acceptable agreements to the long term benefit of both parties.

This Protocol is signed in duplicate in Shanghai, China _____ on _____ 19 _____ .

For and on behalf of
GRAND CHINA IRON & STEEL COR-
   PORATION
(SINO)

For and on behalf of
Easy Steel Mills
(INVESTOR)

_____ (SIGNED) _____   _____ (SIGNED) _____

PROTOCOL
FOR
JOINT CO-OPERATION IN PAPER
MANUFACTORY AND MARKETING

The Harbin Paper Mills of the People's Republic of China (hereinafter referred to as "China") and Foreign Paper Manufacturing Corporation of Switzerland (hereinafter referred to as "SWISS") are now jointly set forth their mutual plans to co-operate in paper manufacturing and marketing.

BACKGROUND .

This protocol follows the various discussions that have been held between the representatives of the ministry of foreign economic relations and trade of The People's Republic of China and "SWISS" which commenced on ___
___ 19 ___ , and have continued at various times both in the PRC and in Switzerland since that date.

PURPOSE

By this protocol, the parties agree to continue their mutual efforts to achieve the following main objectives:

A.   Creation of a planning statement for the development of a jointly owned paper brand (hereinafter referred to as "PRODUCT") having international quality standards.

The planning statement will be a mutually agreed upon program, including scheduling, for the complete development of the product. Such development will involve specific details on the following items:
— Factory site selection and layout.
— Evaluation of and selection of fabrics.
— Required equipment.
— Quality control.
— Supervision and costs thereof.
— Promotion design and trademark.
— Sales analysis and projections.
— Marketing analysis and costs.

B.   Creation of a planning statement for the development of Swiss paper brand / brands to be produced and sold under license or contract manufactured in China.

It is contemplated by the parties that the development of Swiss paper brand / brands under license or contract manufactured in the PRC will proceed simultaneously with the development of the product, upon review and evaluation of the proposal by China, an agreement satisfactory to both parties will be reached.

C.   Execution of an agreement satisfactory to both parties setting forth the basic relationship between the parties and their respective responsibilities.

This agreement will establish the obligations and undertakings of the parties in implementing "A" and "B" of this protocol. This will include a compensation method agreed to by both parties.

SCHEDULE

In order to progress as rapidly as possible in achieving the purpose of this protocol, the parties agree to the following schedule:

1.   By (date: author) China and Swiss representatives will provide each other with the necessary data to formulate the planning statement.

2.   By (date: author) Swiss will provide China with its license or contract manufacturing proposals.

3.   By (date: author) representatives of the parties will complete negotiations and reach a preliminary agreement on the planning statement and license / contract manufacturing.

4.   By (date author) representatives of the parties will execute the agreement referred to in "C" above.

PRELIMINARY FINANCIAL PLAN

To guide their respective representatives in negotiating the planning statement, China and Swiss agree to the following points:

1.   Equipment will be loaned by Swiss to China to produce up to 500 million metric tons of paper annually and will remain in China for the life of the product / license / contract manufacturing project, freight and insurance charges will be repaid by Swiss and reimbursed by China at a later date. Additional equipment for capacity expansion will be negotiated at a later date.

In order to achieve trial production for one Swiss brand in the fourth quarter of 19____ , Swiss will ship the equipment to China as soon as possible and China will ensure that all necessary preparation will be done prior to the arrival of the shipment. If the final contract cannot be signed as described in "C" above, China will pay Swiss the price of the equipment which will be negotiated in China before the shipment.

2.   Should swiss sell paper and packaging materials to China for a licensed brand, payment to Swiss for such paper and materials will be either in foreign currency. In the event Swiss obtained a contract with the China national industrial products corporation for sale of the product or contract manufactured brand, these costs will be included as production costs to be reimbursed in foreign currency.

Should both parties agree to use contract manufacturing instead of licensing, the manufacturing fee payable to China will be determined at a later date.

3. Technical assistance provided by Swiss for the product / license brand will be included in production costs and will be reimbursed from proceeds of sales.

4. Swiss and China will use their best efforts to achieve total production of the product / license / contract manufactured brand of 500 million metric tons of paper in 19____. In order to ensure that sufficient foreign currency will be generated to cover the operating costs, Swiss will use its best efforts to market a portion of product in international markets, and a portion of product / license / contract manufactured brand in foreign currency outlets within PRC China in cooperation with China National Industrial Products Corporation. China agrees to sell the remaining portion of the 19____ production in foreign currency.

5. The operating profit derived through the sale of the product will be shared by the parties on a 50 / 50 basis. Each party shall respect the proprietary nature of the date supplied pursuant to this protocol. In the event that this protocol does not proceed to the execution of an agreement referred to in "C" above, all proprietary date shall be returned to the originator.

This protocol is entered into in the spirit of friendship and in sincere interest in achieving the long-term mutual benefits of cooperation for the Ministry of Foreign Economic Relations and Trade and Foreign Paper Manufactory Corporation of Switzerland.

This protocol is done in both Chinese and English with equal validity.

Executed in Beijing, China on the _____ day of _____ , 19____ .

For and on behalf of:
Harbin Paper Mills of The People's Republic of China

_____

For and on behalf of:
Ministry of Foreign Economic Relations and Trade (PRC)

_____

For and on behalf of:
Foreign Paper Manufacturing Corporation of Switzerland

_____

SHIPBUILDING PROTOCOL BETWEEN CHINA SHIPBUILDING CORPORATION (CSC) AND THE X SHIPBUILDERS

The China Shipbuilding Corporation (CSC) and the X Shipbuilders (XS), motivated by a sincere desire for collaboration, are willing to cooperate in a number of areas of activity on the basis of equity and mutual benefit. After amicable discussions, both sides have concluded this agreement and have determined that initially their collaboration shall consist of the following:

1. Ship Design
    CSC has the right to select any design of vessel from XS standard design range (including all types of offshore vessels, rigs and floating platforms). Both Parties may also cooperate in the development of new designs or in renewing or upgrading the existing ship designs in China to make them internationally competitive.

2. Ship Construction
    The construction of the initial vessels in each series of ship type selected would be undertaken in any of XS merchant shipbuilding yards (the lead yards) and the ensuing vessels of the series would be built in any of the CSC shipyards. This arrangement would apply to both domestic and overseas shipbuilding contracts.
    XS lead yards will undertake to supply to CSC all the necessary design plans, specifications and working drawings free of charge and arrange for the supply for marine equipment not available from CSC sources.
    XS undertakes to train key CSC personnel in the lead yards during the construction period and arrange for similar training for key personnel at the factories where the marine equipment is being manufactured.

3. Sales and Marketing Procedures
    XS will cooperate with CSC to promote the sales of vessels built in China or the _____ for both the domestic and international markets. Both parties shall regularly exchange information concerning the international ship market.

4. Supply of Marine Equipment
    XS and CSC will cooperate in the supply of marine equipment. XS is willing to assist CSC with procuring such equipment in the _____ and also with the promotion of Chinese manufactured equipment in the market.

5. Training
    In addition to the training of technicians at XS lead yards in the _____ , other types of training can be undertaken by XS at its training centres at costs to be agreed upon through consultations by both sides.
    Such training programmes can incorporate the following elements:
    A. Shipbuilding technology and management techniques.
    B. Structured training courses (technical department / production administration / commercial department / production technology / management science).
    C. Visits to XS shipyards and research establishments.
    D. Visits to equipment manufacturers.

6. Research and Development
    Research and development institutions of both sides shall maintain their contacts in order to promote further cooperation in research and development work, and will also exchange regularly information relating to design and marine technology.

7. Other Technical Cooperation
    In addition to the above collaboration terms in respect of shipbuilding and already agreed by the two corporations XS would be willing to provide CSC with the latest ship design and construction methods, scientific research and shipyard management information directed towards mutual benefit on terms and conditions to be agreed.

8. Credit Finance
    XS is willing to provide the collaboration above-mentioned with the backing of ship finance package which will be discussed and determined by both parties in relation to specific business.

9. Collaboration
    XS and CSC acknowledge that the execution of this agreement provides a framework for the collaboration between both parties. The enterprises and institutions of both XS and CSC will henceforth discuss and conclude the practical details of the collaboration in relation to all the areas of activity mentioned herein in relation to specific business.

10. Validity
    The validity of this agreement would in the first instance be for _____ years. But if at a period of _____ months before expiry neither party has proposed alteration or additions to this agreement and / or neither party has requested its termination, then this agreement shall be considered to be fully effective for a further period of _____ years.

11. Languages
    This agreement is written in both the Chinese and English languages, both of which are equally effective.

Dated this the _____ day of _____ .

_____
(SIGNED)
China Shipbuilding Corporation

_____
(SIGNED)
The X Shipbuilders

COMPUTER
INFORMATION EXCHANGE PROTOCOL

At the invitation of the Chinese _____ ,
whose principal address is situated at _____ ,
China, the _____ of _____ ,
visited China during the period _____ to _____
19 _____ ; the visit, discussion were held between representatives
of the _____ of China and representatives of
_____ on matters of developing technology
cooperation on computer science. Both sides exchanged information with
each other. The representatives of the _____
expressed the willingness to provide recommandations concerning transfer of
technology and financing of development, production and application of
computer components, equipments, systems and spare parts; the design of a
and _____ and
related matters.

In recognition of conditions of the computer industry in China, both parties
have expressed the desire that relations will be established to commence
cooperation in the following fields:

1. Provide the design, technology know how for the manufacture and the
    complete facilities for the development and manufacture of large scale
    integrated circuits. This shall include facilities and equipment for computer
    design, mask fabrication, electron beam exposure, ion implantation,
    integrated circuit packaging and testing. Representative products are:
    —list out all the products (author)—

2. Design, technology know how and complete facilities for the manufacture
    of microwave _____
    and _____ devices. Typical products are:
    —list out all the products (author)—

3. Technology and facilities to develop, design and manufacture:
    —list out all the products (author)—

4. Provide expert consulting by an appropriate person or persons from ____
    to visit China to render assistance in advising and teaching design and
    manufacturing techniques for _____

5. Advice of Shipment: Immediately after completion of loading of goods on board the vessel the Sellers shall advise the Buyers by airmail of the Contract number, name of goods, quantity or weight loaded, total value, name of vessel, time of loading. The Sellers have the right to load 5% more or less of the contracted quantity for each lot. The goods' value for the part loaded more or less should be calculated according to the Unit Price stipulated in this contract.

6. Shipping Documents: The Sellers shall present the following documents to the negotiating bank for payment:
   (1) Invoice in one original and 3 copies.
   (2) Two copies of the packing list or weight memos.
   (3) Clean on board Bill of Lading in one original and three copies.

7. Inspection: The Certificate of Quality, Quantity / Weight issued by the Manufacturer or the China Commodity Inspection Bureau shall be taken as the basis of delivery.

8. Force Majeure: The Sellers shall not be held responsible for late delivery or non-delivery of the contracted goods owing to natural disasters or other Force Majeure causes. However, in such a case, the Sellers shall immediately inform the Buyers in due time.

9. Discrepancy and Claim: In case discrepancy on the quality of the goods is found by the Buyers after arrival of the goods at the port of destination, the Buyers may, within 30 days after the arrival of the goods at the port of destination, lodge with Sellers a claim which should be supported by an Inspection certificate issued by a public surveyor approved by the Sellers. The Sellers shall, on the merits of the claim, either make good the loss sustained by the Buyers or reject their claim. It is agreed that the Sellers shall not be held responsible for any loss or losses due to natural cause or causes falling within the responsibility of the Shipowners or Underwriters. In case the Letter of Credit does not reach the Sellers within the time stipulated in the Contract, or if the Letter of Credit opened by the Buyers does not correspond to the Contract terms and that the Buyers fail to amend thereafter its terms in time, after receipt of notification by the Sellers, the Sellers shall have the right to cancel the contract or to delay the delivery of the goods and shall also have the right to lodge claim against the Buyers for compensation of losses.

10. Arbitration: Any dispute arising from the execution of, or in connection with this Contract shall be settled through negotiation. In case no settlement can be reached between the two Parties, the case under dispute shall be submitted to the Foreign Trade Arbitration Commission of the China Council for the Promotion of International Trade or the third country agreed upon for arbitration. The fees for arbitration shall be borne by the losing Party.

This Contract is made out in Chinese and English, both versions being equally authentic, each party holding one of the two originals after signing as evidence.

_____   _____

THE SELLERS   THE BUYERS

THE AGREEMENTS / CONTRACTS:

JOINT VENTURE AGREEMENT BETWEEN YELLOW RIVER CONFECTIONERY (CHINA) LIMITED AND CHINA DRAGON CONSTRUCTION CORPORATION

THIS AGREEMENT is made and entered into this _____ ,
19   ,by and between YELLOW RIVER COMPANY CONFECTIONERY
(CHINA) LIMITED, (hereinafter referred to as "YR") a corporation
organized and existing under the laws of Japan and CHINA DRAGON
CONSTRUCTION CORPORATION, (hereinafter referred to as "CD"), an
entity orgainzed and existing under the laws of the People's Republic of
China.

Witnesseth:

WHEREAS, CD has responsibility for the manufacture of confectionery
products, including candies, in and for the People's Republic of China;
and

WHEREAS, YR and its affiliated companies have experience, knowledge
and capabilities in all aspects of production of candies, and

WHEREAS, CD and YR have previously cooperated successfully in a
venture for the manufacture, distribution and sale of SNAKE brand
candies in the People's Republic of China; and

WHEREAS, CD and YR desire to form a joint venture in the People's
Republic of China for the purposes of producing high quality candies in
the People's Republic of China for export and domestic sale;

NOW, THEREFORE, CD and YR agree to form a joint venture corporation
in accordance with the following terms and conditions:

Article 1   Definitions

1.1   Unless the terms or context of this Agreement otherwise provides, the
following terms shall have the following meanings:

1.1.1   "Jointly Owned Brand" ("JOB") shall mean the brand of 100 gm
candies to be manufactured at the Factory.

1.1.2   "Factory" shall mean that certain factory, [name], locate   in
Yellow River, Dragon Province, in the Territory, used by the JVC
for production of the JOB.

1.1.3   "Territory" shall mean the People's Republic of China.

1.1.4   "JVC" shall mean YR CHINA CANDY CORPORATION, the joint
venture company formed by CD and YR.

1.1.5   "Technology and Know How" shall mean the YR advanced and
up-to-date technology, know-how, formulas, techniques and
methods, provided in written or oral form, to be utilized by the

JVC in producing the JOB.

- 1.1.6 "Feasibility Study" shall mean a written analysis prepared by either CD, YR or both concerning the economic and practical feasibility of the JVC.
- 1.1.7 "Joint Venture Law" shall mean the Law of the People's Republic of China on Joint Ventures Using Chinese and Foreign Investment, and the Regulations promulgated thereunder, as presently in effect.
- 1.1.8 "Company Operating Procedures" shall mean those philosophies, concepts and procedures agreed by CD and YR as the operating procedures of the JVC.
- 1.1.9 "Force Majeure" shall mean all events which are beyond the control of the parties to this Agreement of JVC, and which are unforeseen, or if foreseen, unavoidable and which arise after date of signature of this Agreement and prevent total or partial performance by either party or by the JVC.

Article 2: Structure of the Joint Venture

2.1 The JVC shall be formed in accordance with the Joint Venture Law.

2.2 The Articles of Association and By-Laws of the JVC shall be those attached as Appendices A and B, respectively, to this Agreement.

2.3 The Articles of Association and By-Laws are hereby incorporated into and made part of this Agreement.

2.4 CD's interest in the JVC may be owned by GREAT WALL CORPORATION, a corporation organized and existing under the laws of the People's Republic of China, and wholly owned or controlled by CD.

2.5 YR's interest in the JVC may be owned by SINO-TIGER INC., a corporation organized and existing under the laws of Japan.

2.6 The JVC will be organized with CD holding a 50% interest and YR's holding a 50% interest.

Article 3: Scope of the Joint Venture

3.1 The JVC will produce the JOB for sale within the Territory and for export.

3.2 The JOB produced by the Factory will be sold 60% for export, at prevailing international prices for comparable products, and 40% within the territory, for Renminbi and for Foreign Exchange Certificates, at prices comparable to similar products in the Territory, to ensure profits to the JVC.

3.3 The principal activities of the JVC will include:
- 3.3.1 Development of a high quality 100 gm candy to be manufactured as the JOB.
- 3.3.2 Development of a package design and packaging for the JOB.

31

3.3.3 Conceptual design, detailed engineering, and layout of the Factory.

3.3.4 Establishment and operation of the Factory in the Territory for production of the JOB.

3.3.5 Sales of the JOB produced in the Factory for export and in the Territory.

3.3.6 Development of a marketing, advertising and distribution system, and other services, to ensure maximum sales of the JOB.

3.4 Establishment of the Factory will be undertaken by the JVC following:

3.4.1 The completion of a Feasibility Study regarding the economic viability of the JVC; and

3.4.2 Determination, through the Feasibility Study, that the Factory will provide an equitable return on investment to the JVC.

3.4.3 Issuance of any licenses or approvals which the governments of Japan or the Territory may require as a condition precedent to the execution of this Agreement.

Article 4: Obligations of the Members

4.1 Each party will be responsible for its own costs incurred in connection with the formation of the JVC.

4.2 Initial operation capital required by the JVC after it is formed will be contributed _____ % by CD and _____ % by YRs, provided, however, that it is the intention of CD and YR that:

4.2.1 Initial capital contributions of CD and YRs will be the minimum necessary to begin preliminary operations of the JVC and shall not exceed Pound Sterling 80,000 for each party, unless otherwise mutually agreed; and

4.2.2 Additional operating funds and income will be obtained primarily from revenues generated by sales of the JOB by JVC pursuant to orders from third parties.

4.2.3 Further necessary contributions by CD and YR to operating capital will be in accordance with cash flow projections established by Feasibility Studies.

4.3 CD and YR will make available to the JVC equipment, facilities, technical assistance and manpower on a reimbursable contract basis.

4.3.1 CD will make available, for example:

4.3.1.1 Management and labour personnel as may be required in establishing the JVC and the Factory.

4.3.1.2 Land, buildings, supplies, equipment, labour, and raw materials as may be required and available in the Territory for the establishment of the Factory and the production of the JOB.

4.3.1.3. Liaison services with relevant government author-

32

ities of the Territory.

4.3.2 YR will make available, for example:

4.3.2.1 Management, technical, engineering, production and quality control personnel and services as the JVC may require;

4.3.2.2 Technology and Know-How as may be required for the establishment and operation of a modern and up-to-date Factory.

4.3.2.3 Equipment, supplies and raw materials as may be required by the JVC and not otherwise available in the Territory;

4.3.2.4 Technical assistance, including technical, management and production training in the Territory and elsewhere, as may be required for personnel engaged in operation of the JVC or the Factory; and

4.3.2.5 Business and market development assistance in and outside the Territory to enable the JVC to establish a market for the JOB to be produced in the Factory.

4.3.3 The foregoing services, equipment and other items will be provided by CD and YR to the JVC and the Factory to enable them to achieve the purposes of this Agreement.

4.3.4 Payments by third parties to the JVC for the JOB will be used first to reimburse CD and YR for providing the services, equipment, personnel and other items referred to in Article 4.3.1 and 4.3.2 of this Agreement.

4.3.5 Reimbursement shall be at costs or rates agreed by the parties in advance, and shall include each party's direct and indirect costs, without profit.

4.3.6 Revenues to the JVC in excess of such costs or rates will be used to cover any other costs of the JVC, and the remainder will be shared 50% to CD and 50% to YR.

Article 5: Meeting of the JVC

5.1 CD and YR as the parties of the JVC, in meetings held or decisions taken in accordance with the terms of the Articles of Association and By-Laws, and the Company Operating Procedures, shall have supreme authority with respect to the management of the affairs of the JVC.

5.2 The parties reserve for themselves the exclusive determination, in accordance with the terms of this Agreement, the Articles of Association and the By-Laws of the following matters:

5.2.1 To elect and remove the members of the Board of Directors;

5.2.2 To review and approve the annual financial statements and

33

disposition of the net income of the JVC.

5.2.3   To establish the overall policy and annual operating plan of the JVC;

5.2.4   To authorize the contracting of any loans by the JVC;

5.2.5   To approve any suit or claim of the JVC in any court of law or in any arbitration, whether as plaintiff or defendant, and any settlement agreement resulting therefrom;

5.2.6   To approve any purchase, sale or other disposition of a capital asset of the JVC;

5.2.7   To establish the terms and conditions of employment of officers, staff members and workers of the JVC; and

In all matters set forth in this Article 4, the resolutions and decisions for the Meetings of Members of the JVC shall be adopted by unanimous vote of the Members, except as otherwise provided by the Articles of Association and By-Laws.

Article 6:   Board of Directors and Officers of the JVC

6.1   Directors of the JVC

6.1.1   The Board of Directors of the JVC shall consist of five(5) persons.

6.1.2   Three Directors shall be nominated by the CD and two Directors shall be nominated by YR, and these five persons shall be elected by unanimous vote of the Members.

6.1.3   The following persons shall be nominated and elected at the first Meeting of Members:

6.1.3.1   Nominated by CD:

_____
(Name)

_____
(Title)

_____
(Name)

_____
(Title)

_____
(Name)

_____
(Title)

6.1.3.2   Nominated by YR:

_____
(Name)

_____
(Title)

(Name)

(Title)

6.1.4 If a Board Member dies, resigns or is removed from office, the party which originally nominated such Board Member shall nominate his successor, and that person shall be elected by unanimous vote of the Members.

6.1.5 The following functions shall be the exclusive prerogative of the Board of Directors of the JVC;

6.1.5.1 To elect officers of the JVC;

6.1.5.2 To establish management policies and business objectives of JVC, including annual operating production and sales plans of the JVC;

6.1.5.3 To review the annual financial statements of the JVC; and

6.1.5.4 To make distribution of the net income of the JVC such distribution to YR in all cases to be in Pound Sterling.

6.1.6 The resolutions of the Board of Directors shall be adopted in accordance with the Articles of Association and By-Laws, and all resolutions shall be adopted by unanimous vote.

6.1.7 No resolution of the Board of Directors shall be effective if any Director votes against the adoption of such resolution.

6.1.8 The Board of Directors shall not be precluded from adopting resolutions without a meeting pursuant to an unanimous written consent resolution of the Board of Directors.

6.2 Officers of the JVC

6.2.1 The Board of Directors shall elect as officers of the JVC a President, a Vice President (or more than one Vice President), a Secretary and a Treasurer.

6.2.2 Officers may, but need not, be members of the Board of Director.

6.2.3 The President shall be nominated by CD and the Vice President (or, if there is more than one Vice President, then the senior-ranking Vice President) shall be nominated by YR and these officers nominated shall be elected by the Board of Directors.

6.2.4 The Secretary shall be nominated by CD and the Treasurer shall be nominated by YR, and these officers nominated shall be elected by the Board of Directors.

6.2.5 The Board of Directors shall be unanimous vote decide whether the JVC should have more than one Vice President, and which party shall nominate such additional Vice President(s) for election.

6.2.6 The following persons shall be nominated and elected as the initial officers of the JVC at the first meeting of the Board of Directors to serve in the positions set forth after their names:

Teng Ta	President, to be nominated by CD
Tai Fok	Vice President, to be nominated by YR
Koo Yi	Secretary, to be nominated by CD
Yi Min	Treasurer, to be nominated by YR

6.2.7 The Officers shall perform their functions until their death, resignation or removal by the Board of Directors.

6.2.8 Upon the death, resignation or removal from office of any Officer, the party who originally appointed such officer shall nominate a successor who shall be elected by the Board of Directors without delay.

Article 7: Management Committee and Plant Managers

7.1 The President and Vice President (or, if there is more than one Vice President, the senior ranking Vice President) shall, with the approval of the Board of Directors, appoint a Management Committee consisting of themselves and such other persons as they mutually agree upon, to serve as a Management Committee of the JVC.

7.2 The President shall serve as Chairman of the Management Committee and the (senior ranking) Vice President shall serve as Vice Chairman of the Management Committee.

7.3 The Management Committee shall submit to the first and each annual meeting of the Board of Directors the following plans:

7.3.1 An overall Policy Plan;

7.3.2 An annual Operating Plan; and

7.3.3 An annual Production and Sales Plan.

7.4 The Plans shall be submitted to the Board of Directors annually not later than the 31st day of December of each year.

7.5 The Management Committee shall submit a monthly production and sales report to the members of the Board of Directors, and such report shall also contain recommendations for business to be undertaken by the JVC.

7.6 The Management Committee shall submit a monthly financial report to the members of the Board of Directors, and such report shall be submitted within ten(10) following the close of the month reported.

7.7 The initial Management Committee shall be composed of:

7.7.1 Chairman(and JVC President)

7.7.2 Vice Chairman (and JVC Vice President)

36

6.7.3   Director

6.7.4   Chief Engineer

7.8   The Management Committee, with the approval of the Board of Directors, shall appoint a Manager and Deputy Manager for the Factory.

7.9   The Manager shall be nominated by YR and the Deputy Manager shall be nominated by CD.

7.10   The first managers, to serve for two years from the commencement of operations of the JVC, shall be:

Weng Tai   Manager

Tai Fook   Deputy Manager

7.11   The Manager and Deputy Manager shall be skilled in supervision and management of a factory established for production of candies, and they shall serve full-time at the location of the Factory.

7.12   Compensation and other terms of employment for the Manager and Deputy Manager shall be fixed by the Board of Directors.

7.13   The Manager shall be responsible for the design and layout of the Factory, the day-to-day management of the Factory, and, subject to overall supervision by the Management Committee, the management of the Factory, equipment, staff and workers employed in the Factory.

7.14   The Manager shall also be responsible for establishing and supervising procedures for quality control and production standards, and such other duties as may be specified by the Management Committee.

7.15   The JVC shall bear the full costs of the Manager, including his salary, suitable housing for him and his family, full-time services of a qualified interpreter / translator, automobile, round trip business class air fare between Hong Kong and the Factory in the Territory, and reasonable moving costs for him and his family to and from the Factory.

7.16   The Manager shall be entitled to six(6) weeks annual paid home leave for himself and his family with the cost of business class air fare to and from the Factory to be paid by the JVC.

7.17   **YR shall have the right at any time, upon thirty (30) days written notice to the Board of Directors, to recall the Manager, provided that YR shall have provided a qualified replacement prior to the departure of the said Manager.**

Article 8:   Technology and Know-How

8.1   The JVC may request YR to render to it Technology and Know-How for the operation of the Factory , through consultations at the JVC office at Blue River, at the Factory, or by correspondence or other means, or through visitation by JVC technical personnel at YR facilities in Japan or elsewhere, or through the assignment of one or several YR technical experts to locations in the Territory.

8.2 YR shall be entitled to a fee for Technology and Know-How rendered by it or its personnel to the JVC at an established mutually agreed rate in H.K. Dollars per man-day.

8.3 The JVC shall reimburse to YR the reasonably necessary travel and living expenses of such personnel for the period during which such assistance is being rendered.

8.4 In the event that the compensation derived by technical experts and other persons temporarily assigned by YR to the JVC to impart Technology and Know-How is subject to individual income taxes in the People's Republic of China, such amounts shall be reimbursed to those persons by the JVC.

8.5 CD shall assist YR or non-Chinese JVC personnel to comply with all Chinese Government visa, travel permit and work permit formalities and other local laws and regulations, but all costs for transportation and lodging shall be borne by CD or the JVC, each for its own personnel.

8.6 YR shall assist CD and Chinese JVC personnel travelling to JAPAN with respect to visa requirements, and will assist in obtaining lodging and transportation in JAPAN for such personnel, but the cost of transportation to and within the country, and lodging shall be borne by CD or the JVC, each for its own personnel.

8.7 Technology and Know-How disclosed by YR to CD or the JVC shall at all times remain the property of YR and shall not be disclosed by CD, the Factory or the JVC, or any of their personnel, to third parties, and CD, the JVC and the Factory shall abide by such safeguards against unauthorized disclosure as YR may reasonably require.

Article 9: Supply of Equipment and Raw Material to and Purchase of Local Components by the JVC

9.1 CD and YR shall enter into an Equipment and Raw Material Supply Agreement with the JVC setting forth the general policy, and the terms and conditions, under which the JVC will purchase or lease certain equipment form either party necessary for the Factory.

9.2 YR and CD undertake to cause their respective Boards of Directors, subject to governmental approvals, if any required, to execute the Equipment and Raw Material Supply Agreement upon the approval of this Agreement and its Appendices by the relevant authorities in the Territory.

9.3 The JVC shall be encouraged to procure domestically in the Territory the machinery, equipment, components, parts, raw material, technical information, assistance or services from parties other than YR, provided such procurement does not jeopardize the achievement or maintenance of the quality standards required in the operation of the Factory of the production of the JOB.

Article 10: Operation of the Joint Venture

10.1 Upon the approval by the relevant authorities in the Territory of the Joint Venture Agreement, including the Articles of Association and By-Laws, Company Operating Procedures, and other Appendices, the JVC will establish an office at CD for the following purposes:

10.1.1 To prepare such advertising, marketing or other information as may be necessary or desirable to inform customers and other third parties about the availability of the JOB from the JVC; and

10.1.2 To establish a plan for the preparation of Feasibility Studies or marketing and distribution proposals in response to orders or inquiries from third parties in or outside the territory for the JOB; and

10.1.3 To develop further Feasibility Studies for production of new confectionery products in the Territory.

10.2 Upon the agreement that an economically viable market for the JOB exists in and outside the Territory, the JVC shall commence operations in accordance with this Agreement and the Company Operating Procedures.

Article 11: Use of Land, Equipment, Technology

11.1 The real property, buildings, equipment, Technology and Know-How, and other items to be supplied by CD and YR shall be used by the JVC and the Factory only in the performance of this Agreement.

11.2 To minimize start-up costs of the JVC, facilities and equipment may be initially leased at mutually agreed rates from the parties, or from third parties.

11.3 The ownership and title to each of the items listed in this Article 10 shall at all times remain with the party providing the same.

11.4 In the future it may be mutually agreed that the JVC will construct, develop or purchase such real property, buildings, equipment, Technology and Know-How, and other items, such investment by the JVC being contingent on economic studies of future business conditions and the relevant laws and regulations of the Territory.

Article 12: Mutual Exclusivity

12.1 CD and YR agree that neither will undertake to establish individually nor with other parties any other joint venture, co-production or similar enterprise for the production of the JOB in the Territory.

Article 13: Performance by Subsidiaries or Affiliates

13.1 Equipment, services or other items to be provided by YR to the JVC may be provided by YR or an affiliated or subsidiary company of YR

13.2 Equipment, services or other items to be provided by CD to the JVC may be provided by CD or an affiliated or subsidiary company of CD.

Article 14: Term

14.1 The term of the JVC shall be Twenty (20) years, commencing on the date of approval of this Joint Venture Agreement and its Appendices, by the appropriate government authorities of the Territory.

14.2 The term of the JVC may be renewed by the mutual agreement of the parties hereto, subject to approval of the appropriate authorities of the Territory.

14.3 Either party may, for any reason, give notice of termination of this Agreement or the JVC at any time upon 100 days notice to the other party.

14.4 Upon termination under this Article, YR shall be entitled to reimbursement of its costs hereunder, and any profits due, in Pound Sterling.

Article 15: Arbitration

15.1 All disputes of any kind arising out of or in relation to this Agreement, including the existence or continued existence of this Agreement, which cannot be settled by the parties, shall be submitted to arbitration.

Article 16: Force Majeure

16.1 If the conditions of Force Majeure shall prevail for a period in excess of nine (9) months, then either party, or either Member of the JVC, may cancel this Agreement, the JVC, and all other related agreements, by notice by registered airmail to the other party without any other formality.

16.2 The party claiming Force Majeure shall promptly inform the other affected party or parties and shall furnish appropriate proof of the occurrence and duration of such Force Majeure.

Article 17: Taxes and Duties

17.1 The JVC shall be subject to the Joint Venture Income Tax Law of the Territiory as presently in effect.

17.2 The JVC shall reimburse to personnel of YR such amounts, if any, as such personnel may be required to pay as personal income taxes in the Territory for JVC or other income received under this Agreement.

17.3 The JVC shall reimburse to personnel of CD such amounts, if any, as such personnel may be required to pay as personal income taxes in the Territory for JVC or other income received under this Agreement.

17.4 The JVC shall, with the assistance of CD, apply to the relevant authorities of the Territory for exemption of all import duties or similar charges on equipment, supplies or raw materials imported by or through YR, or the JVC, for the JVC for use in the Factory or otherwise in connection with this Agreement. To the extent such exemptions are not obtained on such equipment supplied by or through YR, such duties or similar charges, if any, imposed on YR shall be reimbursed to YR by the JVC.

17.5 CD shall assist the JVC in making such applications to the relevant authorities of the Territory to obtain the maximum tax exemptions for the JVC as are permitted under the Joint Venture Law and the Joint Venture Income Tax Law.

17.6 To the extent, if any, that YR or the JVC office in the Territory are subject to the Foreign Enterprise Income Tax Law of the Territory, the JVC shall be responsible for reimbursement or payment of such taxes as the case rnay be.

Article 18 :   Labour Relations

18.1 The JVC shall establish all terms and conditions of employment, including wages and benefits, or management, staff members and workers of the JVC, including terms and conditions of employemnt of persons employed in or for the Factory.

18.2 In establishing terms and conditions of employment of management, staff and workers of the JVC, the JVC shall be guided, but not bound, by the provisions of the Labour Management Regulations for Joint Ventures in the Territory as presently in effect.

Article 19:   Trade Marks

19.1 All trade marks, service marks or copyrighted material properly registered by YR or any of its subsidiaries or affiliates anywhere in the work shall at all times remain the sole property of YR or such subsidiaries or affiliates.

19.2 Any disputes under sub-Article 19.1 are not subject to arbitration and shall be resolved solely YR in its own discretion.

19.3 The trade marks or service marks of the JOB shall be owned and registered by the JVC and, upon termination of the JVC, such trademarks or service marks shall be owned by CD.

19.4 If after the termination of the JVC, CD or any other entity continues to manufacturer the JOB, CD or such entity shall pay to YR a royalty of 10% of the wholesale selling price of the JOB for a period of 20 years.

Article 20:   Miscellaneous Provisions

20.1 Waiver.   Failure or delay on the part of either party hereto to exercise any right, power or privilege hereunder, or under any other agreement relating thereto, shall not operate as a waiver thereof; nor shall any single or partial exercise of any right, power or privilege preclude any other future exercise thereof.

20.2 Assignability.   Subject to Article 2.4, 2.6, 12.1 and 12.2 hereof, this Agreement may not be assigned in whole or in part by any party without the prior written consent of the other party hereto.

20.3 Binding Effect.   This Agreement is made for the benefit ot YR and CD and may be enforced by either of them. This Agreement may not be changed orally, but only by a written instrument signed by CD and YR and approved, if required, by the relevant authorities in the Territory.

20.4 Severability.   The invalidity of any provision of this Agreement shall not affect the validity of any other provision.

20.5 Language.   The Agreement is executed in English language original and a Chinese language translation thereof.

20.6 Entire Agreement.   The Agreement and the Appendices 1 & 2 hereto constitute the entire agreement and only understanding of and between CD and YR with respect to the subject matter hereof and supercedes all prior discussions, negotiations and agreements between them.

20.7 Notices.   Any notice or written communicaion provided for herein by either party to the other, including but not limited to any and all offers, writings, or notices to be given hereunder, shall be made by telegram or telex, and confirmed by registered airmail letter, property transmitted or addressed to the appropriate party. The date of receipt of a notice or communication hereunder shall be deemed to be twelve (12) days after its postmark in the case of an airmail letter and two (2) working days after dispatch in the case of a telegram or telex. All notices and communications shall be sent to the address hereinbelow set forth, until the same are changed by notice given in writing to the other party or the Members, as the case may be:

CD:

_____

_____
Telex No.: _____

YR:

_____

_____
Telex No.: _____

Article 21:   APPENDICES

21.1 The Appendices attached hereto are hereby made an integral part hereof. The Appendices are as follows:

   (a)   Articles of Association of Yellow River China Candy Corporation. (Appendix A)

   (b)   By-Laws of Yellow River China Candy Corporation. (Appendix B)

IN WITNESS WHEREOF, each of the parties hereto have caused this Agreement to be executed in three (3) counterparts on its behalf, and its corporate seal, if any, to be hereto affixed by its duly authorized officer as of the date hereinabove provided.

China Dragon Construction Corporation

By: _____

Title: _____

Yellow River Confectionery Company (China) Limited

By: _____

Title: _____

ARTICLES OF ASSOCIATION
OF THE YELLOW RIVER
CHINA CANDY CORPORATION

Article 1:   Name

1.1   The name of the Corporation is Yellow River China Candy Corporation.

Article 2:   Location of Registered Office

2.1   The registered office of the Corporation will be located in Yellow River, Dragon Province, People's Republic of China.

Article 3:   Duration

3.1   The Corporation is established for a period of Twenty (20) years from the date upon which the Corporation is licensed to do business by the General Administration for Industry and Commerce of the People's Republic of China.

3.2   The existence of the Corporation may be extended upon agreement of its Members and the approval of the relevant authorities of the People's Republic of China.

Article 4:   Status and Nature of the Corporation

4.1   The Corporation is a limited liability company established pursuant to the Law of the People's Republic of China on Joint Ventures Using Chinese and Foreign Investment of July 1, 1979, and the Regulations thereunder, as presently in effect.

4.2   The Members of the Corporation are Yellow River Confectionery Company (China) Limited, ("YR"), a corporation organized and existing under the laws of Japan, and the China Dragon Construction Corporation ("CD"), organized and existing under the laws of the People's Republic of China.

Article 5:   Objects of the Corporation

5.1   To produce candies for sale within and outside of the People's Republic of China.

5.2   To establish production facilities in the People's Republic of China for the production of candies including:

    5.2.1   Conceptual design, layout and detailed engineering of production facilities;

    5.2.2   To undertake marketing, advertising and sales of candies manufactured in the production facilities.

5.2.3 To do all such other things as may be necessary, incidental or conducive to the above objects, consist with the laws and regulations of the People's Republic of China.

Article 6:   Limitation of Liability

6.1 The Members have no liability for the debts or obligations of the Corporation.

Article 7:   Registered Capital

7.1 The Members shall contribute investments in the registered capital of the Corporation, and share in the profits (or losses) of the Corporation, in the following proportions:

7.1.1   CD——50%

7.1.2   YR——50%

7.2 Investments by the Members to the registered capital of the Corporation may be in the form of cash, capital goods, industrial property rights, or otherwise.

7.3 The initial investments of the Members shall be made as follows within 60 days after the Corporation is licensed to do business:

7.3.1   CD   :Cash RMB: 10,000,000.00

7.3.2   YR   :Cash US: 7,000,000.00

These Articles are hereby agreed to on this 10th day of November, 1983, by the following Members:

China Dragon Construction Corporation

By: ___Signed_____
(Signature)

_____
(Name)

_____
(Title)

Yellow River Confectionery Company
(China) Limited

By: __Signed_____
(Signature)

_____
(Name)

_____
(Title)

BY-LAWS OF THE YELLOW RIVER
CHINA CANDY CORPORATION

Article 1: Offices

1.1 The principal office of the Corporation shall be in the City of Yellow River, Dragon Province, People's Republic of China.

1.2 The Corporation may also establish offices at such other places as the Board of Directors may from time to time determine.

Article 2: Meetings of Members

2.1 All Meetings of Members shall be held at such places as Board of Directors may determine.

2.2 An Annual Meeting of Members shall be held in the City of Yellow River during the month of May at a time and place to be determined by the Board of Directors.

2.3 Special Meetings of Members may be called either by the Chairman or the Vice Chairman of the Board of Directors.

2.4 Notice of the date, time and place of any meeting of Members shall given by cable or telex to Members at the addresses provided at Article 11 of these By-Laws at least ten (10) days prior to such meeting.

2.5 A representative of each Member present at any meeting shall constitute a quorum.

2.6 The Chairman of the Board of Directors shall preside at all meetings of Members.

Article 3: Board of Directors

3.1 Unless and until otherwise resolved by resolution of the Members, there shall be five Directors of the Corporation.

3.2 China Dragon Construction Corporation ("CD") shall appoint three Directors, one of whom shall be named Chairman of the Board of Director.

3.3 Yellow River Confectionery Company (China) Limited ("YR") shall appoint two Directors, one of whom shall be named Vice Chairman of the Board of Directors.

3.4 Directors shall serve until replaced by the Member appointing them, and either Member may remove and replace a Director at any time.

Article 4: Powers and Duties of Board of Directors

4.1 The Management of all the affairs, property and interest of the Corporation shall be vested in the Board of Directors.

4.2 In addition to the powers and authorities conferred by the Articles of Association and these By-Laws, the Board of Directors shall exercise all powers of the Corporation and do all things as are not prohibited by law.

4.3 Regular or special meetings of the Board of Directors may be held upon notice to all Directors at the principal offices of the Corporation or at such other place as the Directors may designate.

4.4 Meetings of the Board of Directors may be called by the Chairman or the Vice Chairman.

4.5 The presence of at least four Directors is necessary to constitute a quorum for the transaction of business.

4.6 The Chairman of the Board or, in his absence, the Vice Chairman, shall preside at all meetings of Directors.

4.7 No salary or other·compensation shall be paid to Directors, as such, for their services but, by resolution of the Board of Directors, a fixed sum and expenses of attendance, if any, may be allowed for attendance at each regular or special meeting of the Board of directors; provided, that nothing herein contained shall be construed to preclude any Director from securing the Corporation in any other capacity and receiving compensation therefor.

Article 5: Officers

5.1 The Officers of the Corporation shall be a President, one or more Vice Presidents, a Secretary and a Treasurer.

5.2 Officers shall be elected by the Board of Directors for terms determined by the Board of Directors.

5.3 The Board of Directors shall fill vacancies among the officers occurring by death, resignation or removal promptly after such vacancies occur.

5.4 The President shall be the Chief Executive Officer of the Corporation and shall have general supervision of the affairs of the Corporation, shall sign or countersign all certificates, contracts, and other instruments of the Corporation as authorized by the Board of Directors, and perform all such other duties as are incident to his office or as are properly required of him by the Board of Directors.

5.5 Each Vice President shall have such powers or discharge such duties as may be assigned to him from time to time by the Board of Directors. During the absence or disability of the President, the Vice Presidents, in the order designated by the Board of Directors, shall exercise all the functions of the President.

5.6 The Secretary shall issue notices of all meetings, keep minutes of all meetings, shall have charge of the seal and the corporate books, and shall make such reports or perform other duties as may be properly required of him by the Board of Directors.

5.7 The Treasurer shall have the custody of all moneys and securities of the Corporation, and shall keep regular books of account. He shall disburse the funds of the Corporation in payment of the just demands of the Corporation, or as may be ordered by the Board of Directors, taking proper vouchers for such disbursements. He shall render to the Board of Directors from time to time as may be required of him an account of all his transactions as Treasurer and of the financial condition of the Corporation. He shall perform all duties incident to his office, or as are properly required of him by the Board of Directors.

5.8 The Board of Directors may appoint such other officers or agents as it shall deem necessary, who shall hold their offices for such terms, and shall exercise such powers and perform such duties, as shall be determined by the Board of Directors.

5.9 The salaries of all officers and agents of the Corporation shall be fixed by the Board of Directors.

Article 6: Books and Records of the Corporation

6.1 The books, accounts and records of the Corporation shall be kept, in the English and Chinese languages, at such place or places as the Board of Directors may from time to time appointed.

6.2 The books, accounts and records of the Corporation shall be open for inspection by either member or its authorized representative at any reasonable time.

6.3 The Board of Directors shall, by unanimous vote, appoint outside auditors for the Corporation, requesting such auditors to provide semi-annual audited statements, according to accepted international practices, on the financial condition of the Corporation.

6.4 Either Member of the Corporation may at any time and at the expense of the Corporation request and obtain an independent audit of the financial records or books of account of the Corporation and, upon receipt of such request the Corporation shall afford all reasonable facilities and disclose all relevant information in its possession to such Member or the persons appointed by it to make such audit.

Article 7: Fiscal Year

7.1 The fiscal year of the Corporation shall be the calendar year.

Article 8: Bank Account

8.1 The Corporation shall open an account with, and conduct its banking business principally with, the Bank of China.

Article 9: Distribution of Profits

9.1 After deduction of expenses and payment of taxes, profits of the

Corporation shall be distributed to the Members as follows:

To CD   :50%

To YR   :50%

Article 10:   Disputes

10.1 In the event of any dispute arising between the Members, or among the Board of Directors, which cannot in the opinion of any party be resolved through friendly consultation, any party may refer the matter to arbitration, in Hong Kong. The Appointing Authority for the arbitration shall be the China Arbitration Association, and the arbitration shall be conducted in both Chinese and English language.

Article 11:   Notices

11.1 Notices requires or permitted to be given hereunder shall be given personally in writing or by telex to the Members at the following addresses:

To CD:
Address:

To YR:
Address:

Article 12:   Seal

12.1 The Company Seal of the Corporation shall be designed in a manner approved by the Board of Directors, and shall contain the name of the Corporation and the words "Company Seal", all in the English and Chinese language.

Article 13:   Amendments

13.1 Amendments to these By-Laws may be made by unanimous vote of the Board of Directors or otherwise in accordance with the applicable laws and regulations of the Poeple's Republic of China.

SUPPLY HEAVY INDUSTRIAL MACHINERY TO CHINA

MEMORANDUM OF AGREEMENT made this _____ day of 19 _____
between _____
whose principal address is situate at _____

(hereinafter referred to as "the Chinese Organization", which expression shall, where the contexts admits, include the Chinese Organization's associated companies, subsidaries, branch offices, agents or representatives in business as the case may be) of the one part and _____
_____ whose principal address is situate at _____

(hereinafter referred to as "Investor", which expression shall, where the contexts admits, include the Investor's associated companies, subsidaries, branch offices, agents or representatives in business as the case may be) of the other part _____

Witnesseth:
WHEREAS, the Chinese Organization intends Investor to supply — the plant to by supplied by the investor (author) — to the Chinese Organization and have it located on premises owned by the Chinese Organization at — address (author) —; and _____

WHEREAS, Investor represents that it is capable to supply the plant as well as equipment and services to Chinese Organization; and _____

WHEREAS, both parties possess adequate and sufficient authority to enter into this agreement;
NOW, THEREFORE, in consideration of respective undertakings and covenants hereinunder set forth, both parties agree as follows:

Article 1 — Definitions

1.1   Unless the terms or context of this agreement otherwise provides, the following words and expressions shall have the meanings assigned to them.

1.2   "Civil Engineering" shall mean the architectural and civil construction of subfoundations, foundations, buildings, structures, general facilities, temporary construction facilities, and site grading.

1.3   "Agreement" shall mean this document.

1.4 "Contract Date" shall mean Contract Date and Starting Date as stipulated in Article 33.

1.5 "Contractor's Equipment" shall mean all construction, installation, and testing equipment, appliances, materials, tools, facilities, and all other materials that are necessary to the performance of the Investor's scope of undertakings.

1.6 "Electrical Output" shall mean the measured gross electrical power from the generator terminals.

1.7 "Equipment" shall mean machinery, apparatus, and components that will become a permanent part of the Plant to be provided by Investor.

1.8 "Ex Ship" shall be defined and construed in accordance with the provisions of " _____ ".

1.9 "Factory" shall mean the applicable place of manufacture or supply of Investor.

1.10 "Factory Test" shall mean those tests normally performed at the Factory.

1.11 "Field Engineer(s)" means those Investor's. Personnel appointed by ____ to provide technical direction of installation under this Agreement.

1.12 "Plant" shall mean the extension to the electric generating station known as _____ , as described in the Agreement.

1.13 "Government Authorizations" means any and all authorizations, rulings, licenses or other approvals, sanctions, or exemptions required or permitted to be obtained from any governmental body under or in connection with this Agreement.

1.14 "Loan and Return Equipment" shall mean the Investor equipment loaned to the Chinese Organization, which shall be returned to Investor at point of origin. Title shall at all times remain with Investor.

1.15 "Major Component of Equipment" shall mean — list of articles the Investor prepares to supply.

1.16 "Man-month" shall mean the services of one (1) man for one (1) calendar month.

1.17 "Operator" or "Plant Operator" or "Plant Service Operator" or "Installation Operator" means the Chinese Organization or Operator of the Plant.

1.18 "Overtime" means any time of performance in excess of eight ( ) hours a day or (_____) hours a week.

1.19 "The Laws" shall mean the laws of the People's Republic of China related to technology transfer, joint venture and foreign investments as well as other relevant regulations and rules announced by the provincial government where the joint venture is situated.

1.20 "Customs Duties" shall mean the Customs Laws of the People's Republic of China promuglated by the 19th Session of the Standing Committee of the 6th National People's Congress on January 22, 1987 as well as the Import and Export Tariff of People's Republic of China enforced on March 10, 1985.

Article 2 - The Work

2.1 Investor's Duties
Investor shall design and provide the manufacture and supply of the Equipment items.
Investor shall also provide Supervision of Installation for such Equipment and appropriate data relative to the Equipment for Plant design, installation, operation and maintenance.

2.2 Chinese Organization's Duties
In support of Investor's duties, Chinese Organization shall provide the items as required by the Investor to accomplish the purpose of this contract.
Chinese Organization shall provide Investor and its employees and representatives with all custom clearances, visas, foreign exchange permits and any other Governmental Authorizations required within China by Investor in connection with the performance of the Investor's duties.

2.3 Plant Site
Chinese Organization shall provide Investor all site information as required by Investor for the design and supply of the Work no later than (_____) days following the Contract Date. Chinese Organization shall consult with Investor concerning site information needed by Investor. This information will be comprised of results of researches and surveys.

2.4 Plant Installation
Based on the above information for the design of the Works, and prior to scheduled initiation of foundation excavation, the Chinese Organization shall notify Investor in writing that the Site, in the opinion of the appropriate Regulatory Agency, is adequately safe for installation of the Plant. Sole responsibility for selection of the Site and the direct and indirect consequences of such selection rests with the Chinese Organization.

2.5 Plant Construction Petmit
The Chinese Organization shall also provide to Investor copies of the results of all investigations, surveys, reports, and other information developed by The Chinese Organization for purposes of obtaining licenses and permits for engineering and construction of the plant.

2.6 Obligations.

The performance by Investor of its obligations under this Contract is expressly made conditional upon the Chinese Organization performing its obligations under this Contract.

Article 3 - Delivery, Title, And Loss

3.1 Delivery shall occur and title and risk of loss or damage to each item of Equipment shall pass to the Chinese Organization Ex Ship port of entry, as defined in (NAME OF AN INTERNATIONAL SHIPPING CONVENTION — author). In the event of shipment by air, all the provisions of Ex Ship shall apply.

3.2 Within a reasonable time prior to the Equipment's arrival at port of entry, Investor shall notify the Chinese Organization of the location, type of Equipment and the approximate time of its arrival at port of entry.

3.3 If the Chinese Organization delays or fails to take delivery of any item of Equipment when ready, then Investor may place such Equipment into storage, and any demurrage, storage, insurance and / or other charges incident thereto shall be for the account of the Chinese Organization. In such event, delivery shall occur and title and risk of loss or damage to the Equipment shall pass to the Chinese Organization upon issuance of a warehouse receipt, but no later than Ex Ship port of entry.

3.4 Investor at its cost shall prepare Equipment for export shipment and shall adhere to packing requirements recognized by the export trade and shall use its best judgment regarding such packing.

Article 4 - Independent Contractor

4.1 Investor shall be an independent contractor in the performance of this Contract and shall have complete charge of the personnel engaged in the performance of the Investor's duties. Investor shall perform its Scope in accordance with its own methods and have complete authority to direct and control its performance under the Contract without restraint or interference by others.

4.2 The Equipment shall be designed and manufactured in accordance with Investor standard practice, or where Equipment is not manufactured by Investor, in accordance with normal practice of the manufacturer, as approved by Investor.

Article 5 - Price Adjustment

5.1 A Provisional Price adjustment shall be made at the end of each month following the Base Month. This adjustment shall be calculated as above, using provisional indices as determined by Investor. Revisions to all provisional adjustments, if any, shall be made at the time final indices are published.

5.2 In the event of any change in the requirements of the Contract resulting in a change in the price, the price change that is quoted shall be considered as having been in effect during the Base Month for the purpose of this adjustment.

5.3 Should the specified indices be discontinued, or should the basis of their calculations be substantially modified, proper indices shall be substituted by mutual agreement of the parties. However, changes in the base year reporting basis, minor changes in weighting and minor changes in benchmarks shall not be construed as substantial modifications to the indices.

5.4 This adjustment shall apply to all payments due after the date the adjustment is made and evidenced in writing form Investor to the Chinese Organization.

Article 6 - Terms Of Payment

6.1 The Contract price (_____) shall be paid by the Chinese Organization promptly in — insert type of currency (author) —, subject to the conditions specified below.
   a. Portion of Contract Price Other Than Renminbi
      The Contract Price other than Renminbi (_____) shall be paid in monthly payments. Payments shall commence on the first day of the month following the Contract Date and shall continue on the same day of each month thereafter in accordance with the following schedule of payments:
   b. Renminbi Portion of the Contract Price
      The portion of the Contract Prices to be paid in Currency of the People's Repulic of China shall be paid in monthly payments. Payments shall commence on the day of the month following the Contract Date and shall continue on the day of month thereafter in accordance with the following schedule of payments:

6.2 Where items are for the account of the Chinese Organization and are not covered by the schedules of payments set forth herein, it is agreed that within thirty days of identifying the cost of those items, the Chinese Organization shall provide irrevocable Letters of Credit to cover the costs of those items. Said Letters of Credit shall provide for payment upon presentation of Investor invoices.

6.3 Conditions of Payment
   a. All payments due under this Contract shall be paid through irrevocable Letters of Credit upon presentation of Investor invoices

in accordance with the schedules of payment and other terms set forth herein. Said Letters of Credit shall cover the price, plus the estimated price adjustment, plus any other amounts that Chinese Organization is due to reimburse Investor under the Contract, the content and form of which are in all respects satisfactory to Investor.

b.　All Letters of Credit shall remain in full force and effect until all payments due under this Contract have been made and shall provide for payment of termination charges that, in the event of termination of the Contract, shall be paid within (＿＿＿) days from receipt of an invoice signed by Investor stating that the Contract has been terminated in accordance with the provisions of Article 17 - Termination.

c.　Letters of Credit covering any — name of currency (author) — payments shall be confirmed by a U.S. bank acceptable to Investor, and Letters of Credit covering any People's Republic of China or third country payments shall be opened through a prime bank of the People's Republic of China or respective third party country acceptable to Investor.

d.　In the event there should be an increase or decrease in any portion of the Contract Price, such adjustments shall be made with the next scheduled payment to make appropriate corrections for all past under and overpayments. If changes are required to any existing Letters of Credit, such changes shall be made promptly.

e.　All amounts payable herein shall be paid without deduction or retention.

f.　All expenses in connection with the establishment and operation of the Letters of Credit, as well as any other bank charges incurred in making payment to Investor, shall be for the account of the Chinese Organization.

6.4　If payments made by the Chinese Organization under this Article are received after the scheduled receipt date because of causes not attributable to Investor, an amount equal to (＿＿＿) of any foreign Bank prime rate times the payment due plus an additional (＿＿＿) of the payment due shall be for the account of the Chinese Organization each month the payment is late.

6.5　The Chinese Organization shall obtain the necessary authorizations for Investor and its employees to be entitled to the most favourable currency exchange rate between the —name of foreign currency (author) — and Renminbi for the duration of this Contract. Also, such authorizations shall provide for freedom to repatriate any sums received in connection with this Contract.

Article 7 - Technical Direction Of Installation

7.1 Investor shall furnish the services of Field Engineers as specified in this Contract, to give Technical Direction to the Chinese Organization regarding methods and procedures for the installation of the Equipment, and in conducting the performance tests.

7.2 Definition

    a.   The terms Technical Direction of Installation and Technical Direction shall mean the engineering and technical recommendation and counsel furnished by Investor based upon current engineering, manufacturing, installation and operating standards for the Equipment. Technical Direction of Installation and Technical Direction exclude all supervision, management regulation, arbitration and / or measurement of the Chinese Organization's personnel, agents or contractors and work related thereto, and it does not include responsibility for planning, scheduling, monitoring or management of the Work.

    b.   Investor shall not be liable for any loss or injury to persons or property (including the Equipment being installed or maintained) caused, in whole or in part, by acts of the Chinese Organization personnel or acts of the Chinese Organization's subcontractors; and the Chinese Organization agrees to save Investor harmless from any such liability.

7.3 Technical Direction services provided by Investor, in addition to those specified in this Contract, shall be added to Investor's duty at Investor's rates, and terms and conditions in effect at the time the service is performed under the following circumstances, and in accordance with provisions of Article 8 - Revisions and Extra Work.

    a.   If the work schedule requires overtime Technical Direction, i.e., during other than the Standard Work Week; or

    b.   If the work schedule is interrupted or extended, or accelerated, so as not to correspond to the schedule set forth in the Contract; or

    c.   If the Chinese Organization labour force performing the work on the Equipment is not of adequate size and / or composition; or

    d.   If other services of a Field Engineer not specifically provided for in this Contract are required; or

    e.   If it is otherwise reasonably determined by either the Chinese Organization or Investor that additional Technical Direction will be necessary to enhance the proper installation and testing of the Equipment.

7.4 Schedule

    a.   The period of Technical Direction of Installation at the Site shall commence on the date agreed upon by the parties and shall continue until the date upon which Investor gives the Chinese Organization notice that the Technical Direction is complete.

b. The Chinese Organization shall consult with Investor before scheduling any installation work and shall afford Investor reasonable opportunity to perform the services specified herein.

Article 8 - Revisions And Extra Work

8.1 The Chinese Organization and Investor recognize that as of the date of the Contract the detailed design of the Plant will not have been finalized and that revisions to the work may be found necessary or desirable as the design is developed througout the course of the Contract.

8.2 The Chinese Organization may propose revisions in the investor's duties and extra work as provided below:

a. If revisions in the Investor's duties are necessary to comply with changes in the requirements of Governmental Authorities or are caused by the discovery during the performance of the Work of Site conditions or other conditions requiring such revisions.

b. The Chinese Organization may request Investor to make revisions in the Investor's duties. Investor shall have the right to review and comment on any such requests, Investor shall notify the Chinese Organization of the advisability of such requested revisions. Investor may reject any proposed revision that would, in the sole opinion of Investor, adversely affect the safety or operability of the Equipment or the warranties specified in this Contract.

c. If, in the opinion of Investor, revision arising pursuant to Articles 8.2a and 8.2b above, increase the costs of or adversely affect any condition of the Contract, Investor shall so notify the Chinese Organization, specifying the necessary adjustments to the Contract Price and other pertinent provisions of this Contract.

8.3 Investor Revisions

a. Investor may make revisions in the work without changing the Contract Price if such revisions will not adversely affect the technical soundness or the safety of the Plant, the warranties contained in the Contract or the Delivery Schedule or the Chinese Organization's duties.

b. Investor may propose revisions in the Work that increase or decrease the Contract Price or affect other pertinent provisions of the Contract, in accordance with Article 8.4 below.

8.4 All changes to this Contract shall be implemented by a fully executed written change order in form and substance acceptable to Investor, and shall indicate adjustments to the Investor's duties, the Contract Price, the Project Schedule, the Contract warranties, and other relevant terms and conditions of this Contract.

Article 9 Quality.

9.1 Investor shall conduct a Quality Control Program including all tests and inspections of the Equipment at the factory in relation to goods and services supplied by Investor under this Contract and shall have sole authority with respect to implementing such Quality Control Program. This Quality Control Program will encompass the design, procurement, manufacture, and Technical Direction of Installation of the Equipment.

9.2 The tests and inspections for the Equipment shall be the standard commercial tests and inspections generally employed by Investor.

9.3 Investor shall, upon receipt of the Chinese Organization's (_____) week advance written request, admit personnel of the Chinese Organization to observe such standard Factory Tests and inspections of such Equipment as shall be mutually agreed upon by Investor and the Chinese Organization to be major Equipment, insofar as they are permitted to do so by Governmental Authorities, of the ( ) Government, provided further that Proprietary Information shall not be disclosed thereby and that the Chinese Organization shall not disrupt normal Factory operations. Investor shall exert its best reasonable efforts to obtain similar rights of access and observation from its suppliers or subcontractors. Investor shall notify the Chinese Organization, within a reasonable time prior to the test date, of the place where the test is to be conducted. Should the Chinese Organization not be represented at the time of such tests or inspections, Investor may proceed therewith. The Chinese Organization shall have the right to request additional tests and inspections at reasonable times, provided any such additional tests and inspections shall be the suject of an advance written change order acceptable to Investor.

The costs of any such additional tests and inspections shall be payable by the Chinese Organization upon presentation of a Investor invoice therefor.

9.4 Investor will furnish to the Chinese Organization such certified inspection and post certificates as are normally made available by Investor.

Article 10 - Drawings And Documents

10.1 The Chinese Organization shall have the right to review and comment on the drawings and documents as provided by Investor.

10.2 The Chinese Organization comments shall be received by Investor within _____ days after transmittal by Investor to the Chinese Organization of the drawings listed below:

a. _____ .
b. _____ .
c. _____ .
d. _____ .
e. _____ .

10.3 With respect to the drawings and documents listed above, Investor response to comments submitted by the Chinese Organization, in accordance with this Section, shall specify one (1) of the followings:

a. That the comment is accepted for incorporation without changes to the Contract Price and schedule; or

b. That the comment is rejected and the reasons for such rejection; or

c. That resolution will require further discussion between the Chinese Organization and Investor.

10.4 Drawings and Documents for Information Purposes

The following drawings and documents shall be submitted to the Chinese Organization as they are issued for information purposes only.

a. _____ .
b. _____ .
c. _____ .
d. _____ .
e. _____ .

10.5 All submittals in accordance with this Article shall be transmitted with a covering letter.

Article 11 Justifiable Delay

11.1 Investor shall not be liable for any loss or damage due to delay in, or prevention of, the performance by Investor of its obligations under this Contract if such delay or prevention results from any cause beyond the reasonable control of Investor including, but not limited to:

a. Act of God, such as storm, flood, or earthquake; or

b. Civil disturbances, such as riots, revolutions, rebellion, or insurrections; or

c. Accidents or disruptions, such as fires or explosions; or

d. Major Equipment breakdowns not due to the fault or negligence of Investor; or

e. Faulty castings or forgings; or

f. Delays or accidents occurring in the course of transportation, acts, (including delay or failure to act) of third parties such as inland and ocean carriers, stevedores, or warehousemen; or

g. Labour difficulties, such as strikes, lockouts, factory shutdowns, or sabotage; or

h. Inability to obtain, or unforeseen shortages in, necessary labour (including shortage of suitable labour in China), materials, manufacturing facilities, or material from Investor's usual sources of supply, or shorter working hours imposed on Investor or its Subcontractors; or

i. Acts (including delay or failure to act) of the Chinese Organization or of its Subcontractors, agents, consultants, suppliers, or employees; or

j. Any acts, decrees, priorities, orders, or regulations of any governmental authority (federal, state, provincial or local) such as quarantines, embargoes, prohibition of trade, or any delay or failure by such governmental authority to issue any necessary license, permit, work permit, export, or import authorization, etc.; or

k. Any wars (declared or not), hostilities or invasions; or

l. Delays in delivery of materials or work from Subcontractors of Investor, or delays in deliveries of materials or works to such Subcontractors; or

m. Effects of energy shortage; or

n. Default of subcontractors employed in China.

11.2 In the event of delays resulting from any of the conditions specified in Article 11.1 above, the time schedule for delivery of the Investor's duties or any part thereof shall be extended for a period of time reflecting the effect of the justifiable delay. The Chinese Organization shall pay and indemnify Investor against any liability or expense incurred by Investor by reason of such excusable delay within thirty (30) days after receipt of Investor invoices. The investor invoices will be based on actual storage and other costs related to the justifiable delay, plus a monthly project continuation charge of $ _____ for month or part thereof to cover project overhead expenses.

11.3 The Chinese Organization shall reimburse Investor for any liabilities and costs incurred in efforts to recover any time lost in the project schedule resulting from any of the causes set forth in this Article, provided that the attempt to recover such time is requested by the Chinese Organization.

Article 12 - Suspensions And Extensions

12.1 The Chinese Organization shall have the right to suspend the Work upon (_____) days written notice to Investor, if

a. The Work may be deemed extended or suspended at the option of the Investor in the event the Chinese Organization is delayed due to acts or omissions of any occurrence of justifiable delay as defined in Article 11 - Justifiable Delay.

b. The Work may be extended or suspended at the option of Investor in the event that the Chinese Organization payments are not made when due, as defined in Article 6 - Terms of Payment.

12.2 The time schedule shall be extended by periods of time reflecting the effect of the suspensions or extensions. The Chinese Organization shall pay and indemnify Investor against any liability or expense incurred by Investor by reason of such suspension or extension within (_____) days after receipt of Investor invoices. Investor invoices shall be based on actual storage and other charges related to the suspension or extension and at the prevailing rates, terms, and conditions for Field Engineers.

12.3 In the event that any cause for suspension is not removed and Investor does not receive written notice to resume work within (_____) days after the date of any suspension hereunder, or if suspensions exceed in the aggregate, a total of (_____) months, Investor may terminate this Contract, and the provision of Article 13 Termination, shall apply.

Article 13 - Termination

13.1 Termination by The Chinese Organization
In the event that:
a. Investor shall go into liquidation or shall cease to carry on its business; or
b. Investor commits a substantial breach of its undertaking hereunder so as to prevent Completion of the Investor's duties under this Contract and thereafter shall fail (on not less than (_____) days written notice from the Chinese Organization to that effect) to take steps to remedy such breach;
Then the Chinese Organization may, by written notice, terminate this Contract and thereupon may take over the Work and prosecute same to completion, by contract or otherwise, and require Investor to cease and desist from further Work. In the event of such termination, the Chinese Organization's recoveries shall be determined by mutual agreement, or if no agreement can be reached, then pursuant to the provisions of Article 18 - Arbitration.

13.2 Termination by Investor
In the event that:
a. shall go into liquidation or shall cease to carry on its business; or
b. shall commit a substantial breach of any of its undertakings hereunder so as to inhibit performance by Investor of its duties under this Contract and shall fail thereafter(on not less than (_____) days written notice from Investor to that effect) to take steps to remedy such breach; or
c. The Chinese Organization fails to pay to Investor any sum, when due, in accordance with this Contract; or

62

d.   Any event in Article 12 - Suspensions and Extensions, shall have subsisted for a consecutive period of (_____) days or for a total of (_____) months in the aggregate; or

e.   The lending institution suspends or cancels disbursements under or pursuant to the credit agreement between the Chinese Organization and the lending institution.

Then Investor may, without prejudice to any other remedy against the Chinese Organization, by written notice to the Chinese Organization, forthwith terminate the Contract, and the provisions of Article 12.4 and 12.5 below shall apply.

13.4 In the event of a termination under Article 13.2 above, Investor shall be entitled to be paid that portion of the Contract Price corresponding to Work done up to the date of such termination.

In addition, the Chinese Organization shall reimburse Investor any other costs which are reasonably incurred or committed by Investor at the date of such termination in contemplation of Contract performance, together with any costs reasonably incurred by Investor in relation to termination of the Work. A reasonable profit shall be included in the above reimbursable amounts.

13.5 Amounts due to Investor pursuant to Article 13.4 above shall be paid within (_____) days from receipt of Investor invoices.

Article 14 - Insurance And Indemnity

14.1 For the purpose of this Article, wherever the word Investor appears in quotation marks (" Investor ") it shall mean Investor's, its subsidiaries, assignees, and affiliated companies or divisions, as well as the employees and subcontractors, of any tier, of any of them.

14.2 Insurance Provided by Investor
The costs for premiums, deductibles and exclusions for insurances determined by Investor to be necessary as a consequence of doing business in the Chinese Organization's Country and Ocean Marine Insurance covering loss or damage to material and equipment on a warehouse-to-warehouse basis shall be reimbursed to Investor. The supply of such insurances shall not be construed to extend Investor liabilities under this Contract, and the Chinese Organization shall indemnify and hold Investor harmless from any costs or liabilities in excess of those specifically delineated in this Contract as Investor responsibility.

14.3 Insurance Provided by the Chinese Organization
The Chinese Organization shall provide, maintain and be responsible for premium payments for the following insurance and / or financial protection in a manner satisfactory to Investor.

(a)   All Risk Builder's Risk Insurance protecting the Work for its full replacement value against the risks of physical loss or damage, commencing from the agreed date of access to the Site and remaining in effect until all Investor obligations hereunder are fulfilled.

(b) Liability protection against bodily injury, including death resulting therefrom, and property damage to third parties that arise from actions of the Chinese Organization and / or its employees, subcontractors and suppliers. The Chinese Organization agrees to hold the Investor harmless from all claims and litigation costs resulting from bodily injury, including death resulting therefrom, and property damage that arises from actions by the Chinese Organization and / or its employees, subcontractors, and suppliers.

(c) The Insurance policies afford under Article 14.3 (a) and (b) above shall include the interests of "the Investor" as additional named insureds or beneficiaries. The Chinese Organization shall waive all of its rights of recourse against "the Investor" under the preceding insurance policies and shall secure from the companies providing the aforesaid insurance policies their agreement to waive their right to recourse or of subrogation against "Investor." All such waivers and insurances shall be in a form and amount acceptable to Investor.

(d) The Chinese Organization shall have its insurance carriers furnish Investor with certificates evidencing that all insurance required of the Chinese Organization under this Contract is in full force and effect and in form and content acceptable to the Investor.

(e) The Chinese Organization shall be responsible for all policy conditions, exclusions and deductibles under insurance protection provided by the Chinese Organization, pursuant to Paragraph C of this Article.

14.4 Indemnities

(a) The Chinese Organization shall be solely responsible for and shall indemnify and hold "Investor" harmless against any and all claims, including claims of intentional act, liabilities, or expenses, including expenses of litigation, that may occur to any persons or entity, whether or not based on any claim for any cause whatsoever on their part, for any bodily injury, including death resulting therefrom and any property damage including, but not limited to, damage to or loss of use of the Site, the Equipment, the Plant, or any part thereof.

(b) The Chinese Organization shall take such action as is necessary to assure that at all times the laws of China relating to the operations that do or may take place under this Contract or any contract in connection therewith stipulate that the Chinese Organization, not Investor, is the Operator of the Plant.

Article 15   Taxation

15.1 The Investor will assume the payment of all taxes, duties, tariffs, fees, imposts, excise, or other taxes assessed by any taxing authority in

(a) To the extent legally possible, the Chinese Organization shall obtain from the Government of China (or the government of any country through which the Equipment must pass), its subdivisions, agencies, or instrumentalities, of any level, a valid exemption on behalf of Investor and its non-PRC subcontractors from the payment of any and all corporate income taxes, gross receipts or business taxes, duties, tariffs, fees, levies, import deposits, imposts, stamp taxes, payroll taxes, social benefits, or other similar charges of any kind with respect to this Contract or the subject matter thereof. The same exemption from duties, tariffs, fees, levies, import deposits, imposts, stamp taxes and other similar charges shall also be obtained by the Chinese Organization on behalf of non-China employees of Investor, except that such non-China employees will still be liable for payment of any and all individual income taxes, and taxes and other charges on personal property and effects.

(b) To the extent such exemptions referred to abnove cannot be lawfully obtained or maintained for duration of the Contract. The Chinese Organization hereby agrees to pay such taxes and other charges so that the obligations thereby imposed are fully satisfied.

(c) The Chinese Organization further agrees to pay to Investor any amounts paid or to be paid by non-China employees of Investor for China individual income taxes, personal property taxes, occupation taxes or other similar charges. In the event Investor, or any employee or non-China subcontractor employed by Investor is required to remit such charges directly to taxing authorities or other authorities, the Chinese Organization shall fully and promptly reimburse Investor or subcontractor for such remittances.

(d) If the Chinese Organization shall be required under the laws of any jurisdiction to withhold from any payment made to Investor any income taxes or other amounts referred to in Article 15.1 of this Article, then such payment shall be increased so that the net payment, after withholding the appropriate amount, shall be equal to the payment due Investor without regard to such amount.

(e) In the event the Chinese Organization pays directly to any authority any amounts referred to in Article 15.1 of this Article, than the Chinese Organization shall promptly provide to Investor or its subcontractors an original or duplicate original tax receipt and other appropriate receipts evidencing the payment of such amounts to tho appropriate authority.

65

Article 16   Patent Indemnity

16.1 Investor shall, at its expense, defend or, at its option, settle any claim, suit or proceeding brought against the Chinese Organization, so far as based on an allegation that any Equipment, or any part thereof furnished hereunder, or use thereof for its intended purpose, constitutes a direct or a contributory infringement of any claim of any letters of patent existing on the Contract Date of this Contract in China, so long as:

    (a)   There is a patent corresponding to such patent in China in force as of the Contract Date of this Contract;

    (b)   Said allegation of infringment would apply to such patent and set forth a cause of action for infringement under the laws of had the alleged infringement taken place in;

    (c)   The Chinese Organization shall have made all or substantially all payments then due hereunder; and

    (d)   Investor shall have been notified promptly in writing and given authority, information and assistance necessary or appropriate for the defense of said claim, suit, or proceeding.

16.2 In case the Equipment or any part thereof furnished hereunder becomes the subject of any claim, suit, or proceeding for infringement of any patent of China as hereinbefore qualified or, in the event of an adjudication that such Equipment or part infringes any such patent of China or, if the use or sale of such Equipment or part is enjoined, Investor shall at its option and its expense either:

    (a)   Procure for the Chinese Organization the right to continue using said Equipment or part thereof; or

    (b)   Replace it with noninfringing Equipment or part(s); or

    (c)   Modify it so it becomes noninfringing.

16.3 The foregoing indemnity does not apply to the following:

    (a)   Patented processes performed by or with the aid of the Equipment or with another product or equipment produced thereby.

    (b)   Equipment supplied according to a design other than that of Investor and that is required by the Chinese Organization.

    (c)   Combinations of the Equipment with other equipment not furnished hereunder, unless Investor is a contributory infringer.

    (d)   Any matter that is not a necessary consequence of the use of the Equipment as designed and constructed in accordance with this Contract.

    (e)   Any settlement of a claim, suit, or proceeding made without written consent from Investor.

        The foregoing states the entire liability of Investor with respect to patent infringement by said Equipment or any part thereof or use thereof for its intended purpose.

16.4 If a suit or proceeding is brought against Investor solely on account of activities enumerated in Article 16.3 above, the Chinese Organization agrees to indemnify Investor in the manner and to the extent Investor indemnifies the Chinese Organization in Article 16.3 above, insofar as the terms thereof are appropriate.

Article 17   Limitation Of Liability

17.1 Neither Investor, nor its subcontractors or suppliers shall be responsible to the Chinese Organization or to any third party, in contract, in tort or otherwise, for loss or damage sustained as a result of the operation of the Plant / Unit; loss or use; expenses involving costs of capital; claims of customers; loss of profits or revenues; cost of purchases or replacement power, including additional expenses incurred in using existing power facilites; or any other special, indirect, incidental or consequential loss or damage whatsoever.

The remedies of the Chinese Organization as set forth in this Contract are exclusive and the total liability of Investor with respect to any contract or anything done in connection therewith, such as the performance or breach thereof, or from the manufacture, sale, delivery, installation or Technical Direction of Installation, repair or use of any Equipment covered by or furnished under this Contract, whether in contract, in tort (including negligence), or otherwise, shall not exceed the price of the part of the Equipment on which such liability is based.

17.2 Notwithstanding any other provision of this Contract, the total cumulative liability of Investor arising from, or in any way connected with, the performance or breach of this Contract, whether in contract, in tort (including negligence) or otherwise, will not exceed an amount of percent (_____) of the Contract Price. In applying this limitation, any expenses incurred by Investor in the performance of remedies or payment to the Chinese Organization of liquidated damages, expenses for defense of patents, amounts of uninsured losses, and any work done by Investor under this Contract, valued at prevailing market prices for such work, shall be credited against Investor's total liability to the Chinese Organization.

17.3 In any event, Investor liability of any kind under this Contract will terminate upon the expiration of the warranty provisions contained in this Contract.

Article 18   Arbitration

18.1 Any dispute that arises as to the obligation of either party under this Contract or the interpretation of any provision thereof, if not settled by mutual agreement, shall, at the option of either party and upon written notice to the other party, be finally settled by arbitration under the Rules of Consiliation and Arbitration of the International Chamber of Commerce. Arbitration shall take place in   and shall be conducted in the _____ language. In any such arbitration there shall be appointed three (3) arbitrators, one (1) appointed by each of the parties and a third arbitrator who, unless selected by agreement between the other arbitrators within fifteen (15) days after the appointment of the second arbitrator, shall be appointed by the President of the International Chamber of Commerce. If either party fails to appoint an arbitrator within _____ days after notice for arbitration has been given, then such appointment shall also be made by the President of THE LAW SOCIETY OF ENGLAND AND WALES.

18.2 The dispute shall be submitted to the arbitrators in such manner as they deem appropriate; and the decision of the majority of the arbitrators, rendered in writing, shall be final and conclusive and binding on the parties; and the judgment upon such decision may be entered in any court of any country having jurisdiction.

18.3 Each party shall pay its own expenses in connection with the arbitration, but the compensation and expenses of the arbitrator shall be borne in such manner as may be specified in the decision of the arbitrators.

Article 19   Interpretation

19.1 The validity, construction, and interpretation of the terms and conditions this Contract, shall be in accordance with the laws of (_____) not including, however, its laws with respect to choice of conflict of laws.

Article 20   Laws of China

20.1 The Chinese Organization shall advise Investor how requirements of Chinese laws, decrees, codes or regulations affect Investor duties. If such requirements significantly affect Investor's duties, Investor shall notify the Chinese Organization and necessary modifications shall be made. Should Investor be charged with a failure to comply with any of Chinese laws, decrees, codes or regulations related to Investor's duties due to the Chinese Organization's failure to make same known to Investor in a timely manner, then the Chinese Organization shall hold Investor harmless from and indemnify Investor for any loss or damage as the result of such failure.

20.2 Enforceability in China

(a)   The Chinese Organization shall furnish, within _____ days after signature of this Contract, opinions of its legal counsel demonstrating to the satisfaction of Investor that this Contract, its terms and conditions, obligations and warranties, and other documents of legal significance related to the subject matter of this Contract are legal, valid, and enforceable under the laws of China.

(b)   If any approvals or registrations are necessary for the validity and enforceability of this Contract under the laws of China such approvals and / or registrations shall be obtained by the Chinese

Organization prior to furnishing the opinions under this Article.

Article 21   Assignment

21.1 Except as provided below, neither the Chinese Organization nor Investor shall assign this Contract in whole or in part without the prior written consent of the other Party, which consent shall not be unreasonably withheld. This Contract shall be binding upon and shall inure to the benefit of the legal representatives and successors of the Chinese Organization and Investor. Investor reserves the right to assign this Contract in whole or in part, to any subsidiary or affiliate of Investor; however, in such event Investor shall notify the Chinese Organization in writing of such assignment and remain bound as guarantor of the obligations thus assigned.

Article 22   Language And Notices

22.1 This Contract and any notices or other communications, whether written or oral, relating or pursuant to the performance of the Investor's duties shall be in the language.

22.2 All notices or other communications required or permitted to be given between the parties under this Contract shall be in writing and shall, unless otherwise specifically set forth herein, be deemed sufficiently given only when signed by a duly authorized representative of the transmitting party and delivered in person or when deposited in the mail, registered or certified, postage prepaid and addressed to the receiving party, as specified below. Each party shall designate a representative to receive all such communications from the other party, and shall specify the name and address of its representative on the Contract Date. Subsequent notice to change the representative and / or address shall be given as specified above.

Article 23 - This Agreement

23.1 This Contract contains the entire agreement and understanding between the Chinese Organization and Investor as to the subject matter of this Contract, and merges and supersedes all prior agreements, commitments, representations, writings, and discussions between them. Neither the Chinese Organization nor Investor will be bound by any prior obligations, conditions, warranties, or representations with respect to the subject matter of this Contract. This Contract may not be changed in any way except by an instrument in writing executed by both the Chinese Organization and Investor.

Article 24   Heading

24.1 The Article headings appearing in this Contract are for convenience of reference only and shall not control or affect in any way the scope, intent or interpretation of any of the provisions of this Contract.

Article 25   Proprietary Information

25.1 All of the information, know-how, drawings, designs, specifications, and other documents prepared by Investor that may be furnished to the Chinese Organization in accordance with the provisions of this Contract shall be deemed Proprietary Information. Such information, know-how, drawings, designs, specifications, and other documents will not be used by the Chinese Organization other than for construction, operation, or maintenance of the Plant without the prior written authorization of Investor and shall not be copied, published, or otherwise disclosed, in whole or in part, to others. All such drawings, designs, and specifications or other documents which may be furnished shall be returned to Investor upon request. Nothing in this Contract shall be deemed to create any obligation of Investor to furnish to the Chinese Organization or any other third party information that Investor considers to be of a proprietary nature.

Article 26   Contract Date And Starting Date

26.1 The Starting Date of this Contract shall be on the date when the last of all of the following events have occurred:

(a)   The Chinese Organization has established Letters of Credit in accordance with Article 6 - Terms of Payment.

(b)   The Chinese Organization has made initial payments to Investor in accordance with the provisions of Article 6 - Terms of Payment.

(c)   All licenses necessary for commencement of the Work have been obtained by the Chinese Organization for the performance of the Work.

(d)   Free access to the Site has been provided for Investor and its Personnel in accordance with the provisions of Article 2 : The Work.

(e)   Investor has notified the Chinese Organization that Investor has received notice and satisfactory evidence that all of the insurances and Government Authorizations and indemnities contemplated under this Contract have been obtained or will be available at the times required in form and substance satisfactory to Investor.

(f)   The legal opinion called for by Article 19 - Laws of China, has been delivered to Investor.

26.2 Investor shall have no obligation to perform in any manner pursuant to the terms and conditions of this Contract unless or until the Starting Date has occurred, except as mutually agreed between the Parties. If, however, the Starting Date has not occurred within _____ months from the Contract Date, then Investor may, at its sole option, terminate this Contract pursuant to the terms of Article 13 - Termination.

70

IN WITNESS WHEREOF, the Parties have caused this Contract to be executed by their duly authorized representatives on the date and year first written above.

The Chinese Organization
BY_____

Investor
BY_____

COMPENSATION TRADE AGREEMENT ON LICENCE TO MANUFACTURE A SPECIFIC PRODUCT

THIS COMPENSATION TRADE AGREEMENT is made this _____ day of
19 _____ between _____ of China
(hereinafter referred to as "Sino") of the one part and _____ of _____
(hereinafter referred to as "Investor") of the other part.

Whereby it is mutually agreed as follows concerning a compensation
trade project to be set up in _____ ,
a Special Economic Zone as defined by the laws of the People's Republic of
China.

1.   Definitions
1.1   The Site
      shall mean all that piece and parcel of land situate at the present location
      of _____ Factory
      and located inside _____ , a Special
      Economic Zone of China.

1.2   Equipment
      shall mean all those equipments, machines, plants, installations, items
      and spare parts which are deemed to be necessary for the setting up of
      this project.

1.3   The Licensed Products
      shall mean _____ produced and packed on the Site and such other
      products as Investor may from time to time authorize the Sino to
      manufacture and produce on the Site.

1.4   The Improvements
      shall mean any development of or improvements in the Licensed
      Products or their use or their method of manufacture made by Sino
      during the period of this Agreement.

1.5   The Territory
      shall mean the territory of the People's Republic of China.

2.   LICENCES
2.1   Investor hereby grants to the SINO an exclusive licence during the term
      of this Agreement to manufacture the Licensed Products, on the Site
      under the Registered Trade Marks in accordance with the technical
      assistance to be provided by Investor to SINO pursuant to Article 7.1 and
      such of the Improvements as Investor has from time to time approved

solely and exclusively for Investor for sale by Investor in Hong Kong and elsewhere outside the Territory.

2.2 Investor hereby grants to the SINO a further exclusive licence to use and sell to third parties in the Territory under the registered trade marks (but not for resale outside the Territory) such of the Licensed Products manufactured as aforesaid which are in excess of Investor Estimated Volume (as defined) of Investor's requirements of the Licensed Products set forth in Article 7.3.

3. THE SITE

3.1 SINO grants to Investor an exclusive licence during the term of this Agreement to erect or cause to be erected a storey factory building ("the Factory") on so much of the Site as is hereafter set forth for the manufacture of the Licensed Products and any other related purposes at the rental hereafter set forth which rental shall be included in the Surcharge.

3.2 Investor shall complete or cause completion of the erection of the Factory on or before _____ on the Site, and install the Equipment therein in the stages set out in Annex. The total value of the Factory and the Equipment shall be not less than _____

3.3 Investor shall utilize the following area on the Site in connection with the manufacture of the Licensed Products.

19 ____ —19 ____ Total Space Requirement for production of Licensed Products

3.4 Investor shall be entitled to occupy and use the rest of the Site for any other purpose which is directly or indirectly related to Investor's business and / or operations in _____ other than the manufacture of the Licensed Products.

4. SURCHARGE

4.1 Investor shall pay to the SINO a surcharge ("the Surcharge") on such of The Licensed Products as are manufactured for Investor for sale in or elsewhere outside SINO at the following rates:

Period   Surcharge per _____

4.2   After _____ , the amount of the Surcharge shall be renegotiated by the parties in respect of the balance of the term of this Agreement. In the absence of mutual agreement, the Surcharge shall be increased by ____ % for the next period of ____ years over the Surcharge payable during the immediately preceding Period and thereafter increased by the same percentage, based on the rate charged during the immediately preceding Period for each subsequent period of years (or part thereof) unit the expiry of the term of this Agreement.

4.3   The Surcharge shall be payable (monthly / quarterly / annually in arrears) and shall be the total consideration payable by Investor to the SINO during the term of this Agreement inclusive of the rental for the Site referred to in Article 3.1 labour costs, heat, light and power, plant maintenance, breakage and other expenses of whatsoever nature and Investor shall not be required to make any further payments of whatsoever nature to the SINO in connection with the manufacture, sale and delivery of the Licensed Products hereunder by SINO to Investor.

5.   SALE AND PURCHASE OF FACTORY AND EQUIPMENT

5.1   Subject only to Article 11.1(c) hereof, Investor hereby irrevocably agrees to sell to the SINO and the SINO hereby irrevocably agrees to purchase from Investor upon the date of expiration of this Agreement under Article 10.2 (or its earlier termination under Article 10.3 the Factory and all the Equipment for a price equivalent to the actual amount of Investor 's investment referred to in Article 3.2 above plus Interest of _____ (___) per annum on the balance from time to time outstanding. The price aforesaid shall be paid by the SINO in accordance with the payment schedule set out in Annex. Upon, but not before, payment in full of the price, title to and property in the Factory and the Equipment shall be vested in the PRC absolutely. All payment by the SINO pursuant to this Article 5.1 shall be made in to Investor at its principal office or at such other place and in such manner as Investor shall from time to time specify. Investor gives no warranties (express or implied) in connection with the sale of the Factory and the Equipment.

5.2   The sale of the Factory and Equipment pursuant to Article 5.1 does not include a sale by Investor to SINO of any confidential information supplied by Investor to SINO at any time during the term of this Agreement nor any proprietary right or interest (other than by way of mere licence pursuant to this Agreement) in the Registered Trade Marks or any patents or similar rights of Investor in the Licensed Products or any of the Improvements all of which rights and interests shall be (or became pursuant to this Agreement) the absolute property of Investor.

6.   SINO'S UNDERTAKINGS
        The SINO hereby agrees as follows:

6.1 Within _____ days of the completion of the erection of the Factory and the installation of the equipment, to commence the commercial manufacture of the Licensed Products on the Site.

6.2 To manufacture the Licensed Products in accordance with the same standards of merchantable quality and workmanship hitherto used by Investor and in this connection the SINO shall allow Investor or its designated representatives to inspect the Factory, Equipment and methods of manufacture employed in the manufacture of the Licensed Products at all reasonable times.

6.3 Not without the prior written consent of Investor to be involved, concerned or interested either directly or indirectly in:

(a) the manufacture in _____ of any products which compete with or are likely to compete with the Licensed Products, and to manufacture such products exclusively for Investor;

(b) the sale or distribution of the Licensed Products outside the PRC otherwise than to Investor; or

(c) any agreement or arrangement with any third party which is aimed at or likely to present or restrict the manufacture of the Licensed Products in the _____ .

Not at any time during the term of this Agreement or thereafter to disclose or divulge any of the confidential information in relation to the Licensed Products or their method of manufacture or Investor's affairs or business disclosed to SINO by Investor pursuant to this Agreement to any third party other than so far as is necessary to perform its obligations hereunder, nor to use such confidential information for any purpose other than in accordance with Article 2.1 and 2.2. Promptly to supply Investor with full details of the Improvements referred to in Article 9.1 below, and other relevant information relating to the Licensed Products or method of manufacture thereof which comes into its possession or knowledge.

(To carry out at its own expense) (To permit Investor to carry out at its own expense) and without delay from time to time all changes necessary to the Factory and / or the Equipment and / or the manufacturing methods arising from any changes in specifications or standards of quality of the Licensed Products notified to the SINO by Investor. Not to use the Registered Trade Marks or variations or imitations thereof except in connection with the manufacture of the Licensed Products in accordance with Article 2.1 and the marketing thereof in accordance with Article 2.2 and only in the manner from time to time authorised by Investor in writing, nor during the term of this agreement to, directly or indirectly, contest or aid others to contest, the validity of the Registered Trade Marks or to do (or fail to do) anything which may:-

(a) impair the validity of the Registered Trade Marks,

(b)   adversely affect Investor's present or future registrations thereof, or

(c)   challenge the exclusive ownership and / or rights to the use thereof by Investor in any country in the world.

SINO shall promptly notify Investor of any infringement, counterfeiting or passing-off of any of the Registered Trade Marks in the SINO and agrees to fully co-operate with Investor in registering the Registered Trade Marks in the Territory (if Investor so requests) and in taking any other action which Investor may decide to take to protect its rights in the Registered Trade Marks.

6.8   In the event of any of the Licensed Products supplied by the SINO to Investor proving defective, the SINO shall replace the Licensed Products concerned at its expense. SINO agrees to indemnify Investor and hold Investor harmless from and against any claim or suit arising out of alleged defects in the quality, fitness for purpose or workmanship of any of the Licensed Products manufactured by the SINO pursuant to this Agreement (unless arising from any default in the raw materials supplied by Investor). Investor shall promptly notify the SINO of any such claim or suit and afford the SINO the opportunity to defend same at SINO'S own expense.

6.9   At its expense, to maintain the Equipment in good operating condition, repair and appearance and to promptly perform all maintenance and repair work only by qualified persons, and to notify Investor promptly of substantial breakdowns in any of the Equipment.

6.10   To use the Equipment solely in the performance of its obligations under this Agreement.

6.11   At its own expense, to keep the Factory and the Equipment insured at the full insurable value thereof with an insurer acceptable to Investor against fire, theft and other losses in the name of Investor, and to carry adequate public liability against bodily injury (including death) and property damage in the name of Investor.

7.   INVESTOR'S UNDERTAKINGS

7.1   During the term of this Agreement, Investor shall from time to time furnish such assistance as Investor deems necessary to enable SINO to operate successfully under this Agreement in respect of the following:

(a)   technical / skilled / professional personnel specified in to assist in the setting up and the initial operation of the Factory.

(b)   to provide on-the-job training to select local workers at such times and for such periods as Investor shall determine to be mutually convenient after consultations with the SINO; and

(c)   to provide information concerning changes, or improvements to the methods of manufacture and other matters related to the

Licensed Products.

7.2 Investor shall provide all raw materials required for the manufacture of the Licensed Products required to meet its Estimated Volume of requirements referred to in Article 7.3.

8. WARRANTY

8.1 INVESTOR warrants to SINO for the duration of this Agreement as follows:
   (a) be free from defects in material and workmanship;
   (b) be free from defects arising from the selection of materials;
   (c) be free from defects inherent in the detailed design thereof having regard to the state of the art at the date of such design;
   (d) be in conformance to the Specification taking into account the effect of Annex.

The warranty set forth above shall apply to parts manufactured by INVESTOR or any of the Associates or by Subcontractors pursuant to INVESTOR or its Associates' detailed design and detailed specification.

8.2 INVESTOR further warrants, that parts of the Products selected and / or approved by INVESTOR which are not subject to the warranty contained in (8.1), at the time of delivery of the Products shall be installed in the Products generally in accordance with the installation instructions of the manufacturer thereof and be free from defects in workmanship utilized in effecting such installation as not to invalidate any warranties with respect thereto.

8.3 The warranty of INVESTOR as defined in (8.1) and (8.2) above shall extend only to the defects in the products or parts thereof which become apparent to SINO within _____ months after delivery of the Product.

9. DELIVERY:

9.1 INVESTOR shall not be responsible or liable nor be deemed to be indefault under this Agreement on account of any Excusable Delay mentioned in this Article.

Any delay in the delivery of the Product due to any of the following causes shall be deemed an Excusable Delay:

war; warlike situations; armed aggression; insurrection; civil war; riots; fires; weather unfavourable for flying; explosions; accidents; floods; inundations; earthquakes; epidemics; quarantine restrictions; governmental-acts, -statutes, -priorities and -allocation regulations or -orders affecting material, facilities or completed Product; the application of any facilities or personnel, normally or otherwise available for the performance hereof, to the performance of any military production for the Government of the INVESTOR'S respectively the Governments of the Associations; natural disasters; failure of or delay in transportation;

inability after due and timely diligence to procure materials, accessories, equipment or parts; strikes or other labour troubles causing cessation, slow-down or interruption of work; preventive measures to avoid damage to material, facilities or the Product; any other cause beyond INVESTOR'S control or not occasioned by INVESTOR'S fault or negligence.

Furthermore a delay in the delivery of the Product not exceeding (___) calendar month shall be considered an Excusable Delay.

9.2   In the event delivery of the Product shall be delayed by reason of any Excusable Delay set forth in 9.1 above for a period of more than (___) months after the month of delivery.

9.3   (a)   In the event that prior to delivery thereof to SINO the product is lost, destroyed or damaged beyond repair, the time required by INVESTOR to furnish a replacement for the Product shall be deemed an Excusable Delay.

As soon as possible INVESTOR shall notify SINO in writing of the date upon which a replacement product can be delivered, provided, however, that nothing herein shall be deemed to obligate INVESTOR to deliver such replacement Product, of manufacture would require the reactivation of the production line for that product. If such date of delivery is within (___) calendar months after the scheduled month of delivery of the product so lost, destroyed or damaged beyond repair, INVESTOR shall deliver such replacement Product on terms and conditions to be agreed upon.

(b)   If such date of delivery is not within (___) calendar months after the scheduled month of delivery of the Product so lost, destroyed or damaged beyond repair, then SINO shall have the right, exercisable by giving notice in writing to INVESTOR within (___) days after receipt of such notice from INVESTOR to cancel this Agreement in respect to the purchase of the Product so lost, destroyed or damaged beyond repair.

9.4   Any termination under sections 9.2 or 9.3 (a) or (b) shall discharge and terminate all obligations and liabilities of the parties hereunder with respect to the undelivered Product so delayed, lost, destroyed or damaged beyond repair, except that INVESTOR shall refund to SINO any advance payment made by SINO to INVESTOR for the relevant Product.

9.5   Should delivery of the Product be delayed beyond (___) calendar month, as stipulated in Article 9.1. SINO shall have the right to claim from INVESTOR and INVESTOR shall compensate SINO in relation to the Product so delayed in delivery an amount by way of liquidated damages calculated as follows:

(AMOUNT)——for the first calendar month of such subsequent delay or pro rata;

(AMOUNT)——for the second calendar month of such subsequent delay or pro rata;

(AMOUNT)——for the third calendar month of such subsequent delay or pro rata;

(AMOUNT)——for the fourth calendar month of such subsequent delay or pro rata;

(AMOUNT)——for the fifth calendar month of such subsequent delay or pro rata;

(AMOUNT)——for the sixth calendar month of such subsequent delay or pro rata;

The right of SINO to recover such damages in relation to the Product is conditional upon a claim thereto being submitted to INVESTOR in writing by SINO within (___) days after the date that the Product is ready for delivery.

9.6 Should such delay exceed (___) calendar months, SINO shall have the right to cancel this Agreement, provided, SINO does so within (___) days from the end of the said period of the (___) calendar months. This will discharge and terminate all obligations and liabilities of the parties hereunder with respect to the Product.

9.7 INVESTOR shall not in any circumstances be under any liability - irrespective of their nature and cause - in respect of delay in delivery or failure to deliver the Product other than and beyond the liability or liabilities set forth in this Article, except that, in case of termination, INVESTOR shall refund to SINO, any advance payments made by SINO to INVESTOR for the Product.

10. IMPROVEMENTS

10.1 Investor shall be entitled to the full property of and benefit in the Improvements throughout the world without any payment of any consideration therefore.

10.2 The SINO shall at the request and cost of Investor, execute all such documents and do all such things as Investor may require for the purposes of acquiring such property and benefit and of using in the name of Investor, any patent or other protection in respect thereof in any country of the world.

10.3 If Investor shall receive the grant of any patent or other protection within the Territory in respect of any Improvements, Investor shall, if requested by the SINO , grant to the SINO for a nominal consideration, a licence in a term to be agreed between the SINO and Investor.

11. EFFECTIVE DATE, DURATION AND TERMINATION

11.1 This Agreement shall take effect on the date when executed by both parties hereto ("the Effective Date").

11.2 Following the Effective Date, this Agreement shall continue in full force and effect for ____ years (subject to Article 10.6). After ____ years, the licences granted hereunder shall cease and be of no force and effect unless the parties hereto have agreed in writing to a renewal thereof.

11.3 Either party shall have the right at any time by giving notice in writing to the other party to terminate this Agreement forthwith if that other party commits a breach of any of the provisions of this Agreement but should the breach in question be such that the party in breach can effectively remedy then the said notice of termination shall not be effective to terminate this Agreement unless the party in breach fails within (____) days of the date of such notice of termination effectively to remedy the breach complained of.

11.4 This Agreement shall be deemed to be terminated by mutual consent of the parties if either party is unable to carry out its obligations hereunder as a result of any cause beyond its control, natural disaster, rioting, strikes, act of war or legislation or government direction for a continuous period of calendar months.

12. CONSEQUENCES OF TERMINATION

12.1 On the valid termination of this Agreement for whatever reason the SINO shall immediately:

(a) return all originals, copies and translations of the technical data and other confidential information supplied by Investor;

(b) cease to use the Registered Trade Marks or any colourable imitation thereof upon or in relation to any of the Licensed Products or any other similar goods;

(c) SINO shall be obliged to forthwith complete the purchase of the Factory and the Equipment at the price specified in Article 5.1 with interest calculated up to the date of such actual payment by SINO to Investor. Investor shall be entitled to purchase from the PRC all undelivered stocks of the Licensed Products manufactured by SINO for Investor at the price specified in this Agreement and all unsold stocks of raw materials intended solely for use in the manufacture of the Licensed Products shall be returned by SINO to Investor at its expense.

12.2 On the valid termination of this Agreement for whatever reason, neither party shall claim for indemnity, damages, compensation or the like under any applicable law which purports to grant such rights or remedies in respect of or on account of such termination.

13. GOVERNMENT PERMITS

13.1 This Agreement shall be subject to the SINO's obtaining all necessary governmental authorizations, consents, licences and permits from any applicable governmental agency, committee, instrumentality or office which is required under the laws of the People's Republic of China for the execution and performance of this Agreement by either of the parties hereto, and Investor obtaining all such authorizations, consents, licences and permits (if any) required under the laws of Hong Kong.

14. ARBITRATION

14.1 All disputes arising from the execution of, or in connection with this contract, shall be settled amicably through friendly negotiation. In case no settlement can be reached through negotiaton, the case shall then be submitted to Foreign Trade Arbitration Commission of China Council for the Promotion of International Trade, Peking for arbitration in accordance with its Provisional Rules of Procedure. The arbitral award is final and binding upon both parties.

15. TAXATION

In order to induce Investor to enter into this Agreement, the SINO hereby further represents and warrants during the term of this Agreement to Investor as follows:

15.1 All raw materials used in the manufacture of the Licensed Products as well as all items of Equipment (and any additions thereto) supplied by (or on behalf of) Investor pursuant to this Agreement to the SINO shall be imported into the Territory free of import and any other duties, levies, imposts and taxes whatsoever.

15.2 All of the Licensed Products manufactured by the SINO for Investor pursuant to this Agreement shall be exported to Investor free of export and any other duties, levies, imposts and taxes whatsoever.

15.3 Investor shall be free of all taxes (including the Industrial and Commercial Consolidated Tax and the Industrial and Commercial Income Tax) withholdings, levies, assessments and similar charges (other than the Surcharge) in respect of its purchases of the Licensed Products from the SINO pursuant to this Agreement as well as in respect of Investor's sale to the SINO of the Factory and the Equipment pursuant to Article 5.1 hereof.

16. MISCELLANEOUS

16.1 No waiver by either party of any breach of any term or condition hereof by the other party shall be deemed a waiver of any other breach whether of the same or any other provision hereof nor shall any delay or omission on the part of either party to exercise or avail itself of any right that it has or may have hereunder operate as a waiver of any such breach.

16.2 Nothing in this Agreement shall constitute or be deemed to constitute a partnership between the parties hereto or constitute or be deemed to constitute the SINO agent of Investor for any purpose whatsoever and tho SINO shall have no authority or power to bind Investor or to contract in the name of or create a liability against Investor in any way or for any purpose.

16.3 If any provision of this Agreement shall be found by any court of competent jurisdiction to be invalid or unenforceable for any reason whatsoever, the invalidity of such provision shall not affect the other clauses of this Agreement or the licences granted hereunder and all provisions not affected by such invalidity shall remain in full force and effect.

16.4 Any notices or other communications to be served on or sent to either party hereunder shall be sufficiently served or sent if mailed by registered return receipt prepaid airmail to such party at its address set out below and shall be deemed to have been delivered to such party ( ) hours after the time of despatch:

(a)   in the case of the SINO:

(b)   in the case of Investor: at its registered office as shown above.

16.5 The heading to the Articles of this Agreement are included for convenience only and shall not in any way constitute part thereof.

16.6 This Agreement shall be governed by and construed in accordance with the laws of the People's Republic of China.

17.   EFFECTIVENESS OF THIS AGREEMENT

17.1 Unforseen matters shall not affect an execution of this contract

18.   CANCELLATION OF AGREEMENT

18.1 Both parties shall reserve the right to cancel this contract in case there is no effect for (＿＿) months after the effective date of this agreement.

18.2 This contract shall be valid for (＿＿) years after its effective date, and shall be void automatically thereafter.

19.   LANGUAGE USED IN AGREEMENT

This contract is written in both Chinese and English, and both version shall have the equal validity.

SINO

[Authorized Signatures]

Investor

[Authorized Signatures]

PROCESSING AND
ASSEMBLY CONTRACT

MEMORANDUM OF AGREEMENT made this _____ day of
_____ 19 ____ between _____
whose principal address is situate at _____

(hereinafter referred to as "the Foreign Company", which expression shall where the context admits, include the Foreign Company's associated companies, subsidaries, branch offices or representative offices in business as the case may be) and _____

whose principal address is situate at _____

(hereinafter referred to as "the Chinese Organization", which expression shall where the context admits, include the Chinese Organization's associated companies, subsidaries, branch offices or representative offices in business as the case may be) as a result of friendly and thorough discussion between both parties and under the following terms of co-operation and mutual interests:

1) Objectives
    The Foreign Company will supply components, including packing for
        — the type of goods — (author)
    assembly at the Chinese Organization. The Chinese Organization will return the_____ — the same kind of goods mentioned above —
                    (author)
    to the Foreign Company after processed. The Foreign Company will supply all equipment with accessories for the _____ — ditto —
                    (author)
    assembly and the cost of these equipment will be repaid to the Foreign Company within a maximum period of (_____) years by deducting from the assembly cost at the rate of _____ % per payment. In the case of increase of investment, repayment will also be based on the same percentage.

2) Quantity
    1st phase: Monthly quantity will be approximately _____ units.
    2nd phase and thereafter, quantity will be based on volume of business and quantity will be increased step by step upon further discussion by both parties.

3) Scrappage
    Maximum scrappage should not exceed _____ % even within the trial period. All scrapped materials should be returned to the Foreign Company for replacement.

83

4) Assembly Cost

Based on direct labour cost at US$ _____ , including all —name of Products—(author), the Chinese Organization's indirect labour, maintenance staff, tax, rental, etc. (No increase within the first years. Thereafter, increment should be advised _____ months in advance to the Foreign Company and rate not to exceed _____ % and increment should not occur more than once a year.) (In the case of fluctuation of Chinese Yuen and U.S. Currency, further agreement should be made by both parties.) Direct labour and production rate should base on the Foreign Company's calculation formula:

$$\frac{\text{Direct labour of 1100 US\$}}{\text{units / day}} = \text{US\$ / unit}$$

5) Transportation

The Foreign Company will be responsible for transportation of all components, packing, materials, to and fro the Chinese Organization. The Chinese Organization will apply for entry / exit permit for the Foreign Company vehicles to transit through the Chinese Border.

6) Materials and Delivery

The Foreign Company will supply all necessary materials, according to the agreed upon quantity, working week prior to production start and the Chinese Organization will deliver assembled _____ units within working week after receipt of materials.

In case of delayed delivery, the Foreign Company will delay supply of next lot of materials and the Chinese Organization should complete the current lot of _____ assembly before starting production of the next lot. Any loss caused by breach of agreement by either party should be compensated at a rate of not exceeding US$ _____ / unit not according to Direct Larbour cost rate.

However, if parts shortage, wrong parts supplied or delayed material supply or production rate declined, causing loss of less than _____ %, no compensation should be claimed by either party.

7) Payment

The Foreign Company will make payment to the Chinese Organization before the _____ of every month for the delivery of the previous month.

8) Technical Support

The Foreign Company will send technical team to assist the Chinese Organization in the installation of production equipment, production technique and management. The Chinese Organization will arrange all boarding and lodging for these technical teams at the usual standard applied to Chinese officials and arrange for all entry and exit procedures with the Chinese Authorities.

9) Guarantee and Compensation

All losses caused by natural damages, fire, theft, riot, strike, etc. will be responsible by the Chinese Organization and cash compensation to the

Foreign Company be made within _____ days after the loss. OR the Foreign Company to insure for the equipment, etc. stating the Foreign Company as payee of the compensation, and deduct insurance cost from the assembly charges. The Foreign Company will be responsible to replace the damaged equipment, etc. as soon as possible after receipt of compensation.

10) At adverse business seasons, production rate should not be less than __ _____ % of usual time.

11) Miscellaneous
   a) For any extraordinary reasons, if the Chinese Organization has to terminate agreement and the Foreign Company investment has not been fully recovered, the Chinese Organization will cash compensate to the Foreign Company in U.S. Currency the balance cost at the contracted production rate x labour cost.
   If due to extraordinary reasons the Foreign Company has to terminate contract, the Foreign Company will make same compensation but maximum value is limited to the Foreign Company's net asset worth only.
   b) In case of traffic shut-down, worldwide raw material shortage, revision of local / foreign import / export laws and worldwide economic set-back affecting production, both parties should work out a fair and mutual solution.

12) Effectiveness
   This agreement is in duplicate in the Chinese and English languages, both texts being equally authentic. This agreement is valid for a period of years from date of production start. Renewal of agreement should be agreed by both parties _____ months before expiry of present agreement. Any amendment and addition to the above terms should be agreed upon by both parties in writing.

(Signed)	(Signed)
For and on behalf of	For and on behalf of
(The Foreign Company)	(The Chinese Organization)

Author's notes

It is advisable to add an arbitration clause / article to the contract by stating that "Should there be any disputes in connection with this contract, they shall be settled by friendly negotiations between both parties. In case no such agreement can be reached, the matter in dispute shall be decided by arbitration. The place of arbitration shall be agreed upon by both parties in writing and the decision of arbitration shall be final and conclusive."

85

AGENCY SERVICE AGREEMENT

MEMORANDUM OF AGREEMENT made this

day of   19   between

whose principal address is situate at

(hereinafter referred to as "Foreign Company", which expression shall where the context admits, include the Foreign Company's associated companies, subsidaries and branch offices as the case may be) of the one part and _____

_____ whose registered

office is situate at   (hereinafter referred to as "the Chinese Organization", which expression shall, where the context admits, include the Chinese Organization's representatives and agents in business as the case may be) of the other part.

Whereby, both parties after friendly discussions held in Beijing (Peking) Whereby, after friendly discussions held in Beijing (Peking), both parties agreed as follows:

In consideration of Foreign Company introducing the —— name of third party —— (author)

to the Chinese Organization for the negotiation of orders for the purchase of
—— name of the trade deals ——
(author)

the Chinese Organization shall pay to Foreign Company a commission of
  % of all moneys received by the Chinese Organization as a result of such orders, as and when the moneys are received.

The Chinese Organization shall make all payments by banker's draft in currency.

The Chinese Organization assures that it has obtained all necessary government approvals to enter into and consummate the transactions contemplated by this agreement and, in particular, has obtained any necessary approvals from the appropriate government organizations and agencies to remit to Foreign Company the commission payable in   Dollars/Pound Sterling.

Any disputes which may arise between the parties during the term of this agreement will be resolved through friendly discussion or arbitration by third party.

Amendments to this agreement may be made at any time in writing, provided such amendments are agreed to by both parties.

This agreement is done in duplicate at Beijing (Peking) on   19
in the   and Chinese languages, both texts being equally authentic.

(Signed)
For and on behalf of the
Foreign Company

(Signed)
For and on behalf of the
Chinese Organization

JOINT CO-OPERATION IN THE ESTABLISHMENT OF HOLIDAY RESORT

MEMORANDUM OF AGREEMENT made this _____
day of_____ 19_____ between _____ of
_____, whose registered office is situate at
_____ of _____ (hereinafter referred to as
the "Chinese Organization") of the one part and _____
_____ of, _____ whose
principal address is situate at _____
of _____, (hereinafter referred to as the "Investor")
of the other part_____

_____

Whereby both parties, with the assistance of _____
and one Mr. _____ of _____, mutually agreed to
co-operate in the establishment of a holiday rsort in_____,
China as follows:

1. Both parties agreed to co-operate to establish a holiday resort with _____.
    The construction cost will be _____.

2. The Chinese Organization provides site for the construction of the holiday
    resort and shall be responsible for the removal and / or demolition of
    structure on the site (if any).

3. Investor shall be responsible for all the construction capital of the holiday
    resort.

4. The Chinese Organization shall be responsible for the running of business
    of the holiday resort upon completion of its construction and shall
    undertake its profits and loss. The Investor's investment together with the
    interests that ought to be repaid _____ months after the holiday resort
    has been completely constructed and commenced its business. The total
    sum will be divided in to _____ (_____)
    repayments in (_____) years. Each repayment can be itemized as
    follows:

    a. _____ of the total investment amount contributed by the Investor in
        the construction of the holiday resort.

    b. The interests are calculated in accordance with the unpaid capital. The
        guarantee for the above repayment will be provided by, _____China.
        The guarantee shall be irrevocable, non-transferrable and uncondition-
        al. The Chinese Organization may also repay the whole sum
        prematurely. Interest shall cease to be calculated after repayment.
        After the Chinese Organization completely repaid the capital and
        interest, the holiday will be wholly owned by Chinese Organization

without incurring any compensation.

5. Both parties have agreed a fixed profit of _____
   for the Investor. Such profit will be paid by the Chinese Organization by
   _____ ( ) installments within_____ ( ) years
   after the commencement of business of the holiday resort.

6. The Investor shall be responsible for the design, decoration, construction
   management, and tender invitation of the holiday resort until the time
   when the construction of the holiday resort completed. All the expenses
   incurred for these purposes will be paid by the Chinese Organization. The
   exact details of payment will be: _____.

7. The design work of the holiday resort will be carried out by the Investor
   with the co-operation and assistance of _____,
   China. The details for the division of labour will be negotiated separately.

8. Both parties will discuss on what kind of materials which have to be
   imported into China. They will invite tenders for the supply of these
   imported materials. The Chinese Organization shall study the case and
   appoint an appropriate unit to initiate the invitation. The Investor shall
   select, from the tenders given, the most suitable tender for the job. The
   Investor shall undertake the supervision of the tendered project(s) and
   coordination in the progress of the construction of the holiday resort.

9. The issues related to taxes will be dealt with in accordance with the
   taxation laws of China.

10. The Agreement will be executed after the approval from _____,
    the supervisor of the Chinese Organization.

(Signed)   (Signed)

_____   _____
     For and on behalf of   For and on behalf of
the Chinese Organization   the Investor
(_____)   (_____)

89

BILITERAL TRADE AGREEMENT

MEMORANDUM OF AGREEMENT made this _____ day of 19 _____
between _____ of _____
(hereinafter referred to as "the Chinese Organization", which expression shall,
where the context admits, include the Chinese Organisation's associated
companies, subsidaries, or branch offices, appointed nominees as the case
may be) of the one part and _____ of _____
(hereinafter referred to as "the Foreign Company", which expression shall,
where the context admits, include the Foreign Company's associated
companies, subsidaries, branch offices, or appointed nominees as the case
may be) of the other part.

Whereby it is mutually agreed as follows concerning a biliteral trade
arrangement between both parties:

1. The Foreign Company undertakes to supply to the various Chinese a
   wholly subsidaries of the Chinese Organisation (hereinafter referred to as
   "Sub") items from the following list or any other items that may be
   mutually agreed between the two parties to this agreement:

   ——list out the products you want to supply——
   (author)

2. The products listed out above shall be to a value of during the period
   from _____ 19 _____ until the 19 _____ .

3. The Foreign Company will enter into contract for the supply of the above
   items with the appropriate Sub. All conditions of such contracts can be
   entered into between them direct .

4. Sales to be made on a C & F Chinese port basis.

5. Prices will be competitive world market prices at the time of signing
   individual contracts.

6. Equivalent to the C & F value of the items to be supplied by the Foreign
   Company to China, the Foreign Company will purchase from the Chinese
   Organisation the following products:

   ——list out the products you want to purchase——
   (author)

7. The products lists out above shall be to a value of _____
   during the period from _____ 19 _____ until the
   19 _____ .

8. By mutual agreement other Chinese products can be added to the above
   list and the value of which will be negotiatcd accordingly.

9. The Foreign Company will enter into contracts with for the purchase of the above products with the appropriate Sub. All conditions of such contracts can be entered into between them direct.

10. Purchases from the Chinese Sub will be made on an FOB Chinese port basis unless otherwise agreed in the individual contracts.

11. Prices will be competitive world market prices at the time of signing individual contracts.

12. No restriction whatsoever is imposed on these goods as to their destination.

13. It is mutually agreed that if the export of any of the above Chinese items were restricted by any ways or means whatsoever by the Chinese Government, any such restrictions would be applicable against this Agreement provided they are applicable.

14. Should the Chinese Government announce any export incentive scheme or any special export benefit to promote the export of any of the items on the list under 2 above any such incentives will be automatically applicable on the commodities exported within the framework of this Agreement.

15. An account to be opened in the books of the Bank of China in non-convertible US Dollars. This account to be named "ABC Account". Proceeds on this account to be used only for payment of goods under this Agreement.

16. In case of import into China buyers to open a Letter of Credit in favour of sellers.

17. In case of export from China buyers (Sub) to open a Letter of Credit in favour of Chinese sellers. Payment will be made from the ABC Account. Proceeds in both cases i.e. export from or import into China in non-convertible US Dollars.

18. The following payments can be made to and from the ABC non-convertible US Dollar account:
    FOB value of goods to be exported from China
    C&F value of goods to be imported from China
    Local expenses in China incurred in effecting such exports including inspection, controlling and other fees, etc.
    Banking charges and interest when applicable.

19. In order to operate the account an overdraft of 10% (ten percent) is granted either way.

20. An interest of _____ (percent) per annum will automatically be credited by the Bank of China biannually on (month — author) and (month — author) of each year on any outstanding balance in favour of the Bank of China (or their appointed nominees) or BIT as the case may be.

21. At the end of every first calendar year the outstanding balance is automatically payable within twelve banking days in free and convertible

US Dollars to the party in whose favour there is an outstanding balance on the ABC Account by the party in debit, unless the two parties agree to carry forward any such outstanding balance.

22. At the expiry of this Agreement a grace period of six months is granted during which the ABC Account is to be balanced by purchase of goods. If no such purchase takes place the outstanding balance will be paid as per 6(1) above.

23. Party B designates the Bank (first class A1 international bank acceptable to the Bank of China) to operate the ABC Account on their behalf. All expense of this bank for the Foreign Company's account.

24. Bank of China and (the same bank in 7(1) above — author) have to sign an agreement and issue mutually acceptable guarantees in each other's favour covering payment of outstanding balances under this Agreement not later than (date — author).

25. Should any dispute arise between the two parties same shall be settled amicably. In case no such settlement can be reached the dispute will be referred to the Foreign Trade Arbitration Commission whose decision shall be final and binding on both parties to this Agreement.

One in duplicate at Beijing, China on (month____author) in English and Chinese languages - both texts being equally authentic.

(Signed)	(Signed)
Export Company	ABC Company
China	X Country

SELLING A PRODUCTION PLANT TO CHINA

Contract No.: _____

MEMORANDUM OF AGREEMENT made this _____ day of 19 _____
between _____
whose principal address is situate at _____

(hereinafter referred to as "the Buyers", which expression shall where the context admits, include the Buyers' agents and representatives in business as the case may be) as one part and _____

whose principal address is situate at _____

(hereinafter referred to as "the Sellers", which expression shall where the context admits, include the Sellers' agents and representatives in business as the case may be) as the other part agree to sign, as a result of friendly discussion, the contract under the following terms and conditions:

Chapter One   General Principles

1.1 The Buyers agree to buy from the Sellers and the Sellers agree to sell to the Buyers equipment, raw materials, materials, design, technical documentation, licence, knowhow and technical services for a plant with an annual production capacity of _____ (hereinafter referred to as "the Plant").

1.2 For safe and normal operation of the Plant the Sellers shall supply within the battery limits all equipment, such as process equipment, machinery, electrical installations, instrumentation and automatic control devices, special apparatus for laboratory, automatic device for fire fighting system, easy-worn spare parts, and spare parts necessary for _____ year normal operation after acceptance of the Plant (hereinafter referred to as "Equipment"), as well as all materials, such as materials, materials for installations, for instrumentation and for automatic control devices, other necessary materials for erection and catalyst and lubricants (hereinafter referred to as "Materials"). Details of major "Equipment" and "Mateials" to be supplied by the Sellers are for battery limits of the Plant see drawing 1 attached to this Contract.

1.3 The Sellers shall undertake to make all the engineering design work of the Plant according to the basic of design stipulated in Annex _____ to the Contract except the design work to be performed by the Buyers (as stipulated in Annex _____). The Sellers shall supply to the Buyers complete design information and technical documentation (hereinafter

93

referred to as "Technical Documentation"). Details are stated in Annex _____ to the Contract.

1.4   The Sellers shall dispatch their experienced and competent technical personnel to the Plant for technical instructions with respect to erection, mechanical tests, commissioning and performance guarantee test run of the Plant. The service extent and treatment conditions of the Sellers' technical personnel are set forth in Annex _____ .

1.5   The Sellers are responsible to accept and arrange the technical training of the Buyers' personnel free of charge in one of the plants, however the travelling and living costs shall be borne by the Buyers. The training extent and treatment conditions for the Buyers' technical personnel are stated in Annex _____ .

Chapter Two   Price

2.1   In accordance with Articles 1.1, 1.2, and 1.3 of this contract, the total price for the Equipment Materials and Technical Documentation to be supplied by the Sellers, including the licence fee and knowhow fee is

The break down prices of the total price are:
Equipment and Materials _____
Spare parts _____
Technical Documentation _____
Licence and Knowhow _____

2.2   The above total price is a fixed price for a period of _____ years and it will be adjusted by both parties through friendly discussion.

2.3   The prices for the Equipment, Materials and Spare parts are for delivery C.I.F. including all expenses for loading the goods on board the vessel assigned by the Buyers but not including any fee.

2.4   The total price does not include the renumeration and any other expenses for the Sellers' technical personnel to be sent to the Contract Plant for service, but include the expenses with the exception of travelling and living costs, for training the Buyers' technical personnel by Sellers in one of the plants of _____ .

2.5   All expenses for expatriating their personnel for the execution of the Contract shall be borne by the party itself.

Chapter Three   Method of Payment

3.1   All payments by the Buyers to the Sellers under the Contract shall be made by telegraphic transfer in through the Bank of China, and all payments, if any, by the Sellers to the Buyers shall be made by telegraphic transfer in through the. All banking fees incurred in China shall be borne by the Buyers, and those incurred in shall be borne by the Sellers.

3.2   The Buyers shall pay the amount of in Article 2.1 of the Contract to the

Sellers in the following manner and rate:

(a) 10 % of the total price, shall be paid not later than _____ days after the Bank of China, Peking has received the following documents and the Buyers have found them in order:

    (i) An export licence issued by the relevant authorities of the Seller's country authorizing them to export the Equipment or a certificate issued by the relevant authorities stating that an export licence is not neccesary;

    (ii) An irrevocable Letter of Guarantee issued by _____ , in favour of the Buyers, covering ____ % of the total price of the Contract;

    (iii) Proforma invoice covering the total price of the Contract in quadruplicate;

    (iv) Commercial invoice in quadruplicate;

    (v) Sight draft to be drawn on the Buyers to the Bank of China, Peking in duplicate.

(b) _____ % of the total price, shall be paid pro rata shipment within _____ days after the Bank of China, Peking has received the following documents and the Buyers have found them in order:

    (i) Full set of (Ratio——author) clean on board Bill of Lading made out to order and blank endorsed, marked "notifying China National Foreigh Trade Transportation Corporation";

    (ii) Commercial invoice covering the price for the delivered Equipment and Materials, and the proportional amount of Licence and Knowhow fee and Technical Documentation fee in quadruplicate;

    (iii) Detailed packing list in quadruplicate;

    (iv) Quality certificate issued by the manufacturers or the Sellers in duplicate;

    (v) Sight draft to be drawn on the Buyers to the Bank of China, Peking in duplicate.

(c) _____ % of the total price of the Contract, shall be paid within ____ days after the Bank of China, Peking has received the following documents and the Buyers have found them in order:

    (i) Commercial invoice in quadruplicate;

    (ii) Photostatic copy of acceptance certificate of the Plant signed by both parties in quadruplicate;

    (iii) Sight draft to be drawn on the Buyers to the Bank of China, Peking in duplicate.

(d) _____ % of the total price of the Contract, shall be paid within __ days after the expiration of the mechanical guarantee period as set forth in Chapter 9 hereof, and after the Bank of China, Peking has received the following documents and the Buyers have found them in order:

    (i) Commercial invoice in quadruplicate;

    (ii) A letter issued by the Sellers certifying the expiration of the mechanical guarantee period, in one original and three copies;

(iii)   Sight draft to be drawn on the Buyers to the Bank of China, Peking in duplicate.

3.3   In the case as stipulated in Article 4.7, the Buyers shall, within _____ days after receiving and checking up the original documents signed by the warehouse and the insurance company respectively, pay the storage charges and premium for the stored goods from the day commencing with the actual date of the goods' readiness for shipment. At the same time, the Buyers shall pay an interest of _____ % per annum on the ___ % of the shipment value, on the proportional amount of Licence and Knowhow fee, and on Technical Documentation fee counting from the day of the goods' readiness for shipment up to the date of acutal shipment.

3.4   In case of any penalty as stipulated in Chapter 9 hereof in the course of executing the Contract, the Buyers shall have the right to deduct the sum from the payment due or from the next payment when they deem it justifiable.

3.5   In case any document is found incorrect by the Buyers, the Buyers shall cable the Sellers to this effect, indicating the wrong items, within _____ days after the Bank of China, Peking has received such document.

3.6   When making the payment under 3.2(a) the Buyers shall submit to the Sellers an irrevocable Letter of Guarantee issued by the Bank of China, Peking in favour of the Sellers.

Chapter Four   Design

4.1   Within _____ month after signing the Contract, item and questions regarding design conditons of the Plant shall be discussed in China and agreed to be laid down in a protocol signed by both parties.

4.2   The sellers shall within one and a half months after signing the Contract deliver all existing standards and codes of the Sellers' country for the design of the Plant. These documents shall be delivered in English. The Sellers shall deliver at their own expense to the Buyers the said standards and codes in 4 (four) copies C.I.F. Peking Airport.

4.3   After signing the Contract and before the delivery of the preliminary design, the Buyers shall have the right to send at their own expense design liaison personnel to the Sellers' design office to study with the Sellers' technical personnel various technical problems in relation to the Contract, to look into the state of design work and to discuss views on the design with the Sellers. The Sellers shall also arrange their visit to. The purpose of this visit is to give the Buyers' personnel a detailed understanding of plant. The Sellers shall assist them in arranging their living and working and shall provide them free of charge with all necessary technical documentation, drawings and office rooms in the Sellers' office.

4.4 The Sellers shall submit to the Buyers _____ months after signing the Contract the preliminary project and preliminary information of civil engineering. Furthermore, in the month after signing the Contract the Sellers shall dispatch at own expense technical personnel to China. To give explanation on the preliminary project and information of civil engineering design. The review and approval of the preliminary project shall be finished through both parties' efforts within one month after the arrival of the Sellers' personnel, and a protocol shall be signed between both parties as the basis for the final design.

4.5 The final information of civil engineering shall be delivered by the Sellers in the month and the final project in the month to the Buyers after signing the Contract. The Sellers shall dispatch at their own expense, their technical personnel to China at the month after signing the Contract to have a project meeting for explaining and discussing the final project and signing the civil engineering drawings by both parties. Both parties shall make their efforts to accomplish this work and a protocol shall be signed to such effect by both parties.

4.6 The Technical Documentation submitted by the Sellers shall meet the requirements for successful erection, mechanical tests, commissioning, normal and safe operation, as well as maintenance. Should any deficiency or error be found, the Sellers shall make corresponding corrections, improvements or supplements to the Technical Documentation without any delay, and this shall not affect the progress of the construction of the Plant. Should the Technical Documentation be lost or damaged during transportation, the Sellers shall supplement them once again free of charge C.I.F. Peking Airport within _____ (_____)days after receiving the Buyers' notification.

4.7 All Technical Documentation to be submitted by the Sellers shall be worked out in English in 7 (seven) copies, but 9 (nine) copies and 2 (two) reproducible copies for drawings.

4.8 The Sellers shall not, in any case, reveal to a third party the design basis and supplementary ones submitted by the Buyers, unless it is necessary for the Sellers to submit the relevant data required for the execution of the Contract to their relevant authorities and subcontractors.

Chapter Five   Packing

5.1 All Equipment and Materials, and parts to be supplied by the Sellers shall be strongly packed to withstand long distance ocean and inland transportation and numerous handlings in loading and unloading, and protective measures shall be taken to prevent damage from moisture, rain, rust, shock and corrosion according to the different characteristics and requirements of the goods so as to ensure their arrival in good conditions and during storage at the site without any rust, corrosion or deterioration. The Buyers shall handle and store the goods properly according to the requirements given in Article 5.4 and the Sellers' descriptions of packing and transportation. If any Equipment and Materials are damaged or missing due to the Sellers' mistakes the Sellers shall have them repaired, replaced or supplemented.

5.2 All locations in cases and bales shall be labelled by the Sellers indicating Contract number, name of main machine and name of accessory or its position number on assembling drawing. The spare parts shall be marked with "spare parts together with the main machine" or "two-year's spare parts" besides the above particulars.

5.3 The Sellers shall mark the following on the four adjacent sides of each package with indelible paints in conspicuous English printed works of not less than cm (it may be smaller if the package is not large enough).

A. Contract No.
B. Shipping mark:
C. Name of Equipment and item No.
D. Case / Bale No.
E. Consignee code;
F. Port of destination: _____ , China.
G. Gross / net weight (KG).
H. Measurements: Length × width × height (in _____ cm).
I. Centre of gravity or points for slinging (in the case of packing weighing: more than tons).

Each case shall be conspicuously marked with "Handle with Care", "Right Side Up", "Keep Dry" and with other appropriate international trade practice marks according to the special features of different goods and the requirements for transportation, loading, unloading and storage. For the unpacked goods, metal labels with marks as stipulated above shall be put on each side of them, or the above-said marks with indelible paint shall be put on both ends or both sides of each package.

The case containing model of the Plant shall be marked with "model".

5.4 In each case there shall be enclosed following documents:
A. Detailed packing list in triplicate;
B. Quality certificate in triplicate.

5.5 The Technical Documentation shall be properly checked to withstand moisture and rain in long distance transportation and numerous handlings. The surface and inside of the package shall be marked with the following:
A. Contract No.
B. Shipping mark:

C. Consignee: Peking, China.
D. Port of destination: Peking, China.

E.   Weight (KG).

F.   Case / Bale No.

Each package shall contain 4 copies of the detailed list of the Technical Documentation.

Chapter Six   Delivery

6.1   The delivery of Equipment and Materials under the Contract shall be effected by the Sellers F.O.B. in shipments, from the month after signing the Contract and in accordance with the schedule of the construction of the Contract Plant.

Port of destination: _____ , China.

The risk and properties of Equipment and Materials shall be transferred from the Sellers to the Buyers after they have been effectively lifted over the ship's rail of the carrying vessel assigned by the Buyers at the loading port. Equipment and / or machinery shall be delivered in complete set with special tools, special calibrating and testing devices, accessories and easy-worn parts. The foundation jigs and anchor bolts required for the Equipment and machines to be supplied by the Sellers shall be delivered in one lot prior to the first shipment. The Technical Documentation shall be delivered by the Sellers C.I.F. Peking Airport, The delivery schedule and contents are stipulated in Annex to the Contract.

6.2   A preliminary delivery schedule in 6 copies indicating name, item, number, quantity, unit price, manufacturer, approximate weight, approximate measurement, and estimated time of each shipment of the Equipment and Materials shall be sent to the Buyers by the Sellers within _____ months after signing the Contract. Upon mutual consultations and agreement during the preliminary project meeting the said schedule shall be taken as the basis for working out the final delivery schedule for the Contract, and at the same time, both parties shall discuss the special care to be taken for certain goods in transportation and storage.

6.3   Not later than _____ days before the readiness of each shipment, the Sellers shall inform the Buyers by cable of the Contract number, the date of goods' readiness for shipment, approximate total gross weight and approximate total measurement, loading port, as well as the approximate total gross weight, approximately overall dimensions and item number of each large piece exceeding 50 metric tons in weight or m × m × m in measurement.

Within _____ days after despatching the cable the Sellers shall airmail to the Buyers a detailed list of the shipment indicating names, item number and quantity of the Equipment and Materials, a brief transportation description of the Equipment and Materials and a sketch of each large piece exceeding 50 metric tons in weight or m × m × m in measurement each in four copies.

6.4   The Buyers shall advise the Sellers _____ days before the arrival of the carrying vessel at the loading port by cable of the name of the carrying vessel, expected loading date, shipping agent and other information necessary for the shipment. The sellers shall contact the shipping agent for shipment. In case the Buyer shall have to alter the shipping schedule or substitute the vessel, the Buyers or the shipping agent shall duly advise the Sellers to this effect.

6.5 Within _____ hours after the completion of each shipment the Sellers shall inform the Buyer by cable of the date and number of bill of lading, name of the carrying vessel, total weight, total number of cases and Contract number.

The loading date mentioned on the bill of lading shall be the actual delivery date of Equipment and Materials.

6.6 In the event of the Sellers' failure effecting the shipment upon the arrival of Buyers' vessel at the loading port, all expenses thus incurred, including dead freight, demurrage and other charges of the shipping company, shall be for the Sellers' account. Such expenses shall be calculated and settled in accordance with the relevant documents of the shipping company.

6.7 Provided that the loading port is under normal working condition, in case the Buyers' vessel fails to arrive at the loading port within _____ days after the date of goods' readiness for shipment as stipulated under Article 6.3, the storage charges and premium incurred within the said period shall be borne by the Sellers, while the storage charges and premium incurred from the 1st day shall be borne by the Buyers and paid within _____ days after receiving and checking up the warehouse receipt and the original invoice opened and signed by the warehouse and the insurance company respectively. However, the Sellers shall still be obligated to load at their own expense and risk the Equipment and Materials on board the carrying vessel immediately after her arrival at the loading port according to the Buyers' instructions.

6.8 Within _____ hours after delivery of the Technical Documentation, the Sellers shall notify the Buyers by cable of the date of despatch, flight number, airway bill number, number of packages, gross weight and Contract number. The following documents shall be aired by the Sellers to the Buyers within _____ days after the delivery of the Technical Documentation.

A. One copy of airway bill;

B. List of technical documentation in quadruplicate.

The date of airway bill or receipt of post at the Sellers' residence shall be considered the actual delivery date of the Technical Documentation.

6.9 The Sellers shall submit along with the carrying vessel one copy each of the following documents to China National Foreign Trade Transportation Corportation:

A. Bill of lading;

100

B.   Commercial invoice;

C.   Packing list;

D.   Quality certificate;

E.   List of goods shipped, brief transportation description and sketch as stipulated under Article 6.3.

6.10 The Sellers shall airmail to the Buyers five copies each of the A. B. C. D. documents in Article 3.2(b) within two weeks after the C.I.F. delivery of the Equipment and Materials, and two copies each of the ex-works inspection report and detailed records as stipulated in 7.2 within _____ weeks after the C.I.F. delivery of the Equipment ·and Materials.

Chapter Seven   Standards, Inspection and Test

7.1   The Buyers agree that the Sellers will carry out the design, selection of materials, manufacturing, inspection and test for the Equipment and Materials to be supplied by the Sellers according to the existing standards and codes of the Sellers' country. Within one and a half months after signing the Contract the Sellers shall airmail at their own expense to the Buyers the said standards and codes in 4 (four) copies. These documents shall be delivered in English, with an respective indication of item numbers of standards and codes for corresponding Equipment and Materials. The Buyers shall put forward their comments on the submitted standards and codes during the preliminary design meeting, and the final agreement reached between both parties through discussion shall be taken as the basis for the inspection and test of the Equipment and Materials.

7.2   All Equipment and Materials to be supplied by the Sellers shall be inspected by the Sellers and quality certificates and inspection and test records shall be issued by the manufacturers or the Sellers. These documents shall be delivered to the Buyers as a certificate of quality guarantee as stipulated in the Contract. All expenses involved in the inspection and test of the Equipment and Mateials shall be for the Sellers' account.

7.3   The Buyers shall be entitled to send their inspectors at their own expense to the Sellers' or the Sub-contractor's country to join the Sellers' representatives in the quality inspection and test of the Equipment and Materials in the manufacturers' workshops. The Equipment to be jointly inspected shall be fixed between both parties at the preliminary design meeting. The Sellers shall notify the Buyers of the date of inspection and test three months prior to the assembly and readiness of the first main equipment. The Buyers shall within two months after receiving the Sellers' notice inform the Sellers of the list of their appointed inspectors so as to enable the Sellers to render assistance in obtaining their visa. In case the Buyers' inspectors are not present after being notified that the Equipment and Materials are ready for inspection and test the Sellers shall have the right to carry out the inspection and test independently. When necessary, the Buyers' inspectors shall also have the right to join the Sellers in the inspection and test of the Equipment and Materials other than the main ones.

The Sellers shall provide free of charge the Buyers' inspectors with working facilities, all necessary technical documentation, drawings, test rouum, instruments and tools for their inspection and test work. The Buyers' inspectors shall have the right to put forward their opinions for improvement, if they find the Equipment and Materials do not comply with the quality standards and codes stipulated in Articles 7.1 and 9.1 of the Contract. The Sellers shall give their full consideration to the opinions of the Buyers' inpectors and make every endeavour to assure the quality of the Equipment and Materials.

The quality inspection and test jointly done by the Buyers' and the Sellers' inspectors before delivery shall not substitute the inspection and test at the Contract Plant site.

7.4 All Equipment and Materials to be supplied by the Sellers shall be inspected and checked at the Plant site and when it is necessary, tests stipulated in Article 7.1 shall also be carried out. The Sellers are entitled to send their own inspectors at their own expense to the Plant site to join the inspection, check and test, or the Sellers' representatives being on the Plant site will be informed in time about the date of open-package inspection. Such inspection shall be performed as soon as possible after the arrivel of the Equipment and Materials at the Plant site.

The packing list to be supplied as part of the shipping documents as per Clause 4.9 shall be taken as the basis for quantity checkup. Should any shortage, missing, damage or cases which are not in conformity with the quality standards stipulated in Articles 7.1 and 9.1 of the Contract be found with the delivered Equipment and Materials during open-package inspection,check and test in the presence of the representatives of both parties, a detailed record shall be made and signed by them. This record shall be taken as an effective proof for the Buyers to claim replacement, repair or supplement from the Sellers in case the Sellers are responsible. Such replacement, repair or supplement shall be performed as quickly as possible.

If owing to the Sellers' reason the Sellers do not join the inspection, check and test, the Buyers shall have the right to open package and conduct the inspection and test independently. Should any shortage, missing, damage or cases which are not in conformity with the quality standards in Articles 7.1 and 9.1 of the Contract be found, a certificate shall be issued by China National Commodity Inspection and Testing Bureau as an effective evidence for the Buyers to claim replacement,repair or supplement from the Sellers, in case the Sellers are responsible therefor.

7.5 Without prejudice to Articles 7.1-7.4 above, the Buyers may elect to appoint China National Commodity Inspection Testing Bureau as their representative to monitor (according to the existing standards and codes of the Sellers' country) the inspection on, and the test for, Equipment and Materials which are to be supplied by the Sellers, provided that the Buyers inform the Sellers in writing of this decision immediately after they receive the said standards and codes as stipulated under Article 7.1.

7.6 Pursuant to 7.5 above, all Equipment and Materials which are to be supplied by the Sellers shall be jointly inspected by the Sellers and China National Commodity Inspection and Testing Bureau. Quality certificates and inspection and test records shall be issued jointly by the manufacturers and China National Commodity Inspection and Testing Bureau. These documents shall be treated as a certificate of quality guarantee as stipulated in the Contract. All expenses arising out of the inspection and testing of the Equipment and Material shall be shared equally between the Buyers and the Sellers.

7.7 If China National Commodity Inspection and Testing Bureau, after jointly inspecting all the Equipment and Materials which are to be supplied by the Sellers as stipulated in Article 7.7 above, has grounds to prove that such Equipment and Materials do not match the standards and codes of the Sellers' country, no quality certificates and inspection and test records shall be issued. In this respect, China National Commodity Inspection and Testing Bureau will make a report in duplicate to both the Buyers and Sellers. Upon receipt of this report, the Sellers are entitled to improve the said Equipment and Materials and re-submit them for inspection within six months.

7.8 When China National Commodity Inspection and Testing Bureau is to conduct on-the-spot inspection at places of the manufacturers, the Sellers shall provide necessary facilities and convenience for its work.

7.9 China National Commodity Inspection and Testing Bureau is a professional body under the leadership of the State Administration of Import and Export Commodity Inspection of the People's Republic of China. China National Commodity Inspection and Testing Bureau will execute its duties in accordance with the ''Regulations of the People's Republic of China on Inspection of Import and Export Commodities'' promulgated by the State Council of the People's Republic of China on January 28, 1984 as well as any other subsequent legislations thereof. Should China National Commodity Inspection and Testing Bureau be appointed as the Buyers' representative in the execution of inspection and testing for the Equipment and Materials which are to be supplied by the Sellers, the decision of China National Commodity Inspection and Testing Bureau shall be final and conclusive.

Chapter Eight   Construction

8.1 Definition:
Erection refers to the erection work of the Plant. Mechanical tests refer to the running of a single or a series of machines and equipment with electricity, water, air or other media if necessary.
Commissioning refers to the running of the Plant with raw materials, utilities and chemicals in order to produce.
Performance guarantee test run refers to the tests for fulfilling the guarantee figures.
Acceptance refers to the acceptance of the Contract Plant by the Buyers.

8.2 The erection, mechanical tests, commissioning and performance guarantee test run shall be carried out under the organization of the Buyers and the technical instruction of the Sellers.

8.3 Before the erection work starts, the Sellers' technical personnel shall review the civil work and give detailed description of the methods and requirements for the erection, and during the erection they shall give technical instructions and assistance so as to complete the erection satisfactorily.

8.4 If the erection has been finished and the mechanical tests successfully performed as well as the construction is found in full conformity with the requirements of the Technical Documentation a certificate for the finished erection shall be signed by the representatives of both parties at the Plant site.

8.5 The commissioning period shall be _____ months and according to the progress of the commissioning, the date of performance guarantee test run shall be fixed between both parties and both parties will make their best efforts to realize that date.

8.6 During the performance guarantee test run period the production capacity shall reach the guarantee figures every day, the consumption of raw materials and utilities which shall be calculated from the average of the performance guarantee test run period shall reach the guarantee figures and the quality of the product shall reach the guarantee figures every shift.

8.7 If all the guarantee figures stipulated in Annex _____ to the Contract are fulfilled in the performance guarantee test run period as specified in Article 8.6 of the Contract, a certificate of acceptance of the Plant shall be signed by the representatives of both parties within _____ days in four copies, two copies for each party. This shall be deemed as acceptance of the Plant by the Buyer.

8.8 If it is due to the Sellers' fault, the Buyers shall agree to have an extension of _____ months of commissioning. The Sellers shall make corrections and to have further performance guarantee test runs at their own expense. Should the guarantee figures of the Contract are still not reached within _____ months due to the Sellers' fault, the relevant stipulations in Chapter 9 shall be applied. During the extension period of _____ months, all expenses for the Sellers' technical personnel shall be borne by the Sellers.

If it is due to the Buyers' fault, the commissioning period shall be extended by _____ months. During this period, all the expenses for the Sellers' technical personnel shall be for the Buyers' account. The number of the Sellers personnel shall be discussed and fixed by both parties. In case the guarantee figures are still not reached within the period of this further _____ months of commissioning, the Plant shall be accepted by the Buyers and certificate of acceptance shall be signed by both parties.

8.9 In the course of erection, mechanical test, commissioning, and performance guarantee test run, should any damages and losses occur due to the Sellers' mistakes in design and incorrect technical instructions, the Sellers shall indemnify the Buyers for such damages and losses. In case of any defects in the equipment and materials found, both parties shall check them up. If the Sellers are responsible, the Sellers shall supplement the equipment or, if necessary, send any equipment back to the Sellers' country for repair or replacemnt. In such case, the Sellers shall deliver the replacing equipment to the Plant Site, and risks thereof. If the Buyers are responsible, the Sellers shall assist the Buyers to remove the defects. If such supplement or replacement is necessary, the Sellers shall make delivery at port on FOB terms, and the costs involved shall be for the Buyers' account. In performing the obligations specified in the present Article, the Sellers shall do their utmost to ensure the progress of construction of the Plant not to be affected.

8.10 The acceptance of the Contract Plant stipulated in this Chapter of the Contract shall not free the Sellers from their responsibility for the equipment and materials of the Plant during the mechanical guarentee period.

Chapter Nine   Guarantee and Penalty

9.1 The Sellers guarantee that the Plant shall possess the most up-to-date and ripened technology among the relevant plants of the licence owner available at the date the Contract is signed, that the Equipment and Materials are of best quality and that their type selection complies with the requirements of process technology, operation and longterm service. The Sellers shall supply complete and correct Technical Documentation in order to carry out successfully the erection, mechanical tests, commissioning including performance guarantee testruns as well as normal and safe operation and maintenance of the Plant.

9.2 Delay in Delivery

9.2(a)   If owing to the reason of the Sellers the Equipment and Materials are not delivered according to the final delivery schedule as specified in Chapter 6 of the Contract, the Sellers shall pay to the

Buyers penalty for such delay in delivery at the following rates calculated from the date of shipment provided as per final delivery schedule up to the date the delayed Equipment or Materials are shipped:

—for each of the first _____ weeks, _____ % (   ) of the price of the Equipment and Materials delayed.

—for each week after the first _____ weeks, _____ % (   ) of the price of the Equipment and Materials delayed.

For the delayed items, both parties will make their best efforts to effect shipment on board the next vessel assigned by the Buyers.

9.2(b)   The Sellers shall deliver the Technical Documentation on the Schedule in order to ensure that the construction schedule of the Contract Plant will not be influenced. In case the contents and requirements of the Technical Documentation delivered by the Sellers is not in conformity with the requirements specified in _____ to the Contract, the Sellers shall revise them and deliver the correct Technical Documentation as quickly as possible and do their best to see that the progress of the construction of the Plant is not affected.

The payment of the penalty as per the present Article shall not release the Sellers from their obligations of continuous delivery.

9.3   The Sellers shall inform the Buyers as soon as possible of the possibility of any delay in the delivery of Equipment and Materials as well as Technical Documentation, possible length of time to be delayed and any measures be taken to expedite the delivery. When the delay in delivery due to the reasons of the Sellers in over (_____) months, the Buyers shall have the right to cancel the Contract wholly or partially provided no agreement is reached through negotiation between both parties. After the Contract is cancelled, all remaining problems shall be settled through negotiation by both parties.

9.4   The damages occurred in the course of construction, erection, mechanical test, commissioning and performance guarantee test-runs of the Plant, due to mistakes of the Sellers Technical Documentation or due to incorrect instruction of the Sellers' technical personnel shall be remedied at the Sellers' own expense in such a way that the Equipment and Materials shall be corrected, repaired, replaced or completed, which ever necessary.

In case the Buyers' personnel is seriously injured or died during erection, mechanical test commissioning and performance guarantee test-run due to faulty instruction of the Sellers' personnel, the Sellers shall take the responsibility. As to these accidents, the problem should be solved through discussion between both parties.

In case defect of Equipment and Materials is found during erection, mechanical tests, commissioning and performance guarantee test run the defect shall be checked by both parties and if to the Sellers fault, the Sellers correct repair or replace the Equipment or Materials at their own expense. If the Buyers are responsible for the defect, the Sellers, shall give their assistance to remove it and, if necessary, to supply the Equipment and Materials at the Buyers' cost.

In case the Sellers are responsible to remove the defects, the Buyers shall supply the Sellers at their request the necessary personnel, erection tools, cranes, etc. for performing the removal of the defects. The cost thus incurred shall be borne by the Sellers. The removal of defects shall be performed as quickly as possible and the Sellers shall do their best to see that the progress of the construction of the Plant is not effected.

9.5 The Sellers guarantee that the Plant shall reach the guarantee figures provided that the Plant is operated under normal conditions in accordance with the Technical Documentation and the Sellers shall have to prove that the guarantee figures can be reached in the performance guarantee test-run as per Article 8.6. If the guarantee figures cannot be reached owing to the reason of the Sellers the following will apply:

9.6 Mechanical guarantee for Equipment and Materials to be supplied by the Sellers, except consumable materials and normal wear and tear.

9.6(a) Provided that operation and maintenance of the Equipment and Materials of the Plant is done according to the Sellers' Technical Documentation the guarantee period shall be (_____) months from the date of acceptance of the Plant or _____ months after the date of signing the Contract, whichever is earlier. The period of guarantee for repaired or replacing parts of Equipment and Materials shall be (_____) months from the date of readiness for operation or after arrival at the Plant site, or Peking Airport. Should any other equipment be out-of-action because of repair or replacement due to the Sellers' fault then the guarantee period of the out-of-action equipment shall be extended correspondingly, provided such out-of-action exceeds (_____) days.

9.6(b) The Buyers shall notify the Sellers immediately by cable of each defect of the Equipment and Materials occurred during the mechanical guarantee period, and the Sellers shall without delay cable the Buyer whether they will send personnel to the Plant site for the investigation at their own expense, or otherwise the Buyers will entrust the China National Commodity Inspection and Testing Bureau to investigate the reasons of defect, should the Sellers fail to despatch personnel to the Plant site.

The certificate made by the China National Commodity Inspection and Testing Bureau should be considered as the final evidence. The notices of claims shall be still effective when they are sent by cable by the Buyers within (_____) days after the expiration of the mechanical guarantee period.

9.6(c)   If it has been found out that the Sellers are responsible for the defect the Sellers at their own expense shall repair or replace the defective parts of Equipment and Materials within the period agreed upon by both parties. The replacing parts of Equipment and Materials shall be delivered at the plant site. If any defect still remains after repair or replacement, both parties will discuss the matter for settlement.

With regard to the minor defects of Equipment and Materials for which the Sellers are responsible, the Buyers may arrange to make the repairing or replacement at the Sellers' expense with the consent of both parties.

9.7   The total sum of penalty which might occur as provided in Articles 9.2 and 9.6 of the Contract shall not exceed _____ % (percent) of the total contract price as per Chapter 2 of the Contract. (except the costs for removal of defects by the Sellers at their own expense)

Chapter Ten   Licence

10.1 The Sellers, on behalf of _____ hereby grant to the Buyers the nonexclusive license and right to use in China.

10.2 Within (_____) months after signing the Contract the Sellers shall submit to the Buyers (_____) photostat copies of certificates of all of patents pertaining to the above mentioned process registered in _____

10.3 Should any question or claim arise in China from any third party having patents registered in China due to use of the process by the Buyers, the Buyers will handle the matter concerned. Should any question or claim arise outside of China from any third party due to use of the process by the Buyers, the Sellers will handle the matter concerned.

10.4 The Sellers shall inform the Buyers about improvements and new informations on the process up to the acceptance of the Contract Plant. After that date the parties are prepared to exchange informations on experience and improvements of the process.

10.5 Within _____ years after signing the Contract the Buyers shall not disclose in whole or in part to any third party the know-how, Technical Documentation and other information of the process obtained under the Contract. The secrecy does not apply to those parts of the know-how, Technical Documentation or other information of the process which become part of the public knowledge or literature.

10.6 The licence, know-how, Technical Documentation and other information are to be used only for the construction, operation, and maintenance of the Plant.

10.7 The obligations contained in Clauses 10.5 and 10.6 shall neither be affected by the liquidation of the Contract nor by a premature termination of the same.

Chapter Eleven   Force Majeure

In case of force majoure like fire, war, earthquake, typhoon (windstorm), floods, etc. during the period of the execution of the Contract, the problem shall be settled through negotiation between both parties.

Should such case happens, the prevented party shall inform the other party by telex to this effect within one week after the occurrence of force majeure and airmail a certificate issued by the China Council for the Promotion of International Trade in China or the competent Chamber of Commerce in_____ within a period of _____ weeks thereafter.

The prevented party shall not be held responsible for any delay or failure in performing any or all of the obligations caused by force majeure. However, they shall have to continue to fulfil their obligations immediately after the case of force majeure has ceased or the consequences have been removed. The time for implementing the Contract shall be extended by a period equivalent to the effect of the occurrences.

In case the duration of force majeure exceeds _____ months, both parties shall discuss the problems of continuation of the Contract. If no agreement can be reached, the case shall be submitted to arbitration according to Chapter 12.

Chapter Twelve   Arbitration

12.1 All disputes in connection with the Contract shall be settled by friendly consultations between both parties. In case no amicable agreement can be reached, the matter in dispute shall be finally decided by arbitration.

12.2 The place of arbitration is _____ , and the arbitration shall be performed in accordance with the arbitration procedure.

Chapter Thirteen   Taxation

13.1 All taxes, customs, duties and other dues arising in the country of the Sellers in connection with the conclusion and performance of the Contract shall be borne by the Buyers.

Chapter Fourteen   Effectiveness of the Contract

14.1 The Contract is signed between the authorized representatives of both parties on in Peking and shall become effective immediately after signature.

14.2 All previous oral and written statements, documents, letters or others between both parties shall become null and void after signing the Contract.

14.3 The Contract is made out in originals in English _____ originals for each party. All amendments, complements and alternations shall be made in writing and signed by the authorized representatives of both parties, and then they shall form an integral part of the Contract.

14.4 No assignment of any obligation and right under the Contract shall be made by either of the parties to a third party without the previous consent of the other party.

14.5 All correspondence between both parties during the execution of the Contract shall be made in English in three copies.

14.6 Each party shall assist the other to obtain entry and exit visa and to arrange accommodation for their personnel to be sent in connection with the Contract.

14.7 The Contract shall automatically be null and void upon the fulfilment of the Contract, except the provisions in Article 10.7 hereof.

14.8 Copies of original certificates, protocols or minutes of meeting, etc. established during the execution of the Contract shall be handed over to both parties immediately after signature.

14.9 The Contract is made out in (_____) originals in the English and Chinese languages, (_____) originals in both languages for each party, both texts being equally authentic.

(Signed)	(Signed)
For and on behalf of	For and on behalf of
(the Buyers).	(the Sellers).

Author's notes

I   * It is not comprehensive enough to add everything in a single contract, annexus to the Contract may be of help in this aspect. Here are some of the suggested annexus:

Annex 1   Design Plan with Drawing
Annex 2   Range of equipment and materials supplied by the Sellers
Annex 3   Original technical documents
Annex 4   Letter of Guarantee issued by the Buyers' bank
Annex 5   Letter of Guarantee issued by the Sellers' bank

II   Contracted parties in the People's Republic of China prefer to use the word "Article" to the word "Clause", so I used Article throughout the above mentioned sample contract.

THE ESTABLISHMENT OF
A JOINT VENTURE MACHINERY
CORPORATION IN CHINA

The Agreement on The Establishment of A Joint Venture Machinery Corporation in China

_____ (hereinafter referred to as "SINO")
and _____ (hereinafter referred as "Investor")
and _____ (hereinafter referred to as "Co-investor")
Hereinafter joinly referred to as the parties on the establishment of a joint venture _____
Corporation in the Republic of China (PRC).

Whereas, the parties to this agreement are willing to cooperate in order to increase the capacity of the Chinese industry, up-date and up-grade its products and manufacturing methods, generate products suitable for domestic and export use in order to generate foreign exchange, improve installation and maintenance methods, carry out appropriate research and development in the field of _____

Whereas, this objective can best be achieved by the formation of a joint venture company for the purpose of manufacturing, developing, selling, installing and maintaining _____
parts and components thereof (all or any of which are hereinafter included under the designation the PRODUCTS').

Now therefore, in accordance with the principle of equality and mutual benefit, the three parties enter into the following agreement:

1) INCORPORATION
    1.1 The parties agree to incorporate a joint venture (hereinafter referred to as 'the VENTURE') with limited liability in the territory of PRC within the framework of the law of the People's Republic of China on Joint Ventures using Chinese and Foreign investments ('the LAW') and other Chinese laws concerned.
    1.2 The name of the VENTURE shall be Limited.
    1.3 The participants shall have no liability of any sort for the debts or obligations of the VENTURE. The liability of the participants is limited to making the contributions to the capital required pursuant to this agreement and the Articles of Association of the VENTURE.
    1.4 The principal purposes for which the VENTURE is established are the manufacture, development, sale, installation and maintenance of the PRODUCTS

2) CONTRIBUTION AND EQUITY SHARES

2.1 **The parties shall contribute to the VENTURE and share equity participation in VENTURE in a ratio of per cent (SINO) and per cent Investor Co-investor in following manner:**

SINO shall inject the Factory (buildings, machinery, inventory but excluding land) and the old Factory (machinery, inventory but excluding buildings and land) whose injection shall be valued for the purposes of participation at dollars million.

For accounting and other purposes, however, the abovementioned current assets and liabilities are those actually shown in the balance sheet as per incorporation date attached hereto as Appendix. The future financing of the VENTURE'S working capital shall basically remain the same as in the past.

2.2 The foreign parties shall inject a total of dollars million in cash, Investor to contribute the sum of dollars million and Co-investor to contribute the sum of dollars million.

2.3 All parties shall inject all their respective contributions within _____ days after the issuing of the operation's licence for the VENTURE.

2.4 If so required, Investor agrees to provide additional financing in the form of a long-term loan at most favourable market conditions in an amount equal to Renminbi yuan million which shall be made in payments of Renminbi yuan million in the 2nd and of Renminbi yuan million in the 3rd year of the VENTURE and totally repaid in the year.

3) OTHER SERVICES BY FOREIGN PARTIES AND ADDITIONAL AGREE-MENTS

3.1 The VENTURE, through the agreements mentioned below, shall have access to the entire present and future technology and know-how in respect of the design, manufacture, installation and maintenance of Investor's _____

_____ To ensure the complete transfer to know-how, Investor will provide
— Product design
— Manufacturing Techniques and methods
— Production and quality control methods
— Factory design and remodelling
— Factory organization methods
— Installation and maintenace methods
— Engineering assistance

3.2 The following agreements which are annexed hereto and form an integral part of the present agreement shall be signed immediately after the incorporation of the VENTURE among the VENTURE and Investor, respectively:
— Licence agreement

- Consulting agreement
- Maintenance franchise agreement
- Export agency agreement.

4) DURATION AND TERMINATION

4.1 The corporate existence of the VENTURE will commence on the issue of an operations license under Article 3 of the Law and will continue for an initial period of _____ years but may be extended for further periods of _____ years by the written agreement of all of the then participants.

4.2 Not less than _____ years prior to the expiration of the initial period of years of any subsequent extended period of years, the then participants in the VENTURE shall commence discussion regarding the extension of the period of existence of the VENTURE and in the event of their agreeing upon such extension, they shall record such agreement in a written document signed by all of them not later than three years before the expiry of the then current period or by such later date as all of them may agree.

4.3 If a written agreement for the extension of the period of existence of the VENTURE is not signed by three years prior to the expiration of the then current period of existence (or by such later date as all of the then participants may agree), the VENTURE shall terminate at the end of such current period of existence and the provision of clauses 4.5 and 4.6 shall then apply.

4.4 Notwithstanding the foregoing, it shall be open to the then participants to agree at any time to extend the period of existence of the VENTURE for more than one period of years or for a single period longer than years if they so agree and if the law then permits.

4.5 Upon termination of the present agreement, the shares of the foreign parties will be repurchased by SINO. The repurchase price for the foreign parties' share shall be the net equity (_____) of the VENTURE to be determined by a balance sheet effective on the date of termination multiplied by the share factor plus a percentage to be negotiated and to reflect the future profitability of the VENTURE. This final percentage shall take into account the degree of smoothness of the VENTURE progress.

4.6 After termination of the present agreement, the name of the VENTURE shall be changed to exclude any allusion to Investor or Co-investor. SINO agrees not to use any Investor or Co-investor trademark after termination of the present agreement without written consent by Investor or Co-investor respectively.

5) EXTENSION OF THE VENTURE

5.1 It is agreed that a further objective is to incorporate the operation

113

within the VENTURE at a later stage when circumstances permit to do so.

5.2 The parties shall work together with a view to making (＿＿＿＿＿＿) a manufacturer and supplier to the Investor under sub-licence from the VENTURE as soon as practicable. All sales of the products made by(＿＿＿＿＿＿＿＿)under such sub-licence shall be made through the VENTURE organisation and, if overseas, in the manner set out in the export agreement. If ( ) agrees to become a sub-license of, and manufacturer and supplier to the VENTURE, the VENTURE shall grant the necessary sub-licence to ( ) and ( ) engineers will have the opportunity of taking part in the training courses and programmes.

5.3 Further participants may be included in the VENTURE with the consent of the then participants of the VENTURE.

6) SALES, INSTALLATON AND MAINTENANCE

6.1 The VENTURE shall sell the products within the PRC and abroad. Sales targets shall be arranged in accordance with the production objectives contained in the joint proforma (Appendix).

6.2 During the period of validity of the present agreement plus an additional and consecutive period of years, Co-investor and Investor shall be the exclusive agent for VENTURE for the sale outside of PRC of the PRODUCT manufactured by VENTURE. Common target of all parties is the highest possible market share in the Co-investor for products manufactured by VENTURE in order to acquire as much export business as possible. By unanimous decision of the board of the VENTURE, the VENTURE may export directly to countries in which neither Co-investor nor Investor are represented. All export activities of the VENTURE shall be governed by the export agency agreement.

6.3 The VENTURE shall carry out installation and maintenance within the PRC. In order to strengthen on the VENTURE, the VENTURE shall have the exclusive right for installation and maintenance for the machine proposed to be manufactured within the PRC which is imported under the direct control of or under a contract with SINO unless the clients install and / or maintain the products completely with their own personnel.

The VENTURE shall with the help of SINO assist clients and organizations to acquire INVESTOR products to be installed in their buildings. If or a particular contract Investor and Co-investor require sales assitance from the VENTURE commission to be negotiated shall be paid to the VENTURE.

6.4 Installation and maintenance abroad will be the responsibility of Co-investor or Investor. It is intended to up-grade qualified VENTURE and SINO technicians for work abroad.

114

Co-investor or Investor, respectively, shall pay an annual mainte-nance fee for each elevator or its equivalent experience for the average contract life of ( ) years paid in foreign currency according to the export agency agreement appended. Herto (Appendix).

7) DIVIDENDS, REINVESTMENT POLICY

7.1 The gross profit (profit before tax) of the VENTURE shall be determined according to acknowledged accounting principles as applied in the joint proforma (Appendix). The income tax of the VENTURE shall be paid out of this gross profit.

7.2 After payment of the income tax, the payment to the bonus and welfare fund shall be made as from time to time determined by the board of directors of the VENTURE in accordance with the articles of association. The remaining proceeds shall be available for declaration as dividends.

7.3 For the first (____) years, the parties agree to reinvest in the VENTURE (____) per cent of the dividends derived and for the following (____) years, (____) per cent of the dividends in order to expand the VENTURE. At the end of the (____) years the participants will reconsider the reinvestment policy.

8) TAXES

8.1 The VENTURE shall be exempted from income tax for the first three profit making years in accordance with Article 7 of the LAW.

8.2 For a minimum period of (____) years the income tax shall not exceed per cent including local taxes if the after tax profit does not exceed (____) per cent on net equity.

8.3 For a minimum period of (____) years withholding tax on dividends actually paid to the parties shall not exceed (____) per cent. However, no withholding tax shall be levied on the dividends reinvested into the VENTURE according to Article 7 above. Furthermore, income taxes levied from the VENTURE shall be restituted to the VENTURE in proportion of the dividends rein-vested into the VENTURE in accordance with Article 7, paragraph 3 of the LAW.

8.4 No tax shall be levied by the PRC on any income of expatriate executives not paid by the VENTURE. To the extent that the income of expatriate executives is paid by the VENTURE, the tax rate thereon shall not exceed either the rate applied to Chinese natural persons resident and employed in China or the rate of income tax applied to the VENTURE.

8.5 There shall be no other taxes for VENTURE and the three parties.

8.6 All fees and royalties are net of tax.

8.7 There are no other tax liabilities, nor are there any other liabilities of the VENTURE, than those shown on the balance sheet as per incorporation date (Appendix).

9) LEASES OF LAND, BUILDING AND MACHINERY

9.1 Factory land shall be leased to the VENTURE. The VENTURE shall lease the buildings of the old factory and the new factory owned by SINO to the extent made necessary by production requirements. Part of the machinery necessary for production also shall be leased by the VENTURE.

9.2 The leasing rate of the land shall be at a rate of Renminbi yuan (__ __) per square metre per year for a minimum period of (____) years.

9.3 The leasing rate of the buildings shall be at a rate of (____) per cent of the agreed value per year for a minimum period of (____) years.

9.4 The leasing rate of machinery shall be at a rate of (____) per cent of the agreed value per year for a minimum of ten years.

9.5 The VENTURE reserves the right to purchase the buildings of the new Beijing factory at a price to be negotiated.

10) JOINT PROFORMA, RAW MATERIAL, WATER AND ENERGY SUPPLY

10.1 The joint proforma (Appendix) sets binding targets for the VENTURE concerning units produced, installed and maintained and their costs. Domestic prices shall be as low as is consistent with ensuring the VENTURE a reasonable profit, i.e. not exceeding and not less than per cent net profit after tax on total turnover of the VENTURE. Export prices shall be set according to the export agency agreement.

10.2 In order to attain the goal of doubling the present production within five years and quadrupling it within eight years, SINO shall secure the adequate supply of the raw materials, including the raw materials needed for the purposes mentioned in Article 6 before and Appendix.

10.3 Raw materials, energy and water supply shall be available to the VENTURE at the same price as to Chinese public corporations.

11) DOMESTIC LOANS AND TRANSFER OF FOREIGN CURRENCY

11.1 Domestic loans shall be available to the VENTURE at the same interest as they are given to Chinese public corporations.

11.2 Transfer of foreign currency to PRC shall be free from any restriction and tax whatsoever.

11.3 Transfers of foreign currency out of the PRC in connection with agreements shall be free from any restriction. If required by law an amount, not exceeding (____) per cent, may be levied on the following categories.
— Licence fee
— Royalties
— Interest on debt
— Consulting fee

The VENTURE will make every effort to minimize such levies.

12) ORGANS AND MANAGEMENT OF THE VENTURE

12.1 The VENTURE board shall consist of members, of which, including the chairman, shall be appointed by SINO, one by VENTURE to act as vice-chairman and one by Co-investor. Decisions regarding changes to the Articles of Association or board instructions as provided in the Articles of Association shall require majority approval of two thirds of the votes whereby one of the approving votes has to be by the representative of Investor or Co-investor.

12.2 An engineering, production and administration management shall be established in the factories, aided by a standing Investor project team in Australia.

12.3 VENTURE head office shall be established in to manage the VENTURE affairs and handle communications with Investor, Co-investor and the factories.

13) EMPLOYMENT, DISCHARGE AND WAGES OF LABOUR FORCE

13.1 The board of directors shall have the right to employ and dismiss workers and executives of the VENTURE and shall give consideration to the advice and proposals of the INVESTOR project team when taking decisions on the employment and discharge of workers and executives of the VENTURE.

13.2 The labour force of the VENTURE shall be yearly adapted to the needs of the VENTURE regarding the number and the quality of work and in reference to Footnotes 1 and 2 of the Joint Proforma (Appendix _____).

13.3 The wages paid by the VENTURE shall be in reference to Footnotes 1 and 2 of the Joint Performa (Appendix _____).

14) INSURANCE

All insurable risks of the VENTURE shall be insured in the PRC.

15) VISA, WORK PERMITS AND IMPORT LICENSES

SINO agree to be responsible for procuring the timely issue of all visas, work permits, import licences and the like which are necessary for the purposes of the VENTURE.

16) SETTLEMENT OF DISPUTES

16.1 Any disputes arising among the parties to this agreement shall be settled by the board of the VENTURE.

16.2 If the board should fail to resolve such a dispute, it shall be brought in principle before the ordinary court of the domicile of the actual defendant.

16.3 However, if one of the parties to the dispute so desire it shall be determined by arbitration in (_____) in accordance with the arbitration rules of the (NAME OF INTERNATIONAL ARBITRATION CONVENTION——author).

17) CONTRACTUAL LANGUAGE

This agreement is made in both Chinese and English. The Chinese and English version of this agreement shall have equal status in law. This agreement is subject to approval by the respective boards of SINO, Investor and Co-Investor.

Dated this the _____ day of _____ 19 ____ .

For and on behalf of _____ (SIGNED)
    (SINO)

For and on behalf of _____ (SIGNED)
    (INVESTOR)

For and on behalf of _____ (SIGNED)
    (Co-INVESTOR)

CONTRACT FOR
TECHNOLOGY TRANSFER
AND
IMPORTATION OF EQUIPMENTS
AND
MATERIALS

Preamble

China Broadcasting Products Import Export Corporation and Better Broadcasting Products Factory of _____ Province, People's Republic of China (hereinafter referred to as "SINO") as the first part, and Foreign Advance Broadcasting Ltd of _____ , Holland (hereinafter referred to as "INVESTOR") as the second part, and Good-Trade Trading Ltd of _____ . Italy (hereinafter referred to as "GTT")

Whereas, the above three parties have entered into contract with the terms and conditions as follows:

Chapter 1   Technology Transfer

[1]   SINO shall introduce the technology necessary to produce INVESTOR'S. A type and B type products at SINO. These products are referred to "PRODUCTS", hereinafter.

[2]   INVESTOR shall offer, at SINO'S request in accordance with this contract, the technology and information possessed by INVESTOR which are necessary to PRODUCTS.

[3]   Actual names and specifications of PRODUCTS are referred to Appendix _____ .

[4]   INVESTOR shall offer SINO the information concerning trade secret, manufacturing technique and know how which is necessary to produce PRODUCTS.

Details of the information offered by INVESTOR to SINO are shown in Appendix _____ .

Chapter 2   Facility Plannings

[1]   SINO shall prepare the facility for production of PRODUCTS in accordance with INVESTOR'S suggestions.

[2]   In order to assist preparation for production facility at SINO, INVESTOR shall provide assistances including supply of the following data and ·information. These data and information will take international customary

119

examples as standard.

(1) Plan for production line
(2) Plan for production manpower arrangement
(3) Plan for equipments layout
(4) Plan for infrastructure, e.g. water supply, electricity, air-conditioning, transportation, communication
(5) Plan for installation and operation of equipments
(6) Plan for production management.
(7) Plan for market promotion.

Above date and information shall be offered to SINO by INVESTOR within 100 days after the effective date of this contract.

[3] Production line is subject to the production schedule attached to this contract which is named as Appendix _____ .

[4] SINO shall prepare production planning by itself, but shall be able to request for INVESTOR'S cooperation if it deems to be necessary.

Chapter 3   Payment of Royalty

[1] The royalty concerning technology transfer from INVESTOR'S to SINO shall be as follows:-

(1) SINO shall pay INVESTOR US$ _____ as _____ payment for buying the production rights from INVESTOR.

(2) SINO shall pay INVESTOR 3% of the sales prices on each product sold.

[2] All payments shall be made in accordance with this contract and the agreements relating to this clause.

[3] All payments shall be made through Bank of China.

[4] Method of payment shall be by the Irrevocable Letter of Credit payable at sight, in U.S. CURRENCY.

[5] SINO shall open the Irrevocable Letter of Credit for the above _____ payment payable to INVESTOR, within two months after the effective date of this contract.

[6] Within 10 days after the arrival of the above Letter of Credit, SINO shall supply all the technical data specified in this contract.

[7] When SINO places purchase order to INVESTOR for the materials stipulated in this contract, SINO shall add the royalty equivalent to 3% onto the amount of Letter of Credit, each time , or shall open a separate Letter of Credit equivalent to the royalty, at the same time of payment for purchase order.

[8] SINO shall be responsible for induced fees arising in China, and INVESTOR shall be responsible for such fees arising outside China.

Chapter 4   Marketing

[1]   INVESTOR shall assist SINO concerning marketing of PRODUCTS produced by SINO, by means of trade show, seminar, advertisement, etc. However, expenses incurred shall be borne by SINO.

[2]   INVESTOR logo shall be allowed for use in advertisement, etc., if SINO necessitates. However, INVESTOR shall not participate in SINO profit or loss relating to it, nor shall be responsible.

Chapter 5   Quality Control

[1]   Qualtiy of PRODUCTS finished at SINO shall be judged in accordance with INVESTOR'S quality control standards, _____ .

[2]   Quality check for the PRODUCTS produced at SINO at the initial stage of INVESTOR engineers' stay at SINO shall be carried out jointly by SINO and INVESTOR engineers. Details are shown in Appendix IV.

[3]   Quality of product shall be done twice, if needed. In case PRODUCTS quality does not meet the targetted specifications at the second inspection, and if causes are judged to be at INVESTOR'S side, INVESTOR shall solve the problem at INVESTOR'S cost.

[4]   In case quality inspection of PRODUCTS are satisfactory, both SINO and INVESTOR engineers shall sign the inspection certificate in duplicate and each party shall keep one copy.

Chapter 6   Delivery of Equipments

[1]   SINO shall purchase, from INVESTOR, equipments necessary to produce the PRODUCTS.

[2]   INVESTOR shall deliver, at SINO'S request in accordance with this contract, the needed equipments to GTT.

[3]   Details of items and specifications of equipments are shown in Appendix _____ .

[4]   Details of items and prices of equipments, which SINO shall purchase from INVESTOR, shall be determined during SINO'S visit with INVESTOR, subject to INVESTOR'S recommendation and mutual discussion, whilst contract(s) for equipments shall be signed separately.

[5]   Equipments delivered by INVESTOR shall be of latest type and brand new.

[6]   Settlement for the cost of the equipments delivered by INVESTOR to SINO shall be by the Irrevocable Letter of Credit at sight, CIF a China port in US currency.

[7]   INVESTOR shall deliver equipments as per delivery schedules, in accordance with the contract.

[8]   INVESTOR shall offer SINO the technical information concerning the

equipment, as per stipulated by this contract.

[9] Many and various original vendors of the equipments delivered to SINO are involved, and it may happen that equipment's operational manual(s) be in Japanese language. INVESTOR shall, however, make its effort to offer manual(s) in English.

[10] Official delivery dates of equipments shall be the dates and numbers on bills of lading / airway bills. INVESTOR shall inform SINO the airway bill / bill of lading numbers, execution dates, packing list, arrival dates, etc. without delay. At the same time, INVESTOR shall send duplicate of the documents on which above information are described.

[11] In case equipments and technical information, which are requested in the contract, are found missing, SINO shall be able to request INVESTOR for a fulfilment supply or replacement.

[12] INVESTOR shall deliver equipments by rigid packings enough to endure a long distance transportation.

[13] INVESTOR'S packing list for the deliveries shall bear the following:-
(1) Contract No.
(2) Consignee's name
(3) Destination
(4) Shipping mark
(5) Weight
(6) Carton numbers
(7) Consignee mark

[14] INVESTOR shall include duplicate of details of the content in the packing.

Chapter 7 Acceptance of Equipment

[1] SINO shall prepare facility and place to receive the equipment delivered from INVESTOR and store them.

[2] INVESTOR shall despatch engineers to SINO within three weeks after SINO'S request for installation and testing of the equipments which arrived. In this instance, SINO shall provide necessary assistance like interpreter, etc. for INVESTOR.

[3] INVESTOR'S engineers' stay at SINO, in this instance, shall be two (2) weeks.

[4] Acceptance test of the delivered equipments shall be carried out by engineers from SINO and INVESTOR as well as surveyor from China. Details are shown in Appendix _____ .

[5] In case initial test is unsatisfactory, the second test shall be carried out. If the second test is again unsatisfactory, INVESTOR shall replace the equipment involved at INVESTOR'S cost, within two months after the second test. However, SINO shall realize and accept, delay in delivery

may be involved, duration of which will depend on equipment that needs to be replaced.

[6]   In case test results are satisfactory, SINO and INVESTOR shall sign test certificate in duplicate and each party shall keep one copy.

[7]   Stay expenses of INVESTOR'S engineers despatched to SINO for installation and test shall be all borne by INVESTOR.

Chapter 8   Training for Operation and Maintenance of Equipment

[1]   INVESTOR shall implement training programs concerning the operations and maintenances of the equipments, when engineers are despatched to SINO for installation and test. In this instance, SINO shall provide necessary assistances like interpreter, etc. for INVESTOR, _____ .

[2]   Duration of training shall not exceed two weeks including the time for installation and test referred in the previous item.

[3]   Training programs shall be conducted mainly in English language, with Chinese as a supportive language. SINO shall prepare interpreter (Chinese-English) at SINO'S cost, if such arrangement is needed.

[4]   Stay expenses of INVESTOR'S engineers at SINO for training of operation and maintenance of the equipments shall be all borne by INVESTOR.

Chapter 9   Guaranty for Equipment delivered

[1]   In accordance with the international customary standards, _____ , warranty period for the equipments delivered shall be eight (8) months after complete date of acceptance inspection at SINO.

[2]   In case defect of the delivered equipment within the warranty is found, INVESTOR shall take an appropriate settlement without delay, upon SINO'S request.

[3]   In the above instance, INVESTOR shall request SINO for payment of actual costs of transportation and stay, if any, when such defect is judged due to inexperienced operation by SINO , or due to inappropriate handling, or due to an article of consumption.

[4]   INVESTOR shall offer its maximum services to SINO concerning the equipments delivered.

[5]   Maintenace of the equipment after the warranty period shall be at cost, however, INVESTOR shall endeavor to offer its maximum cooperation and lowest cost.

Chapter 10   Procurements of Materials

[1]   SINO shall purchase, from INVESTOR, materials necessary to produce PRODUCTS in accordance with this contract

[2] INVESTOR shall deliver the necessary materials at SINO'S request in accordance with this contract.

[3] INVESTOR shall endeavor to supply these materials at the cost as low as possible.

[4] ACTUAL AND DETAIL ITEMS OF Materials to be purchased by SINO shall be determined by separate purchase contract(s).

[5] INVESTOR shall supply newest materials and guarantee their quality.

[6] SINO shall present INVESTOR its monthly production plan and monthly materials' ordering quantities eight months in advance, so that materials' delivery may be guaranteed.

[7] INVESTOR shall endeavor to deliver the materials ordered by SINO as per specified delivery schedules. However, SINO shall understand and accept such a case that INVESTOR cannot deliver as per the schedules due to unforeseeable and unavoidable causes related to ill-balance of supply against demand on market, etc.

[8] Payment for the materials supplied by INVESTOR to SINO shall be by the Irrevocable Letter of Credit in US currency.

Chapter 11   Exportation Methods of Materials

[1] Official delivery dates of materials shall be the dates and numbers on bills of lading / airway bills. INVESTOR shall inform SINO without delay, airway bill / bill of lading numbers, execution dates, packing list and arrival dates, etc. At the same time, INVESTOR shall send duplicate of documents on which above information are described.

[2] Missing and defective items, if any, of the materials delivered by INVESTOR to SINO shall be fulfilled at INVESTOR'S cost.

[3] INVESTOR shall deliver the materials to SINO by rigid packing enough to endure a long distance transportation.

[4] INVESTOR shall deliver with the packing (list) stating the following:-
(1) Contract No.
(2) Consignee mark
(3) Destination
(4) Shipping mark
(5) Weight
(6) Carton numbers
(7) Consignee mark

[5] INVESTOR shall include duplicate of details of the content in the packing.

Chapter 12   Acceptance of Materials

[1] SINO shall prepare facility and place to receive materials delivered from INVESTOR and store them.

[2]   INVESTOR shall deliver materials with quality accured by due inspection.

[3]   SINO shall carry out acceptance inspection of materials delivered, and shall notify INVESTOR, without delay, about defective or missing item(s) if any.

SINO shall send replacement to SINO at INVESTOR'S cost when INVESTOR acknowledges such notice is reasonable.

INVESTOR, however, shall realize and accept delivery of some items may require a long delivery.

[4]   In above case, when defect is judged due to wrong handling by SINO, INVESTOR shall request SINO for payment of actual costs.

[5]   In case materials delivered are damaged or lost due to a wrong procedure of storage or handling. INVESTOR shall deliver replacements without delay at SINO'S notice. However, expenses involved shall be at SINO'S cost.

Chapter 13   Training of SINO Engineers

[1]   INVESTOR shall accept ten SINO engineers, and provide three-month technical training at INVESTOR.

[2]   In above regard, INVESTOR shall bear costs of lodges and foods for SINO engineers during their stay in Italy, excepting round-trip expenses between China and Italy.

[3]   SINO engineers to be despatched to INVESTOR shall be able to comprehend reasonably _____ English, with fundamental knowledge of electronic engineering.

[4]   Educational programs shall be carried out mainly in English language with English as a supportive language. INVESTOR shall prepare an interpreter (Chinese-English) at SINO'S request and at SINO'S cost.

[5]   INVESTOR shall compile educational programs promptly and shall notify SINO in advance. Items relating to technical education programs are shown in Appendix _____ .

[6]   GTT shall despatch, at the same time, one engineer to attend the above educational programs together.

Chapter 14   Despatch of INVESTOR Engineers

[1]   INVESTOR shall despatch plural engineers to SINO, twice.

At first time, two engineers _____ shall be despatched to SINO for two months in order to effect this project.

At second time, four engineers shall be despatched to SINO for three months in order to achieve production target.

[2]   Tasks of INVESTOR engineers at SINO shall be carried out mainly in English language, with Chinese as a supportive language. SINO shall proparo an intorprotor (Chinoso English) at SINO'S cost, if neccessary.

[3] In above regard, SINO shall bear expenses for stay and trip within China of INVESTOR'S engineers, excepting round trip expenses between China and Italy.

[4] SINO shall be able to request for continued technical support from INVESTOR, if necessary. even after completion of the above two time despatch of INVESTOR engineers. However, in this instance, INVESTOR shall be able to request SINO for the cost of such additional technological cooperation. Terms and conditions shall be subject to mutual discussion and agreement between SINO and INVESTOR, in future.

[5] Details of the technical services requested by SINO from INVESTOR are shown in Appendix _____ .

Chapter 15   Technological Cooperation in Future

[1] INVESTOR shall cooperate with SINO as for future technological developments including high resolution display, etc.

[2] Terms and conditions of the above technological cooperation, including its cost, shall be determined by the separate contract which shall be discussed in future among SINO, INVESTOR and GTT.

Chapter 16   Role of GTT

[1] GTT shall be responsible for information transfer, communication intermediary, etc. between SINO and INVESTOR, and shall offer necessary assistance to SINO.

[2] GTT shall be rewarded reasonably for such activities by SINO.

Chapter 17   Duties of GTT

[1] GTT shall act as a bridge between SINO and INVESTOR.

[2] GTT shall assist SINO in marketing in China of products finished by SINO by means of trade show, seminar, technical training program, etc.

[3] GTT shall consider to market such finished products to Europe and Africa (excluding South Africa) when the quality becomes satisfactory.

[4] GTT shall provide free facility for engineers when SINO despatches them to Europe for product development. However, SINO shall be responsible for all costs for engineers in Europe.

Chapter 18   Arbitration

[1] SINO and INVESTOR shall solve any problems arising from the Contract(s) in a cooperative manner, otherwise arbitration shall be final.

[2] Arbitration shall take place in Stockholm, Sweden.

[3] SINO and INVESTOR shall be bound by the final decision made by the arbitration.

[4] Expense for arbitration shall be borne by the failed party.

[5] This contract shall be carried out as separate from the matters in arbitration, if any.

Chapter 19   Taxes

During the effectiveness of this contract, SINO shall be responsible for any taxation arising in China, whilst INVESTOR and GTT shall be responsible for any taxation arising in Europe respectively.

Chapter 20   Effectiveness of this Contract

[1] Unforseen matters shall not affect an execution of this contract.

[2] SINO, INVESTOR and GTT shall apply for permissions to import / export the related products from their own governments. The effective date of this contract shall be the date of the last party being approved.

Three parties shall try their best to obtain approval within eighty (80) days.

Chapter 21   Cancellation of Contract

[1] Three parties shall reserve the right to cancel this contract in case there is no effect for eight months after the effective date of this contract.

[2] This contract shall be valid for two years after its effective date, and shall be renewable for any two years thereafter.

Chapter 22   Languages used in Contract

This contract is written in both Chinese and English, and both versions shall have the equal validity.

Chapter 23   Documents attached to this Contract

[1] In case any amendment occurs in this contract, the three parties concerned shall agree and sign official documents and shall consider same as a part of this contract.

[2] Appendices shall be valid and form a part of this contract.

Dated this the _____ day of 19 _____ .

For and on behalf of:
China Broadcasting Products
Import Export Corporation and
Better Broadcasting Products Factory
(SINO)   (Signed)

For and on behalf of:
Foreign Advanced Broadcasting Ltd.
(INVESTOR)   (Signed)

Good-Trade Trading Ltd
(GTT)   (Signed)

TECHNOLOGY TRANSFER
AND
TECHNICAL ASSISTANCE
AGREEMENT

MEMORANDUM OF AGREEMENT made this _____ day of 19 _____ between _____, of _____ (hereinafter referred to as "FOREIGN PRO") as the one part and _____ of __ ____ (hereinafter referred to as "CHINA") acting on its own behalf and on behalf of _____ (hereinafter referred to as "AFF.CO.") of the other part.

WITNESSETH THAT:

WHEREAS, FOREIGN PRO has been engaged since _____ in the development, design, manufacture, and sale of certain containers, packaging, and closures and in the development, manufacture, sale, and leasing of machinery and equipment to design, manufacture, apply, and feed such containers, packaging, and closures;

WHEREAS, FOREIGN PRO has, through substantial expenditures of time, effort, and funds, formulated, developed, and / or acquired valuable proprietary and confidential technical data and know-how relating to the manufacture of certain closures and of machinery and equipment to manufacture, apply, and feed such closures;

WHEREAS, FOREIGN PRO is the sole and exclusive owner of all rights, title, and interest in and to such technical data and know-how relating to such closures and the related machinery and equipment and is entitled to convey such technical data and know-how and to grant the right to manufacture and sell such closures and related equipment to third parties;

WHEREAS, _____ CHINA and the AFF.CO desire to obtain the technical data and know-how relating to such closures and related equipment and to be granted by FOREIGN PRO the right to manufacture and sell same in Chinese Territories; and

WHEREAS, it is understood by FOREIGN PRO that all activities concerning the manufacture and sale of such closures and related equipment within Chinese Territories will be performed by the AFF.CO. hereunder and that all activities concerning payments or imports concerning such closures and related machinery and equipment will be performed by CHINA hereunder;

NOW THEREFORE, in consideration of the premises and mutual covenants set forth herein and in order to be legally bound hereby, the parties hereto agree as follows:

ARTICLE 1.   DEFINITIONS

1.1   The "Licensed Products" as used herein shall mean metal closures of different diameters, with _____ sealing **mumbers** or proprietary coatings (other than proprietary coatings which are not owned by FOREIGN PRO), known as " _____ ", for the vacuum sealing of _____ containers, which are manufactured by FOREIGN PRO as of the Effective Date of this Agreement and during the term hereof, as well as any modifications and improvements of same developed during the term of this Agreement.

1.2   The "Equipment" as used herein shall mean:

(a)   type _____ closing equipment, in accordance with FOREIGN PRO'S current designations, designed and used to apply the different diameters of the Licensed Products;

(b)   type _____ feeder equipment, in accordance with FOREIGN PRO'S current designations, designed and used to feed the different diameters of the Licensed Products; and

(c)   replacement parts for the closing equipment and the feeder equipment described in paragraphs 1.2(a) and (b) hereof, respectively.

1.3   The "Machinery" as used herein shall mean the machines, including subassemblies and spare parts, designed and used to manufacture the Licensed Products.

1.4   "Technology" as used herein shall mean all _____ confidential, and proprietary technical data, know-how, engineering, technical, and other drawings and designs, processes, specifications, bills of materials, descriptions of assembly and manufacturing procedures, inspection standards, instructions, and other technical data, documentation, and information, relating to:

(a)   in the case of the Licensed Products and the Equipment, the design, manufacture, handling, assembly, operation, use, testing, quality control, and maintenance of the Licensed Products and the Equipment; and

(b)   in the case of the Machinery, the handling, operation, use, testing and maintenance of the Machinery,

which are owned by or in the possession of FOREIGN PRO (other than such information relating to proprietary coatings which are not owned by FOREIGN PRO, or may be available to or hereafter acquired by FOREIGN PRO from third parties (unless same are subject to secrecy agreements precluding disclosure by FOREIGN PRO to others), as may be updated and improved by FOREIGN PRO from time to time during the term of this Agreement, regardless of whether same are patented (or patentable) or not, and based on which FOREIGN PRO as of the Effective Date of this Agreement and during the term hereof manufactures the Licensed

130

Products and the Equipment or operates and maintains the Machinery. "Technology" shall also mean any patents and patent applications and other industrial property rights (except trademarks and trade names) covering the Licensed Products and the Equipment (but not the Machinery) owned or utilized by FOREIGN PRO at any time during the term of this Agreement.

1.5 "Technical Assistance" as used herein shall mean any assistance, training, and consultation, whether technical in nature or otherwise, relating to the manufacture, handling, assembly, operation, use, testing, quality control, and maintenance of the Licensed Products and the Equipment and to the handling, operation, use, testing, and maintenance of the Machinery provided by FOREIGN PRO to CHINA and / or the AFF. CO. during the term of this Agreement.

1.6 The "CHINESE Parties" as used herein shall mean CHINA and the AFF.CO.

1.7 The "Effective Date" as used herein shall mean the date determined under Article 12 hereof.

ARTICLE 2.   TRANSFERANCE AND GRANT OF RIGHTS

2.1 FOREIGN PRO hereby conveys and grants to the AFF.CO. the exclusive and perpetual right to manufacture, use, and sell the Licensed Products and the Equipment and to use the Machinery in Chinese territories in accordance with, pursuant to, and under the Technology. Said conveyance and grant shall encompass all elements of the Technology relating to the Licensed Products, the Equipment, and the Machinery in Chinese Territories _____ owned by FOREIGN PRO as of the Effective Date of term of this Agreement. In addition, FOREIGN PRO shall furnish to the AFF. CO. all coating codes and information concerning sources of supply with respect to proprietary coatings which are not owned by FOREIGN PRO but which are used by FOREIGN PRO in its manufacture of the Licensed Products, such that the AFF.CO. will be able to purchase such proprietary coatings directly from said sources of supply.

2.2 FOREIGN PRO hereby declares that it has the unrestricted right to convey and grant to the AFF.CO. the rights described in paragraph 2.1 hereof and FOREIGN PRO further declares that it shall not grant similar rights to any other person in Chinese territories during the term of this Agreement.

2.3 The AFF.CO. may sublicense or subcontract in Chinese territories in whole or in part, the production of the Licensed Products and the Equipment under the Technology and may disclose the Technology and sell or lease the Equipment to any sublicensee or subcontractor in _____ for such purpose, provided that such disclosure and sale or leasing shall not purport to confer upon said sublicensee or subcontractor any rights other than those granted to the AFF.CO. hereunder and shall

131

be restricted in the same manner as FOREIGN PRO disclosure or the Technology to the AFF.CO. hereunder, in particular as described in the Confidentiality provisions of Article 4 hereof. It is understood and agreed that the _____ Parties shall be responsible jointly and severally with any sublicensee or subcontractor for the carrying out of the provisions of this Agreement.

2.4 It is expressly understood and agreed by the parties that FOREIGN PRO'S conveyance and grant of rights to the AFF.CO. with respect to the Technology relating to the Licensed Products, the Equipment, and the Machinery under this Article 2 does not in any manner constitute, imply, or result in the conveyance or grant of any rights to the AFF.PRO. or to CHINA to manufacture the Machinery.

The AFF.CO. hereby agrees that it shall use the Machinery only to manufacture and test the Licensed Products hereunder. The AFF.CO. further agrees that it shall use the Technology relating to the Machinery only to handle, operate, use, test, and maintain the Machinery for the sole purpose of manufacturing and testing the Licensed Products. The AFF.CO. hereby also agrees that it shall not use the Technology, or otherwise act, to copy, imitate, or in any way reproduce and manufacture the Machinery or any copy of facsimile thereof.

2.5 Any developments, improvements, modifications, or inventions concerning the Licensed Products and the Equipment made by FOREIGN PRO during the term of this Agreement shall become part of the Technology and shall be disclosed and conveyed by FOREIGN PRO to the AFF.CO. at no additional charge in accordance with the terms and conditions of this Agreement promptly after FOREIGN PRO'S use of same in its commercial manufacture of the Licensed Products and the Equipment.

2.6 Any developments, improvements, modifications, or inventions concerning the Licensed Products and the Equipment, whether patentable or unpatentable, made by the TRUST or its sublicensee(s) or subcontractor(s) during the term of this Agreement shall be disclosed by the AFF.CO. to FOREIGN PRO at no charge, except for the royalty which must be paid by a licensee to the inventor of an invention as a matter of _____ law. The AFF.CO. shall also grant to FOREIGN PRO the exclusive (other than the _____ Parties) and the perpetual right to manufacture, use, and sell the Licensed Products and the Equipment under same outside _____ and to sublicense others to do so. It is understood and agreed by the parties, however, that the AFF.CO. shall not make any modification of FOREIGN PRO'S standard design of any of the Licensed Products and the Equipment without the prior written consent of FOREIGN PRO thereto, provided, however, that such consent by FOREIGN PRO shall not be considered a representation or undertaking on the part of FOREIGN PRO with respect to the results to be achieved by the TRUST as a consequence of such modification.

2.7 Promptly after commercial use, FOREIGN PRO shall disclose and convey to the AFF.CO. and the AFF.CO. shall disclose and license to FOREIGN PRO, on the bases set forth in paragraphs 2.5 and 2.6 hereof, respectively, any developments, improvements, modifications, or inventions concerning the handling, operation, use, testing, and maintenance of the Machinery made during the term of this Agreement.

2.8 It is understood and agreed that neither party shall be required to convey or disclose to the other party any developments, improvements, modifications, or inventions unless same are directly related to the Licensed Products, the Equipment, or the Machinery in the manner described in this Article 2.

2.9 The parties hereby agree that FOREIGN PRO shall have the absolute right, in its sole discretion, to discontinue to manufacture, use, sell, or otherwise do business with respect to any of the Licensed Products, the Equipment, or the Machinery at any time during the term of this Agreement and, consequently, to eliminate said Licensed Product, Equipment, or Machinery from this Agreement upon _____ days prior to written notice of same to the Chinese Parties. Upon such elimination herefrom, neither FOREIGN PRO nor the Chinese Parties shall have any further obligation hereunder with respect to such eliminated Licensed Product, Equipment, or Machinery except that, notwithstanding any such discontinuance and elimination by FOREIGN PRO of any Licensed Product, Equipment, or Machinery, FOREIGN PRO shall perform all of its obligations hereunder with respect to all the Licensed Products, Equipment, and Machinery for a minimum period of at least _____ (___) years after the Effective Date hereof. The AFF.CO. shall not be precluded from continuing to manufacture, use, and sell any such eliminated Licensed Product or Equipment or to use any such eliminated Machinery in Chinese territories on the basis of the Technology already conveyed to the AFF.CO. at the time of such discontinuance and elimination by FOREIGN PRO, provided, however, that the AFF.CO. shall continue to comply with the provisions of this Agreement.

2.10 The written notice of discontinuance and elimination of any of the Licensed Products, the Equipment, or the Machinery, described in paragraph 2.9 hereof, shall:

(a) describe the Licensed Product, the Equipment, or the Machinery which FOREIGN PRO has determined to discontinue and to eliminate from this Agreement;

(b) be signed by an officer of FOREIGN PRO; and

(c) be deemed conclusive evidence of FOREIGN PRO'S determination to discontinue its manufacture, use, or sale of, or its otherwise doing business with respect to said Licensed Product, Equipment, or Machinery.

ARTICLE 3.   TRANSFER OF TECHNOLOGY AND TECHNICAL ASSIST-
              ANCE

3.1   FOREIGN PRO shall deliver the tangible materials constituting the Technology, in accordance with the schedule set forth in Exhibit A hereto, by prepaid air mail or air freight C.I.F. to CHINA or to such other party in Chinese territories which the Chinese Parties will designate. FOREIGN PRO shall provide six (6) copies of said materials in a form capable of being copied, in _____ measurements, and in the _____ language. The Chinese Parties may, at their own expense, convert such materials to the metric system and translate same into the Chinese language, subject to the Confidentiality provisions of Article 4 hereof.

3.2   FOREIGN PRO shall provide Technical Assistance in the form of training and consultation by FOREIGN PRO'S personnel with respect to the Technology for management, engineering, production, and other personnel of the AFF.CO. at FOREIGN PRO'S plant(s) in _____ AUSTRALIA, EUROPE OR MIDDLE EAST, at FOREIGN PRO'S sole discretion and as designated by FOREIGN PRO within a reasonable time after FOREIGN PRO'S receipt of a written request for same from the Chinese Parties. Only those Chinese personnel employed by the AFF.CO., who are familiar with plant operations and able to understand technical manufacturing discussions, shall be eligible for such training and consultation. FOREIGN PRO shall provide up to _____ (_____) man / working days of such training and consultation during the _____ year after the Effective Date hereof. The Chinese Parties shall bear all the costs of such training and consultation in the Middle East, including the providing of adequate translators and the indemnification of FOREIGN PRO against any claims for injury to person or property made by any of said Chinese personnel. FOREIGN PRO shall evaluate the competency of the Chinese personnel after such training and consultation and shall report said evaluation to the AFF.CO. within _____ (_____) days after the completion of such training and consultation. In the event that the _____ will desire training and consultation in addition to that set forth above, then FOREIGN PRO shall provide, subject to the availability and other commitments of its personnel, additional training and consultation at a cost to the Chinese Parties to be mutually agreed upon by the parties, payable by the Hungarian Parties, within _____ days after their receipt of FOREIGN PRO'S invoice therefor, by bank transfer to an account in a __ ____ bank designated by FOREIGN PRO. The site for such training and consultation shall be either in the Middle East or in Australia, at FOREIGN PRO'S sole discretion.

3.3   FOREIGN PRO shall provide, within a reasonable period of time after the request of the Chinese Parties therefor, Technical Assistance at the plant(s) of the AFF.CO. in Chinese in the form of advice and other technical services by FOREIGN PRO'S engineering or production personnel who are experienced in the manufacture of the Licensed Products and the Equipment. In particular, FOREIGN PRO'S personnel shall:

(a) furnish and explain the technical assistance, know-how, instructions, and other technical data and information constituting the Technology; and

(b) train the employees of the AFF.CO. in the assembly, operation, and maintenance of the Machinery and in the production and use of the Licensed Products and the Equipment. FOREIGN PRO shall provide up to _____ (_____) of FOREIGN PRO'S personnel. In the event that the AFF.CO. will desire such advice and other technical services in Chinese territories in addition to that set forth above, then FOREIGN PRO shall provide, subject to the availability and other commitments of its personnel, additional man/working days of such advice and other technical services at a cost to the Chinese Parties to be mutually agreed upon by the parties, payable by the Chinese Parties, within ____ (_____) days after their receipt of FOREIGN PRO'S invoice therefor, by bank transfer to an account in a _____ bank designated by FOREIGN PRO. With respect to all Technical Assistance provided by FOREIGN PRO'S personnel in Chinese territories, the Chinese Parties shall:

    (i) reimburse FOREIGN PRO for the costs of the round-trip tourist-class air travel of FOREIGN PRO'S personnel from the Middle East to China and return;

    (ii) provide to FOREIGN PRO'S personnel the best available hotel accommodations near the site;

    (iii) provide round-trip transportation of FOREIGN PRO'S personnel between the hotel and the plant facility;

    (iv) provide directly to FOREIGN PRO'S personnel the amount of Reminbi (_____) per calendar day for meals and other out-of-pocket expenses;

    (v) provide all necessary translator services to FOREIGN PRO'S personnel free of charge;

    (vi) provide safe and adequate facilities at the AFF.CO'S plant and the necessary tools (other than special tools) to FOREIGN PRO'S personnel for the purpose of rendering Technical Assistance hereunder;

    (vii) be responsible for and bear the cost of any medical treatment required by FOREIGN PRO'S personnel in Chinese territories as a result of any personal injury substained while rendering Technical Assistance or while travelling to or from or being present at the AFF.CO'S plant; and required permissions for FOREIGN PRO'S personnel to travel to and remain in China and to bring in any special tools for the purpose of rendering Technical Assistance:

behalf of FOREIGN PRO hereunder.

3.4 FOREIGN PRO may, at its option, substitute personnel of any of FOREIGN PRO'S subsidiaries for FOREIGN PRO personnel in the rendering of the Technical Assistance described in paragraph 3.3 hereof.

ARTICLE 4.   CONFIDENTIALITY

4.1 It is understood and agreed by the parties that the Technology and any other information which FOREIGN PRO considers _____ proprietary to itself and which will be conveyed and disclosed by FOREIGN PRO by its carrying out the provisions of this Agreement is and shall remain _____ confidential during the term of this Agreement and after the expiration or termination hereof for any reason whatsoever, until such time as same shall enter the public domain or otherwise become generally known without any breach of this Agreement by the Chinese Parties.

4.2 The Chinese Parties agree that they shall maintain the _____ confidentiality of the Technology and said other information conveyed and disclosed by FOREIGN PRO hereunder and shall not, without the prior written consent of FOREIGN PRO, disclose same or allow same to be disclosed to anyone, except to their management and employees and to any of the AFF.CO'S sublicensee(s), subcontractor(s), agents, suppliers, or customers in Chinese territories, and then only to the extent required for the proper and authorized use of the Technology hereunder, unless the Technology and said other information.

(a) are contained at the time of disclosure by FOREIGN PRO hereunder or thereafter in a patent or patent application or other printed publication made by a third party without any breach of this Agreement by the Chinese Parties; or

(b) are acquired by the Chinese Parties from a third party lawfully in possession of same and not subject to any contractual or fiduciary obligation to FOREIGN PRO to maintain the secrecy of same.

The Chinese Parties agree that, prior to any disclosure of the Technology and said other information, they shall enter into _____ agreement, containing in substance the provisions of this Article 4, with their management and employees and with any of the AFF.CO'S sublicensee(s), subcontractor(s), agents, suppliers, or customers to whom such disclosure is to be made.

4.3 The Chinese Parties agree that any reproductions, notes, summaries, conversions, translations, or similar documents containing or relating to the Technology shall themselves become, immediately upon their creation, a part of the Technology and, thus, subject to the confidentiality provisions of this Article 4.

4.4 The parties hereby agree that they shall keep secret and confidential and shall appropriately safeguard and not disclose to any unauthorized person, during the term of this Agreement and after the expiration or termination hereof for any reason whatsoever, all secret and confidential information which they may acquire pursuant to this Agreement in relation to any other party or any part of its business.

ARTICLE 5. INDUSTRIAL PROPERTY RIGHTS, WARRANTIES, AND QUALITY CONTROL

5.1 The Chinese Parties shall not at any time or in any manner question, contest, or dispute the right, title, or interest of FOREIGN PRO in and to, or the validity of, any of the patents, patent applications, unpatented inventions, or other industrial property rights of FOREIGN PRO covering the Licensed Products and the Equipment and constituting the Technology, and shall not aid or encourage others to do so.

5.2 FOREIGN PRO hereby declares that, to the best of its knowledge, the rights of any third parties will not be infringed by the parties' performance of this Agreement, by the AFF.CO'S use of the Technology, by the AFF. CO'S manufacture, use, or sale of the Licensed Products or the Equipment, or by the AFF.CO'S use of the Machinery in Chinese territories under this Agreement. FOREIGN PRO makes no representation or warranty, implied or otherwise, as to whether the Technology conveyed hereunder to the Chinese Parties and embodied in the Licensed Products or the Equipment, the methods of manufacture or use of the Licensed Products or the Equipment, the methods of operation or maintenance of the Machinery, or the sale of the Licensed Products or the Equipment in Chinese territories will infringe the industrial property rights of any third party.

5.3 In the event of any suit or threatened suit or claim against the Chinese Parties by any third party for infringement of industrial property rights, resulting from the manufacture, use, or sale of the Licensed Products or the Equipment or the use of the Machinery, the Chinese Parties shall forthwith, upon receiving knowledge thereof, give written notice of any such suit or threatened suit to FOREIGN PRO and FOREIGN PRO shall make available to the FOREIGN PRO all relevant information, evidence, and particulars in FOREIGN PRO'S possssion which may assist the Chinese Parties in defending or otherwise dealing with such suit or threatened suit.

5.4 It is understood and agreed by the parties that the Chinese Parties shall have the sole and exclusive right in Chinese territories to enforce, or to enjoin or to recover damages for the infringement of, any patent of FOREIGN PRO concerning the Licensed Products or the Equipment in _____ which is conveyed to the Chinese parties hereunder.

5.5 Each party shall advise and submit to the other party a copy of each patent application or patent renewal covering any development, improvement, modification, or invention applicable to any of the Licensed

Products or the Equipment, described in paragraphs 2.5 and 2.6 hereof, which is filed or acquired by or for it in its own country during the term of this Agreement by written notice to the other party _____ (_____) days after any such filing or acquisition. The party filing such patent application or patent renewal shall file a correspondent patent application or patent renewal in the country of the other party at the latter's written request and expense. Each party shall advise the other party of any issuance or acquisition during the term of this Agreement of any patent covering any such development, improvement, modification, or invention by written notice to the other party _____ (_____) days after any such issuance or acquisition.

5.6 This Agreement shall remain in full force and effect regardless of whether FOREIGN PRO shall at any time own or control patents in Chinese territories covering the Licensed Products or the Equipment. Either party shall, however, have the right to file any patent application in Chinese territories relevant to the Licensed Products or the Equipment. Any patents which may be granted to FOREIGN PRO or to the Chinese Parties in Chinese territories with respect to the Licensed Products or the Equipment during the term of this Agreement shall be considered part of the Technology and shall be promptly conveyed to the AFF.CO. in accordance with the terms and conditions of this Agreement.

5.7 Any patents which may be granted to the Chinese Parties outside Chinese territories with respect to the Licensed Products or the Equipment during the term of this Agreement shall be licensed to FOREIGN PRO outside Chinese territories on an exclusive basis (other than for the Chinese Parties themselves) and at no charge to FOREIGN PRO, except for the royalty which must be paid by a licensee to the inventor of patent as a matter of Chinese law.

5.8 FOREIGN PRO represents that the Technology to be conveyed to the AFF.CO. hereunder shall be the same Technology on the basis of which FOREIGN PRO itself manufactures the Licensed Products and the Equipment and that the Technology, together with the Technical Assistance to be furnished to the AFF.CO. hereunder, shall be sufficient for the manufacture of the Licensed Products and the Equipment. Therefore, the AFF.CO., utilizing the Technology and the Technical Assistance, should be able to manufacture the Licensed Products and the Equipment with the same quality as those manufactured by FOREIGN PRO, equal to world standards, in compliance with the relevant regulations of the United States Food and Drug Administration. FOREIGN PRO agrees to provide additional Technology, if same is available to FOREIGN PRO, and Technical Assistance to clarify the Technology, if requested by the AFF. CO., to facilitate the AFF. CO'S achieving the standard of quality of the Licensed Products and the Equipment contained in the Technology, at a cost to the Chinese Parties to be mutually agreed upon by the parties. However, nothing containing in this Agreement shall be construed as a warranty by FOREIGN PRO that the AFF.CO., will in fact be able to manufacture the Licensed Products and the Equipment at the level of quality or in the quantities or with the efficiencies as those of FOREIGN PRO, since the parties recognize and agree that the manufacture of the Licensed Products and the Equipment by the AFF.CO. is within the complete control of the TRUST and that the TRUST is not dependent upon FOREIGN PRO in any way except as expressly set forth in this Agreement.

5.9   The AFF.CO. shall use its best efforts to maintain a standard of quality and workmanship in its manufacture of the Licensed Products and the Equipment equal to that of FOREIGN PRO and shall manufacture the Licensed Products and the Equipment out of materials which, in FOREIGN PRO'S opinion, are equal in technical suitability and quality with those used by FOREIGN PRO or out of materials approved by FOREIGN PRO. The Chinese Parties shall permit representatives of FOREIGN PRO, upon reasonable advance notice and during normal business hours, to inspect the manufacturing facilities of the AFF.CO. used for the manufacture of the Licensed Products and the Equipment. In particulars, FOREIGN PRO'S representatives shall be permitted to inspect and monitor the quality control procedures to be used by the AFF.CO., as well as to inspect samples of the Licensed Products and the Equipment manufactured by the TRUST, in order to ensure the compliance of the AFF.CO. with the quality standards for the Licensed Products and the Equipment contained in the Technology.

5.10   Upon the completion of the rendering of the Technical Assistance by FOREIGN PRO'S personnel, as provided in Article 3 hereof, but not more than _____ (_____) months after FOREIGN PRO'S completion of the delivery of the tangible materials constituting the Technology, described in paragraph 3.1 hereof, representatives of FOREIGN PRO, in the presence and under the observation of representatives of the Chinese Parties, shall conduct a quantity production test by means of a production run of the Licensed Products, performed by personnel delegated for this purpose by FOREIGN PRO at the plant site of the AFF.CO., with the parameters of said test being set forth in the Machinery Purchase and Sale Agreement described in Article 6 hereof. The AFF.CO. shall furnish, at its expense, the materials, power, and other auxiliary services required for the performance of said test. In the event that said quantity production test is not successfully completed in the first instance, said test shall be repeated by FOREIGN PRO, with the cooperation of the Chinese Parties, at the earliest opportune time. Upon the successful completion of said test, the parties' representatives shall sign a protocol of acceptance in _____ (_____) copies certifying the completion of FOREIGN PRO'S performance of its obligations hereunder.

5.11 In the event that FOREIGN PRO will fail to deliver the Technology in accordance with the schedule set forth in Exhibit A hereto, as provided in paragraph 3.1 hereof, FOREIGN PRO shall pay to the Chinese Parties a penalty in the amount of _____ percent (_____ %) of the total purchase price (described in paragraph 7.1 hereof) for each week or partial week of delay in said delivery up to a maximum of _____ percent (_____ %) of the total purchase price hereunder. Said penalties shall not be subject to reduction by any legal procedure by FOREIGN PRO and the Chinese Parties shall not claim or be entitled to any other remedy or damages with respect to said delay or any other failure of performance under this Agreement by FOREIGN PRO, whether at law or otherwise, with all such rights, remedies, and damages hereunder hereby being waived by the Chinese Parties in substitution for the penalties described in this paragraph 5.11.

ARTICLE 6.   PURCHASE AND SALE OF THE MACHINERY

6.1 FOREIGN PRO hereby agrees to sell and deliver specified amounts of the Machinery and the Equipment exclusively in Chinese territories to the Chinese Parties and to provide Technical Assistance concerning the assembly, installation, commissioning, operation, use, and maintenance of the Machinery and the Equipment and the training of the AFF.CO.'S personnel to perform same at the plant site of the AFF. CO., in accordance with a separate Machinery Purchase and Sale Agreement of even date among the parties.

ARTICLE 7.   CONSIDERATION

7.1 In Consideration of the exclusive rights granted, the Technology conveyed, and the Technical Assistance to be provided hereunder (subject to payment of the additional consideration expressly set forth in Article 3 hereof), CHINA shall pay to FOREIGN PRO the total purchase price in the amount of _____ (_____ $ _____), payable in the following lump-sum fixed payments:

(a) percent (_____ %) of the total purchase price, i.e., _____ dollars (_____), shall be paid by CHINA by bank transfer to an account in a _____ bank designated by FOREIGN PRO, within _____ (_____) days after the Effective Date hereof or, if later, upon notification of the opening by FOREIGN PRO at a _____ bank acceptable to the _____ Bank of a confirmed irrevocable letter of credit in said amount in favor of CHINA as a guarantee of the performance of FOREIGN PRO hereunder, with said letter of credit being released automatically upon delivery of the tangible materials constituting the Technology as provided in paragraph 3.1 hereof;

(b) percent (_____ %) of the total purchase price, i.e., _____ ($ _____), shall be paid by CHINA under a confirmed irrevocable divisible letter of credit, to be opened by CHINA with the _____ Bank and confirmed by a _____ bank designated by FOREIGN PRO and acceptable to the _____ Bank, within _____ (_____) months after the Effective Date hereof, allowing partial shipments and corresponding partial payments, with a validity of _____ (_____) days, and providing payment upon delivery of the tangible materials constituting the Technology, as provided in paragraph 3.1 hereof, against FOREIGN PRO'S presentation of the following documents:

(i) detailed commercial invoice in _____ (_____) copies;

(ii) copy of air mail receipt or air freight waybill and a statement of the forwarding agent certifying that shipment was irrevocably effected to Chinese territories; and

(iii) copy of receipt signed on behalf of the Chinese Parties certifying the receipt of the tangible materials constituting the Technology at the office of CHINA [at the Budapest airport]; and

(c) percent (_____ %) of the total purchase price, i.e., _____ _____ (_____), shall be paid by CHINA, by bank transfer to an account in a _____ bank designated by FOREIGN PRO, within _____ _____ (_____) business days after the signing by the parties' representatives of the protocol of acceptance, described in paragraph 5.10 hereof.

7.2 In the event that the AFF.CO. will manufacture in excess of a total of _____ _____ (_____) units of the closing equipment as stated in paragraph 1.2(a) hereof or in excess of _____ (_____) units of the feeder equipment described in paragraph 1.2(b) hereof during the first _____ (_____) years of this Agreement, then CHINA shall pay to FORIEGN PRO a royalty in the amount of _____ (_____) for each such excess unit of the closing equipment and a royalty in the amount of _____ (_____) for each such excess unit of the feeder equipment, by bank transfer to an account in a _____ bank designated by FOREIGN PRO within _____ _____ (_____) days after the AFF.CO.'S completion of the manufacture of each of said excess units of the Equipment.

7.3 All taxes, duties, levies, custom fees, assessments, and charges of any kind, present and future, on the Technology or the Technical Assistance furnished hereunder or on any payments, payment instruments (e.g., orders of payment, letters of credit), or receipts effected or issued hereunder, imposed by any governmental authority or official body in Hungary shall be borne by the Chinese Parties.

7.4 All taxes, duties, levies, custom fees, assessments, and charges of any kind, present and future, on the Technology or the Technical Assistance furnished hereunder or on any payments, payment instruments (e.g., orders or payment, letters of credit), or receipts effected or issued horoundor, impocod by any govornmontal authority or officiol body in the

141

Middle East shall be borne by FOREIGN PRO.

7.5 Each party shall bear the costs of any payment orders or letters of credit issued or opened by it, including the costs of any extensions of validity and any bank commissions and fees.

ARTICLE 8.   DURATION AND TERMINATION

8.1 Unless earlier terminated, this Agreement shall have an initial term of ____ (_____) years commencing on the Effective Date hereof. In the event that this Agreement is not terminated earlier than said full initial term, then the AFF.CO. may thereafter continue to manufacture, use, and sell the Licensed Products and the Equipment and to use the Machinery under the rights granted herein without the obligation of paying any additional consideration to FOREIGN PRO, including the right to manufacture, use, and sell under any patents included in the Technology covering the Licensed Products or the Equipment, provided that the Chinese Parties shall make no claims against FOREIGN PRO with respect to the Licensed Products or the Equipment.

8.2 The Chinese Parties shall have the right to extend the initial term of this Agreement for _____ (_____) additional periods of _____ (_____) year(s) each upon notice given to FOREIGN PRO at least _____ (_____) days prior to the expiration of the term then in effect. All the terms and conditions of this Agreement shall apply to any such extension, with the exception that the consideration to be paid by CHINA to FOREIGN PRO in accordance with Article 7 hereof shall be negotiated by the parties at the time of each such extension.

This Agreement shall terminate prior to the expiration of the initial term described in paragraph 8.1 hereof, or any term extension described in paragraph 8.2 hereof, whenever any of the following events occur:

(a) the terms and conditions of this Agreement are breached by either party and said breach is not cured within _____ (_____) days from the receipt by the breaching party of written notice of such breach from the nonbreaching party; or

(b) the liquidation, dissolution, bankruptcy, insolvency, or entering into receivership of either party takes place without its business being taken over and carried on by another enterprise of the same standing, which enterprise agrees to be bound by the terms and conditions hereof.

8.4 The early termination of this Agreement for any reason shall not affect any accrued rights or obligations of the parties as of the effective date of' such termination, nor shall it affect any rights or obligations of the parties under this Agreement which are intended by the parties and agreed herein by them to survive any such termination, especially the secrecy provisions of Article 4 hereof, nor shall it preclude any claim for damages or other remedy of the party effecting such early termination against the other party hereto.

8.5 The AFF.CO. agrees that, upon the early termination of this Agreement attributable to breach by the AFF.CO.:

(a) all rights granted hereunder shall revert to FOREIGN PRO;

(b) the AFF.CO., its sublicensee(s) and subcontractor(s) shall cease to use the Technology and to manufacture, use, and sell the Licensed Products or to manufacture and use the Equipment; and

(c) the AFF.CO. shall forthwith deliver to FOREIGN PRO (or its designated subsidiary or affiliated corporation) all original and copied materials embodying the Technology (either in their original form or in a form translated into another language or converted into metric measurements) or, at the request of FOREIGN PRO, shall destroy same.

ARTICLE 9.   ARBITRATION AND APPLICABLE LAW

9.1 All disputes and differences of any kind arising under this Agreement, including the existence or continued existence of this Agreement, which cannot be settled amicably by the parties, shall be submitted to the _____ established by the _____ . _____ in order to settle the dispute in an amicable manner under the _____ Rules adopted by said _____ .

9.2 Failing a settlement in this manner, all disputes and differences of any kind arising between the parties out of, in relation to or in connection with this Agreement, its application or interpretation, or any breach hereof or default hereunder (including disputes concerning the existence or continued existence of this Agreement or the validity of this arbitral provision), shall be submitted to arbitration. The arbitration shall take place in _____ , _____ , and shall be conducted in English. Therefore, each arbitrator shall be fluent in the English language.

9.3 The arbitration court shall consist of _____ (_____) arbitrators. FORE-IGN PRO shall appoint one (1) arbitrator and the Chinese Parties shall appoint one (1) arbitrator. The two (2) arbitrators shall appoint the third arbitrator who shall act as the chairman of the arbitration court. If the two (2) arbitrators appointed by the parties do not agree on the person of the third arbitrator within _____ (_____) days after the appointment of the last of the two (2) arbitrators, then the third arbitrator shall be appointed by _____
at the request of one of the parties.

9.4 The party desiring to submit a dispute to arbitration (including the existence or the continued existence of this Agreement) shall notify the other party in writing to that effect, indicating the name and address of the arbitrator appointed by it. The party which will receive such notification shall appoint an arbitrator within _____ (_____) days from its receipt of the notification and shall notify the claimant party in writing to that effect. If within said _____ (_____) day period such appointment will not have been made and notice will not have been given to the claimant party, then the second arbitrator shall be appointed by _____ at the request of the claimant party.

9.5 The arbitrators shall resolve any disputes in accordance with the wording and the spirit of this Agreement and, if necessary, where there are no relevant provisions covering the questions in dispute and the arbitrators will determine that reference to a particular law is required in making a decision, then they shall refer to _____ the _____ law of _____.

9.6 The award of the arbitrators shall be given by majority vote and shall state in writing the reasons for the rendering of their decision. The arbitrators shall give their award promptly, if possible within _____ (__ ____) months from the date of the full constitution of the arbitration court.

9.7 The award of the arbitrators shall be final and executory with respect to all controversies arising under this Agreement, including the existence or continued existence of this Agreement.

9.8 The costs of arbitration shall be decided by the arbitrators. They shall likewise decide which party shall bear same, or if all parties should share same, and, if so, in what proportion.

9.9 The award of the arbitrators shall be enforceable by any court having jurisdiction over the party against which the award has been rendered, or where assets of the party against which the award has been rendered can be located.

9.10 Each of the parties hereby agrees to pay the amount of any arbitral award and / or of any costs of arbitration which the arbitrators determine that it is required to pay within _____ (_____) days after the arbitrators' award has been notified to it.

ARTICLE 10.   FORCE MAJEURE

10.1 If a case of force majeure prevents the total or partial performance by a party of any obligation resulting from this Agreement, then the party claiming force majeure shall notify the other party in writing by a registered air mail letter within _____ (_____) days from the occurrence of the conditions causing the force majeure, both at the beginning and at the end of the respective case of force majeure. Said party shall attach to said notice a confirmation from the competent authorities in its country as to the veracity and correctness of the facts and dates stated. In the event that no notice is given to the other party, then a party shall not be entitled to invoke force majeure in such instance and shall bear all the costs, risks, and consequences of said case of force majeure.

10.2 Force majeure shall be understood to mean all events beyond the control of the parties, unforseen or, if foreseen, unavoidable, which arise after the Effective Date of this Agreement and prevent the total or partial

144

performance by the parties of any obligation set forth herein, including, but not limited to, strikes or other labor difficulties, acts of God, acts of governments (in particular with respect to restrictions on foreign currency exchange), and other similar events, acts, or omissions, but not including a lack of materials or labor caused by an event which is not itself force majeure.

10.3 When a case of force majeure shall be notified in accordance with paragraph 10.1 hereof, then the terms of the contractual obligations of the parties for the period of delay caused by the force majeure shall be automatically extended.

10.4 For any delays or noncompliance with obligations due to force majeure, no party shall claim any right of cancellation, damages, interest, or any other compensation from any other party. No party shall bear the damages which any other party may incur due to force majeure.

10.5 If delay due to a case of force majeure continues in excess of _____ (_____) months, then the party against whom force majeure has been invoked shall have the right, if the parties are unable to agree otherwise, to cancel this Agreement by a registered airmail letter to the other party without any other formality. In such an event, the consequences of such a liquidation of the parties' contractual obligations shall be determined by arbitration as provided in Article 9 hereof.

ARTICLE 11.   GENERAL PROVISIONS

11.1 Succession.   It is agreed by the parties that the respective rights and obligations of the parties under this Agreement shall pass to the legal successor or successors in interest of any of the parties hereto, with due notice being given of any such succession.

11.2 Assignment.   Neither party shall have the right to assign its respective rights and obligations under this Agreement to any third party without first obtaining the advance written approval of the other party, which approval shall not be unreasonably withheld, except that FOREIGN PRO shall have the right in all circumstances to assign this Agreement to any of FOREIGN PRO'S whollyowned subsidiaries. In addition, FOREIGN PRO may assign this Agreement in connection with the transfer of its business relevant to this Agreement but, in such an event, FOREIGN PRO shall remain responsible as a coprincipal debtor with its assignee of any claims of the Chinese Parties arising under this Agreement.

11.3 Language of the Agreement.   The English language version of this Agreement shall be controlling, notwithstanding the translation of this Agreement into Chinese or any other language.

11.4 No Partnership or Agency.   The parties hereby agree that the parties' relationship shall be that of independent contractors and that nothing contained in this Agreement shall be construed as constituting the parties as partners or joint venturers, or the AFF.CO. as an agent of FOREIGN PRO.

11.5 No Waiver.   The failure or delay of any party to enforce at any time any of the provisions hereof or any rights in respect thereto or to exercise any option provided herein shall in no way be construed to be a waiver of such provisions, rights, or options in the future or in any way to affect the validity of this Agreement.

11.6 Separability.   In the event that any provision of this Agentment is declared void or unenforceable or becomes unlawful in its operation, such provision shall not affect the enforceability of the rights and duties of the parties with regard to the remaining provisions of this Agreement, which shall continue as binding.

11.7 Exhibits.   The various Exhibits to this Agreement, which are attached hereto, are hereby made an integral part of this Agreement.

11.8 Authorized Signatures.   Each of the representatives of the parties signing this Agreement shall have the necessary authority to be able to sign in full compliance with the legal requirements of his country and with the effect of authoritatively binding the party which he represents.

11.9 Notices and Correspondence.
(a)   All notices and communications made pursuant to this Agreement shall be made in English and in writing and shall be deemed to have been properly given if sent by registered air mail, telex or cable, or by hand delivery to the intended receipient through any possible means.

11.10 Entire Agreement.   This Agreement expresses the complete and final agreement and understanding of the parties and supersedes and automatically cancels any other or prior agreement or understanding between the parties, written or oral. This Agreement shall not be altered, amended, or supplemented in any way except by an instrument in writing signed by the properly authorized representatives of all the parties hereto.

ARTICLE 12.   EFFECTIVE DATE OF THE AGREEMENT

12.1 The Effective Date of this Agreement shall be the date on which the last of the following events shall take place:
(a)   the signing of this Agreement by the representatives of the parties; and
(b)   each party's receipt of a notification from the other party of the approval of this Agreement by the competent authorities of its government.

12.2 On the Effective Date, this Agreement shall come into force and shall become legally binding on the parties hereto.

12.3 Each party shall diligently seek to obtain any necessary government approval and shall immediately inform the other party upon obtaining same.

12.4 In the event that all of the events described in paragraph 12.1 hereof have not taken place within _____ (_____) days after the parties' signing of this Agreement, then any party may notify the other party in writing of its intention not to pursue the undertakings set forth herein and _____ (_____) days from said notice, any express or implied undertakings set forth herein shall terminate. In such case, no party shall have any claim for damages or other compensation from any other party and this Agreement shall be considered null and void ab initio.

IN WITNESS WHEREOF, the parties hereto have caused this Agreement to be duly executed as of the date herein below written

name of the foreign party
(FOREIGN PRO)

Date: _____   By: _____
Place: _____

name of the Chinese
party
(CHINA)

Date: _____   By: _____
Place: _____

name of the party
represented by the Chinese
party
AFF.CO.

By: _____

Date: _____
Place: _____

COMPENSATION TRADE AGREEMENT

THE CHINA _____ CORPORATION, _____ Branch (hereinafter called "SINO", which expression shall, where the context admits, include SINO'S agents, representative associated companies or affliated companies in business as the case may be) of the one part and _____
_____ (hereinafter called "INVESTOR", which expression shall, where the context admits, include INVESTOR'S agents, assigns or representatives in business as the case may be) of the other part.

Whereby after friendly negotiation, it is mutually agreed as follows:

1.   MATERIALS:

INVESTOR shall be responsible for providing SINO equipment, moulds and tools for production as required under this agreement (details in exhibit 1). INVESTOR shall prepay the costs transportation and miscellaneous charges of these equipment, moulds and tools. SINO will repay INVESTOR in installation by products shipped under purchase orders or invoices prepared under this agreement (details to be arranged). SINO will pay back the interest charges advanced by INVESTOR in accordance with interest rates announced by Bank of China, _____ Branch.

2.   Quantity:

In 19 _____ , a trial quantity of _____ (_____) pieces will be supplied. In 19 _____ , _____ (_____) pieces will be supplied, INVESTOR will propose orders, with delivery time and specifications to be confirmed.

3.   Quality and Inspection:

SINO will manufacture in accordance with technical standard agreed upon. Both parties will inspect the goods under a mutually agreed standard. SINO shall guarantee that the products will meet the standards specified, namely the _____ standard, INVESTOR can raise claims against SINO who will be responsible for losses and charges incurred therefrom. In the case of force majeure, the issue can be settled through mutual consultation.

4.   Payment:

Purchase orders should be proposed by INVESTOR and confirmed by SINO. INVESTOR should open an irrevocable Letter of Credit in favour of SINO days prior to the delivery of the goods.

5.   Prices:

CIF _____ . After INVESTOR has proposed the order size, the prices will be determined by Corporation and INVESTOR.

6. Packing:

    Wooden cases or cartons with waterproof paper inside. Bulk packing. In cases / cartons of _____ kg. In pallets of about _____ tonne.

7. Claim period:

    Within _____ days after arrival of goods in _____ , INVESTOR can raise claims against SINO.

8. **Style of materials**

    For style of materials provided by INVESTOR under this agreement, SINO cannot sell to other clients in _____ .

9. **Correspondence**

    To facilitate execution of this agreement, all correspondence and cable copies despatched by both parties for the fulfilment of this agreement should be sent to Corporation, _____ the sole agent of SINO in INVESTOR'S COUNTRY.

10. **Related matters**

    For matters not included in this contract, both parties agree to discuss them in _____ 19 _____ in China. This contract has two original copies, one for each party. It will be valid for _____ (_____) year commencing on the date of signing. Two months prior to the expiry of this agreement and upon consent by both parties, the agreemnt can be renewed.

11. **Exhibits**

    This agreement and Exhibits attached hereto shall be equally binding.

12. **Languages**

    This agreement was prepared in both Chinese and English languages, both texts being equally authentic.

(Signed)   (Signed)
For and on behalf of   For and on behalf of

_____   _____

(SINO)   (INVESTOR)

Exhibits:

1. List of materials supplied by Investor.
2. Details of technical standards and procedural requirements.
3. Schedule for trade talks during the agreement period.

PROCESSING AGREEMENT

MEMORANDUM OF THIS agreement is made between CHINA X X X Import & Export Corporation (hereinafter referred to as "the SINO SELLER") of the one part and Y Ltd of _____ (hereinafter referred to as "FOREIGN BUYER") of the other part. Both parties hereby agree on the following terms and conditions after negotiation:

1. The SINO SELLER agrees to process the _____, _____, and _____, to be supplied by the FOREIGN BUYER to produce _____, the SINO SELLER shall pay the FOREIGN BUYER the processing charges. The design, specification, quantity of each batch and the amount of processing charges shall be detailed in the agreement(s) for sale and purchase to be entered between both parties.

2. The SINO SELLER agrees to furnish in advance the FOREIGN BUYER with the major production equipment and the equipment for manufacturing and repairing the moulds. The cost of the equipment is about (Amount: _____). The type, model and quantity of this equipment shall be determined jointly by both parties or by the SINO SELLER and Corporation of (on hehalf of the FOREIGN BUYER.)

3. In consideration of the purchaser furnishing the FOREIGN BUYER with the above-mentioned equipment, the FOREIGN BUYER agrees to sell the finished products to the SINO SELLER at a special discount of (percentage _____ %) of the invoice value of the finished products until the total amount so deducted equals the cost of the above-mentioned equipment. The materials and moulds shall be provided by the SINO SELLER free of charge.

4. The SINO SELLER agrees to deliver in batches the above-mentioned equipment to the Vendor at Shanghai before the end of the year 19 _____. The SINO SELLER further agrees to send technical personnel to China to assist in the installation of the above-mentioned equipment and to provide technical guidance. The SINO SELLER further agrees to provide the FORIEGN BUYER with adequate materials which include _____ and _____, allowing a reasonable quantity of wastage. Such materials shall be required to be delivered at China within _____ days after the arrival of the above-mentioned equipment so as to enable the FOREIGN BUYER to commence production on time.

5. Both parties agree to process the first lot of materials _____ and _____ into _____ types of and _____, with quantities not less than _____. The standard of quality of finished products shall be that of the samples. (Both parties shall each retain a set of the samples.) The FOREIGN BUYER shall begin to deliver finished products to the _____ within _____ days after the materials arrive at China.

6. At the request of the FOREIGN BUYER, the SINO SELLER agrees not to supply and sell the finished products manufactured according to the designs specified by the SINO SELLER to other countries or territories.

7. This agreement shall become effective from _____ 19 _____ for a term of _____ year. Both parties shall enter into negotiation to extend or amend the agreement upon its expiry.

Dated this the _____ day of _____ 19 _____ .

China XXX Import & Export Corporation	Y LTD.
(SINO SELLER)	(FOREIGN BUYER)

By: _____   By: _____

JOINT CO-OPERATION IN THE MANUFACTURING OF MOTOR VEHICLE SPARE PARTS

A G R E E M E N T

According to the Letter of Intent dated _____
and basing on the details there stated, it is hereby agreed BETWEEN CHINA ____
CORPORATION, BRANCH OF _____ ,
_____ , _____ , China and
_____ FACTORY, _____ COUNTY of
_____ , China (hereinafter
respectively and individually called "SINO CORP" and "THE WORKS" and
collectively called "CHINA") and _____
OF _____ , _____ Branch of _____ ,
_____ (hereinafter called
"INVESTOR") _____ as follows:

1. CHINA shall set up the works as a high quality motor vehicle spare parts factory at _____ County to produce motor vehicle spare parts the design of and raw material for which are supplied by INVESTOR. The annual production of the motor vehicle spare parts which will include radiator carburetor, shock absorber, clutch and other similar items (hereinafter called "the Products") shall not be less than one million dozens (1,000,000 dozens). Actual details of items to be produced, quantities, prices or production charges and delivery dates shall be set out in individual production orders to be given from time to time which orders shall form part of this Agreement.

2. All designs, machinery, facilities and moulds (hereinafter called "the Equipment") required by the works to produce the Products shall be supplied and installed by Investor free of charge. The works shall be responsible for the safety, up-keep, repair and maintenance of the Equipment. Apart from damage to the Equipment resulted from fair wear and tear and breakdown during normal usage, the works shall be responsible for the well being of the Equipment and will compensate INVESTOR for any damage to the machinery both by human beings or otherwise and the SINO CORP shall ensure that the works do compensate INVESTOR with the costs of the Equipment.

3. All technical personnel required by the works in directing the installation and operation of the Equipment, quality control and packaging of the Products shall be provided by INVESTOR. All expenses incurred by the provision of these technical personnel shall be borne by INVESTOR.

4. The Equipment shall remain the absolute properties of INVESTOR throughout and after the duration of this Agreement.

5. CHINA shall provide all land, factory buildings, warehouse facilities and the necessary labour force for the commercial production and operation of the works to the satisfaction of INVESTOR.

6. THE WORKS guarantees that the wastage of raw material shall not exceed the limited prescribed in the Directives to be given by INVESTOR regarding the cutting of the _____ materials and injection moulding of the _____ materials. CHINA shall be the absolute owner of all scrap metal and waste material produced by THE WORKS and shall be entitled dispose of the same at its sole discretion.

7. INVESTOR shall have the right to control the quality of all the Products and shall be entitled to reject and refuse to pay for any items which do not meet with the standard set down by INVESTOR. In the event that total rejects of any one consignment or order exceeds percent (_____ %) of the total consignment or order, CHINA shall have the right to deduct from future payments due to CHINA, the costs of the raw material of the rejects.

8. INVESTOR shall be responsible for all transportation charges and insurance premia payable for delivering all raw material and finished Products between Chinese territories and _____ . THE WORKS shall be responsible for all transportation charges and insurance premia payable for delivering the raw material and finished Products between Chinese territories and THE WORKS.

9. All packaging material required shall be supplied by INVESTOR and THE WORKS shall provide the necesary packing facilities and labour force.

10. CHINA shall be jointly responbsible for and shall indemnify INVESTOR against all duties, taxes and other government levies imposed by the Chinese Government both national or provincial on the Equipment, the raw material, the packaging material and the finished Products or on INVESTOR in the performance of this Agreement.

11. INVESTOR shall pay for all the finished Products which have passed the quality control tests administered by INVESTOR in accordance with the detailed terms regarding items, quantities, prices or production fees, delivery dates at the time of delivery on a D / P basis. The documents required to effect payment shall include the following:

    (a) Commercial Invoice issued by CHINA or THE WORKS as appropriate;

    (b) Packing Lists issued by CHINA or the WORKS as appropriate;

    (c) Bills of Lading or Railway Cargo Receipt issued by carrier concerned;

    (d) Inspection Certificates issued by INVESTOR;

    (e) In the event that the International General System of Preference is applicable to China, the relevant Certificate of Origin Form A required by the System.

Both parties agreed that for the duration of this Agreement, the prices or production fees to be charged by THE WORKS shall not be more than the price or production fee for each item as set out in Schedule A annexed to this Agreement unless with prior written agreement of the parties hereto.

12. In the event that raw material of equivalent quality is available in the Chinese territories at market prices not higher than those applicable to similar raw material in _____ , INVESTOR shall purchase such raw material within the Chinese territories and shall pay for same at the time when the finished Products are paid for. However, the Factory shall be responsible for arranging and paying for transportation of the raw material from its places of production within the Chinese territories to THE WORKS.

13. This Agreement shall commence on the _____ day of 19 _____ and shall have an initial duration of _____ years from the commencement date. CHINA and THE WORKS shall not·produce items similar to the Products for other parties in the Province of _____ . INVESTOR shall not place orders for the manufacture of items similar to the Products with any other factories in the Province of _____ (other parts of the Chinese territories and the world excepted). This is in order to protect the respective sole and exclusive production and distribution rights of the parties.

14. If neither party objects, this Agreement shall automatically continue for a further _____ year period upon the expiration of this Agreement.

Party A   Party B

_____   _____

AGREEMENT OF GUARANTEE
AND INDEMNITY

THIS GUARANTEE AND INDEMNITY is made the ___ day of _____ 19 _____
BETWEEN: _____ LIMITED of _____ Street, _____ in _____ ("the Guarantor") of the first part, _____ LTD. of _____ Road, Province, China ("the
Customer") of the second part and the BANK OF CHINA. ("the Bank") of the
third part.

WHEREAS the Bank has granted certain Credit Accommodation to the
Customer at the request of the Guarantor.

NOW THEREFORE IN CONSIDERATION OF THE PREMISES THIS DEED
WITNESSETH AND THE PARTIES AGREE AS FOLLOWS:

1. The Guarantor hereby guarantees to the Bank:
    (a) The payment of each and all sums of money interest and damages
        in which the Customer now or hereafter be indebted or liable to the
        Bank under pursuant to or in connection with the transaction
        referred to in the Schedule and also
    (b) Due and prompt observance of all covenants obligations terms and
        conditions on the part of the Customer to be performed or
        observed under pursuant to or in connection with such transactions
        and / or guarantees (alone or jointly with any person or corporation)
        (all of which obligations (being the payment of each and all sums of
        money interest and damages as aforesaid and also the observance
        and performance of all covenants obligations terms and conditions
        as aforesaid) are hereinafter collectively called ("the Guaranteed
        obligations").

2. This Guarantee shall be a continuing Guarantee for the purposes of
    securing the whole of the Guaranteed Obligations notwithstanding any
    partial payment or performance thereof and shall be without prejudice to
    nor shall the Guarantor be exonerated in whole or in part nor shall the
    Bank's rights and remedies against the Guarantor be in any way
    prejudiced or adversely affected by any of the following:
    (a) Any indulgence granted by the Bank or any other person in
        connection with the transaction;
    (b) The insolvency bankruptcy liquidation or receivership of the
        Customer, any release variation or modification of the transaction;
    (c) The liquidation receivership or insolvency of the Guarantor;

3. This Guarantee shall not be in any way effected by the fact that any of
    the Guaranteed Obligations or any part thereof may not be or may cease
    to be enforceable or that the Customer or any other person purportedly

155

primarily liable to pay such moneys may be discharged and to give effect to this covenant this Deed shall be treated and construed as an indemnity and the Guarantor HEREBY INDEMNIFIES the Bank in respect of any failure by the Customer to make any payment or perform an obligations.

4.   This Deed shall be governed by the law of the State of Victoria.

5.   The parties hereto mutually COVENANT AND AGREE that in the event that the Guarantor shall satisfy the whole of the Guaranteed Obligations or any part of the Guaranteed Obligations shall be entitled to a Mortgage or Charge over all the assets of the Customer over which the Bank holds any security and that such security granted to the Guarantor shall rank in respect of all moneys paid by the Guarantor to satisfy the Guaranteed Obligations together with the Guarantor's costs and expenses of enforcement in priority to any security held by the Bank. The Customer covenants with the Guarantor that it will do all such acts and execute all such documents as will vest the aforesaid security in the Guarantor.

IN WITNESS WHEREOF the parties hereto have duly executed this Deed the day and year first hereinbefore written.

THE SCHEDULE

THE TRANSACTION :

The grant by the Bank of a Guarantee / Performance Bond / Letter of Credit to Export Finance and Insurance Corporation in respect of the Customer's obligations under an Agreement between _____ Limited and the Customer relating to the sale of certain equipment by _____ Limited to the Customer.

_____ LIMITED   (SIGNED)

(THE GUARANTEE))

_____ LTD.)   (SIGNED)

(THE CUSTOMER))

_____ BRANCH, BANK OF CHINA   (SIGNED)

(THE BANK)

CONTRACT
ON
SETTING UP A SPINNING MILL
IN
CHINA

In order to fully utilize the rabbit fur resources of   Province, expand and strengthen the production capability of   Province's wool textile industry, and develop foreign trade, the   Textile Industrial Corp., the industrial department of   Prefecture Zhejiang Province, the   Wool Textile Mill (hereafter referred to as Party A) and   Enterprises Ltd of   (hereafter referred to as Party B) under the introduction and consultation of the China National Textiles Import-Export Corp (CHINATEX)   Branch, and after having undergone cordial negotiations, hereby enter into compensation trade wherein Party B will provide two carding machines and necessary related equipment and implement the import of raw goods for processing to fulfill the following agreement:

Article 1.   Party A undertakes to provide a portion of an empty factory building in the existing   Machinery Factory, to be used for Party B to install the two machines and related equipment that it imports for Party A (Appendix 1). Party A undertakes to upgrade the factory building by the end of   . Sometime between July and August of this year, Party B undertakes to ship the aforesaid equipment from its various places of manufacture to Shanghai and advance funds for the said and other equipment.

Article 2.   Party A undertakes to handle the procedures for the duty-free import of the equipment.

Article 3.   Expenditure for the installation of equipment will be undertaken by Party A. Party B agrees to dispatch technicians to supervise the installation of equipment and trial spinning of yarn. Living accommodations, food, transportation costs for the said and other personnel at the site shall be borne by Party A. Their salaries and transportation to and from   and   will be borne by Party B.

Article 4.   Equipment insurance. Starting from the formal commencement of production, Party A will assume the insurance cost on the already repaid portion of the equipment, and Party B will assume the insurance cost of the unpaid portion of the equipment.

Article 5.   Both Party A and Party B agree that Party B's advance of loans will be for the following equipment. (Appendix 2):

(1)   total c.i.f. cost of the two carding machines and other related

equipment and parts;

(2)   total cost of air-conditioning equipment and expenditures for the Hong Kong company undertaking packaging, shipping, and installation;

(3)   bank charges for procuring the preceding two items;

(4)   interest due on the first through third items of this article from the beginning of packaging the equipment through its shipment to the factory;

(5)   interest due on the first through fourth items of this article from the approximately six-month period in which the equipment arrives and is installed at the factory and formal production starts;

(6)   insurance costs for fire and natural disaster coverage on the first and second items for the first six months before formal production begins.

Article 6.   Party A agrees, once formal production has begun, to use the processing fee and / or rabbit fur to repay the loans advanced by Party B as described in Article 5 and the interest due on those loans within a one-year period. (If Party A wishes to extend the period for repaying the loan, it must notify Party B six months prior to the end of the loan repayment period.) Party A undertakes to repay the principal and interest advanced by Party B, the repayment schedule will be settled once every six months, and accrued interest is to be calculated according to the prevailing prime rates as quoted by the Bank of China's   branch.

Article 7.   Party A agrees to process the raw goods imported by Party B for five years from formal commencement of production. During this time, the equipment that comes under the articles of this agreement may not be used for production purposes of any other factory, firm, or individual other than Party B.

Article 8.   The equipment that comes under the articles of this agreement will be used for the production of 14-16 count rabbit fur and a mixture of natural and synthetic fiber yarn. Yearly production capacity is set at approximately   pounds. Under certain circumstances and after discussion and approval by both parties, other kinds of yarn may be produced.

Article 9.   Party A and Party B agree to use an internationally acceptable ratio of finished goods to raw materials and a wool content of 16.5% and a 4% oil content. The ratio of yarn to raw materials shall be no lower than 95%; otherwise, Party A must compensate Party B for damages and losses. The method of compensation will be negotiated [between the two parties]. Within the initial six-month period after the start of production, the completed yarn ratio may be no lower than 90%. Under these circumstances, Party A must make proper arrangements for warehousing the produced, returned fibers / threads; Party A and Party B must negotiate means of disposing of them.

Article 10.   Party A guarantees that the quality of the yarn meets acceptable standards of the buyers from   and   knitting factories (see Appendix 3). Party A assumes responsibility if the quality does not meet these standards and consequently results in the return of merchandise or the filing of claims.

Article 11. During the repayment period, Party A undertakes to provide rabbit fur for production using the prevailing f.o.b.   prices as quoted by the China National Native Produce and Animal By-Products Corp (CHINATUHSU) for such rabbit fur as the basis for calculating the value of such inputs to function as a portion of the raw materials supplied by Party B for processing; Party B undertakes to supply the necessary wool, nylon, and other synthetic fibers for the production of rabbit fur and synthetic fiber yarn. If Party A is unable to supply sufficient quantities of rabbit fur, or if Party B is unable to supply sufficient quantities of raw materials and other orders, subsequently causing the other party to suffer losses, the issue will be resolved through negotiations between both parties.

Article 12. An independent internationally recognized third party will inspect the weight of the raw goods and the certificate of inspection will be sent by Party B to Party A for inspection; Party A has the right to require Party B to have the weight of the imported goods reinspected by the China Commodities Inspection Bureau at the port of entry and to send the certificate of reinspection to Party A for its examination.

Article 13. Party A undertakes to handle the import of raw goods (including the import of any duty-free items) and the procedures for exporting the finished product (including the duty-free export of the finished product).

Article 14. The import of raw materials shall use the c.i.f.   terms for delivery of goods. Exports of finished products shall use f.o.b.   . All delivery of goods, as well as internal transportation costs in the storage period (raw materials within a production period of three months, and finished products within a production period of two months) and safeguarding [of the said material] shall be borne by Party A. Party B thus assumes responsibility for the insurance costs covering storage and goods in transit.

Article 15. If Party B succeeds in selling the completed yarn to a unit within the country, and the location that the buyers have directed to receive such goods is within the boundaries of   Province, Party A undertakes to deliver the said yarn to the point of delivery. If the point of delivery is outside the boundaries stated above, then the goods will be handled according to the conditions of the mill / warehouse.

Article 16. Partry A undertakes to provide the materials for packaging the finished product that are suitable for long-distance transport; Party B undertakes to provide the mutton tallow necessary for processing.

Article 17. In as much as Party B is importing raw materials on behalf of Party Λ, and, after processing, the finished products are exported by Party A, the increases in cost arising from this (such as shipping and interest, etc.) shall be partially offset by a subsidy, which shall not exceed Renminbi   annually, given by Party A to Party B.

Article 18.   Using the rate of   per pound, Party B will pay Party A the processing fee for the equivalent spinning of wool yarn. Party A, according to the actual invoice for the delivery of goods at that time, together with the bill of lading, and by using D / P   terms, will collect payment from the bank. The processing fee schedule shall be adjusted once every six months after the start of production and shall be based on the rate of increase of such production in

Article 19.   After the trial yarn has been successfully produced and after the finished product has attained a level of quality that is satisfactory to both Parties A and B, Party B will gradually withdraw all personnel sent to supervise the installation of machinery and trial spinning. If necessary, Party B will give suggestions concerning management in an advisory capacity.

Article 20.   Party A and Party B agree that when the conditions of this agreement have been cordially and satisfactorily implemented, Parties A and B, under mutually beneficial principles and before the   deadline described in Article 7 of this agreement, shall negotiate further on other forms of cooperation.

Article 21.   Party A and Party B agree, after the formal start of production and when production has reached the standard described in Articles 9 and 10, that Party B, using similar methods, may again import two sets of carding machines and related equipment and machinery for dyeing raw materials on behalf of Party A and may, under appropriate conditions, gradually increase the necessary equipment in order to produce wool sweaters using the produced wool yarn.

Article 22.   After Party A repays the loans and interest advanced by Party B as described in Article 6, and within the stipulated time limit as stated in Article 7 of this agreement, Party B entrusts to Party A the rabbit fur and raw materials necessary for processing synthetic and rabbit fur yarn which will be supplied in principle by Party C [China Light Industrial Products Import-Export Corp (INDUSTRY)   ]. The supply schedule, pricing, and foreign exchange calculation, together with the items to be processed, shall be negotiated every six months between parties C and B.

Article 23.   The China National Textiles Import-Export Corp plans to establish a jointly financed company in Hong Kong with Party B that is expected to replace Party B in this agreement and is expected to assume the rights and obligations of Party B in this agreement.

Article 24.   If this agreement contains any areas of uncertainty, Parties A and B will resolve those areas through discussion.

Appendix 1: Machinery and Equipment

Quantity and description.

(1) Spinning machines

    1.1 One carding willow, type AB5B, 1,200-mm working width; by

    1.2 Two three-swift woolen cards, type CR 313, two-meter working width, 192 good ends; by

    1.3 Two self-acting mules, type DFV 872, 552 spindles each, 54-mm gauge, 2.5-meter run; by

    1.4 One No.7-11   automatic cone winder, 20 drums; by

    1.5 2 2/3 sets of card clothing; by

    1.6 One card clothing mounting and grinding equipment; by

(2) One lot testing equipment for spinnig, including one each tensile tester, moisture meter, beam balance, hygrograph, 12G semiautomatic knitting machine, etc.

(3) One lot tools, machine parts and accessories, etc.

(4) One job air conditioner with / without cooling, with air ducts to be made on spot and with other components from various countries

(5) One van; by

I. Breakdown of the loan agreement covering the equipment (estimated value):

    (1)   Cost of the two sets of carding machines (Appendix 1) ...... HK$XXX

    (2)   Air-conditioning equipment (including installation fee) .... HK$XXX

    (3)   Bank charge for purchases of items 1 and 2 .... HK$

    (4)   Interest on equipment from shipment to unloading at the factory (annual interest rate 13%)

          [European equipment in approximately three months, Japanese equipment in approximately one and a half months] ...Total HK$XXX

    (5)   The interest on the equipment from the time it arrives at the factory to the commencement of formal production (approximately six months) (annual interest 13%) .... HK$XXX

    (6)   The insurance cost on the equipment from the time it arrives at the factory to the formal start of production (approximately six months) .... HK$XXX

          Advance on the equipment .... HK$XXX

II. Interest on the advance for the two sets of equipment (estimated value):

    Five years from the commencement of formal production (annual interest 13%) .... HK$XXX

III. Total of principal plus interest on the advance for equipment (estimated value) .... HK$XXX

IV. Monthly payment due (estimated value) .... HK$XXX

    Repaid in five years time .... HK$XXX

V. To repay the advance on equipment (both principal and interest), processing fee per pound: equipment (two sets) after the trial production period should attain a monthly production capacity of rabbit fur and synthetic fiber yarn of   lb; HK$XXX÷   =

                                       HK$XXX per pound

Appendix 3

The accepted quality standards for yarn, according to the
weaving factories, are as follows:

(1)   Deviations in the average count of the yarn may not exceed 5%.

(2)   Sweaters made with the yarn may not have especially coarse or thin sections.

(3)   A batch of yarn (usual lot not exceeding 1,000 kg) may not be mixed with other batches during the dyeing process.

(4)   The yarn must not contain any fibers of an obviously peculiar color.

(5)   The tensile strength of the yarn must not be too weak (the tensile strength standards will be determined by the weaving factories, and details concerning these standards will be investigated further).

(6)   Woolen yarn must not contain any widespread grease stains.

(7)   The colors of the yarn may not be uneven or peculiar.

(8)   When a batch of yarn has been made into a sweater, the sweater must not have sections of differing colors.

(9)   Any slight variation in the feel of the yarn after it has been made into sweaters is acceptable.

(10)   The actual composition of the wool yarn shall closely correspond to the standards specified here.

AGREEMENT
ON
CONSIGNMENT AND OTHER SERVICE(S)

China National Product Import & Export Corporation, Province Branch (hereinafter referred to as "SINO") and Foreign Investor Ltd., China Representative Office (hereinafter referred to as "INVESTOR") have concluded this agreement based on the principle of equality and mutual benefit, to do good freight forwarding service as follows:

1.   TRANSPORTATION ROUTES

Within the scope of feasibility, SINO will deliver export freight to be carried by INVESTOR. INVESTOR is responsible for the entire transport route of transporting to the destinations listed on the bill of consignment.

2.   CONSIGNMENT OF FREIGHT

SINO'S consignment of freight will generally not be later than 15 days before the date of loading for shipment on the letter of credit. SINO will give the bill of consignment to INVESTOR in quintuplicate 15 days before the date of settlement to facilitate the arranging of suitable means of transport for loading and shipment. Special circumstances will be resolved through consultation at the time.

3.   CONSIGNMENT BILL

If upon receipt of the consignment bill INVESTOR thinks that it cannot undertake the carriage, it must give it back to SINO within 3 days. If INVESTOR accepts the carriage, it is within 3 to 4 days to list on the consignment bill the bill of lading number (s), and fill in the name of the ship, the sailing date and freight charges and give a copy to INVESTOR to facilitate the handling of insurance and related documents.

4.   WAREHOUSING

SINO'S freight is to be delivered at Warehouse. INVESTOR is to arrange for a container vehicle to collect the freight at Warehouse for shipment, and will give one working day's notice to SINO before it dispatches the container vehicle to the warehouse. If INVESTOR requests SINO to transport the freight to other places in the city for loading and shipment, the costs of so doing will be borne by INVESTOR.

5.   INVESTOR'S DUTIES OF SHIPMENT

INVESTOR shall be responsible for the safe and rapid transport of the carried freight to its destination and delivery to the recipient. The ship arranged for loading and shipment must accord with China's present foreign policy and related regulations. Cargo ships of Israeli, South African, or South Korean nationalities should not be used.

6. BILL OF LADING

After shipping the cargo, INVESTOR is promptly to issue the clean bill of lading for the entire transport route to SINO. From the time freight given by SINO to INVESTOR for carriage is loaded onto the vehicle, if there is any damage or loss INVESTOR will be responsible to make recovery or compensation.

7. CHARGES

INVESTOR will list in a schedule and give to SINO the relevant methods of calculation of the freight charges and the rates of the charges, the transport charges for the entire transport route from start to finish including all miscellaneous charges and supplementary charges. The standards for the charges shall not be higher than those standards currently used by authorized shipping companies of the Chinese Government. If at a later time there are changes in the freight charges, appropriate adjustments can be effected through consultation between the parties.

As regards the portion of the freight charges which shall be paid by SINO. In transactions concluded with CIF or C & F price terms after the cargo is loaded and shipped, INVESTOR is to make a list of freight charges, and along with 3 copies of the original bill of consignment, transfer _____ calculated in foreign exchange from the account of SINO in the Bank of China _____ branch to the account of INVESTOR. If INVESTOR entrusts SINO to remit the funds to _____ on its behalf, the costs of so doing will be deducted from the amount of the freight charges.

As regards the portion of the freight charges which are to be paid by the recipient INVESTOR is to make a list of the freight charges and collect them from the recipient. At the same time, INVESTOR is to fill in the amount of the freight charges on the original bill of consignment and give a copy to SINO to facilitate the calculation of the commission.

8. FREIGHT ON TRANSIT

If the freight of SINO is loaded on a ship from the interior of _____ for shipment to _____ , INVESTOR is responsible for collecting the cargo from such ship and transferring it to a big ship. INVESTOR is also to issue a combined transport bill of lading for the entire route. The freight charges will be based on the freight price for cargo delivered for shipment in _____ less US _____ per each cubic metre.

9. COMMISSION

INVESTOR will give SINO back a per cent commission from the gross amount of the freight charges for each lot of carried freights.

Settlement is to be made once every month and paid in foreign exchange.

10. EFFECTIVENESS

This agreement takes effect from the date of signing. If in the process of carrying out the agreement there are _____ matters inadequately covered, supplementations or amendments may be effected through consultation between the parties.

If during the period of carrying out the agreement, conflicts with China's foreign policy or related regulations arise and the business of consignment for carriage cannot be continued, this agreement shall cease to be effective.

(SIGNED)   (SIGNED)

For & on Behalf of   For & on Behalf of
China National Product   Foreign Investor Ltd.
Import & Export Corporation China Representative Office
Province Branch

CONTRACT ON SELLING TECHNOLOGY KNOW HOW TO CHINA

MEMORANDUM OF AGREEMENT made this _____ day of 19 _____ between _____, International Corporation (hereinafter referred to as ' INVESTOR ') of the one part and _____ Production Corporation of China (hereinafter referred to as ' CHINESE PARTY') of the other part.

RECITALS

1. INVESTOR has substantial expertise in the design, research, manufacture, promotion and marketing of paper.

2. The CHINESE PARTY has under construction a paper mill in _____ Province, China, with a planned capacity of One Million (1,000,000.00) tons per year.

3. The CHINESE PARTY intends to receive information, assistance and advice with respect to the design review, construction and operation of this paper mill and INVESTOR is ready and willing to provide such information, assistance and advice on certain terms and conditions as stiuplated hereunder.

IT IS AGREED AS FOLLOWS:

1. INVESTOR will provide the following information, assistance and advice on an exclusive basis in _____ Province, China, to the CHINESE PARTY:

   (A) A research and analysis of the existing environmental factors, design, machinery and labour force for the paper mill, including but not limited to recommendations for improvements as appropriate and feasible, such as installation of floater, fluffer, distributer, evener, foam breaker, gas heater and glie bond tester. Also a thorough study of the proposed production plan, with recommendation of modifications, if any, including but not limited to the production target within the next five years and the types of paper to be produced.

   (B) The selection, sourcing and ordering of imported technology know-how, including but not limited to Pandia chemipulper, plating machine, plate glazing calender, potcher, precipator and precision balance. In addition, INVESTOR will try its best to obtain, on behalf of the CHINESE PARTY, the lowest price for any neccessary equipment for modern paper mill from countries like West Germany, Switzerland, Italy ctc., provided, however, that all transactions will be directly dealt with between the above mentioned foreign suppliers and the CHINESE PARTY.

167

(C) Appropriate manufacturing, processing techniques and procedures, including but not limited to preconditioning devices, print
bonding, primary screening operation, automatically controlled
continuous process, corona controlled process, fluidization process, tower reclaiming system, transportation device and system
storage.

(D) The development of high quality papers, including but not limited to
advertising paper, air knife coated paper, archival paper, asphalting
paper, autocopy paper, antique book paper, brocade paper, cable
insulting paper, cigar brand paper and cheque paper, with special
emphasis on ' minimum cost ' formulations in order to maximize of
utilization of local resources while maintaining a high standard of
producing the followings:
i.   culture paper
ii. crystal paper
iii. crumpled paper
iv. corrugated paper
v.   cotton paper
vi. cord paper
vii. cork paper
viii. creping paper
ix. China paper
x.   composite paper
In the event that local resources are not available in sufficient
supply or quality to produce an adequate amount of the above
listed papers, INVESTOR will assist in the importation of any
such resources for the manufacturing of these papers, again,
INVESTOR shall get the cheapest price available in market.

(E) The development of a quality control program for commercial and
packaging paper, including the operation of the equipment necessary for the testing of dipping, distillation and dissolution.

(F) The specifications and standards of packaging materials for the
finished products, including recommendations as to methods of
shipment.

(G) The resolution of those operational manufacturing problems which
may occur from time to time, in the event such problems are
submitted to INVESTOR.

(H) The training at the —— Papermill of papermill operating personnel
and also the training of up to fifty (50) people for a period not to
exceed six (6) months, at INVESTOR facilities in _____ ; provided,
however, that the transportation of such personnel shall be paid by
the CHINESE PARTY, which shall also have the responsibility for all
travel documents, including exit and entry visas. INVESTOR will
pay reasonable living expenses, not to exceed (AMOUNT OF

MONEY IN CASH — AUTHOR) in the aggregate, while the trainees are in _____ .

(l)   The training in _____ Province, China of a reasonable number of people, not to exceed one hundred (100), designated by the CHINESE PARTY, in the marketing and distribution of paper, for a period of three (3) months. To assist such marketing efforts, INVESTOR will make available at no cost to the CHINESE PARTY the promotional and marketing materials which _____ INVESTOR has developed for the feeds in question; proded, however, that the CHINESE PARTY shall have the responsibility for translating such materials and shall bear the costs thereof. Nothing herein shall give any rights to, or beneficial interest in, any INVESTOR trademark, including those trademarks which may be incorporated in the promotional and marketing materials referred to above.

2.   In addition to the foregoing, INVESTOR will, for a fee in addition to that referred to in Paragraph 3 below, and subject to separate agreement between the parties hereto, use its best efforts to do the following:

(a)   Adapt the technology provided pursuant to this Agreement to local customs and the long established habits of Chinese printers.

(b)   Educate farmer's Chinese printers through training programs and seminars, conducted by INVESTOR'S personnel or otherwise, in the areas of printing and publication house management.

3.   In compensation for the information and assistance provided by INVESTOR to the CHINESE PARTY pursuant to this Agreement, the CHINESE PARTY shall pay to INVESTOR a fee of (AMOUNT OF MONEY IN CASH — AUTHOR), payable as follows:

(a)   Within sixty (60) days of the effective date of this Agreement, the CHINESE PARTY shall pay _____ (_____); INVESTOR a disclosure fee in the amount of _____ .

(b)   The balance of said fee in ten (10) equal payments of _____ each, on or before January 1 of each year, the first payment due on January 1, 19 _____ , and the final payment due January 1, 19 ____ __ .

4.   For the fee referred to in Paragraph 3(a) and (b) above, INVESTOR will make available, at its expense, such INVESTOR'S personnel as INVESTOR deems necessary or advisable to be present in _____ . _____ Province, China _____ , in order for INVESTOR to provide the information and assistance pursuant to this Agreement, limited, however as follows:

	Number of Trips	Duration Each Trip
First Year	8	10 - 20 days
Second Year	8	10 - 20 days
Third Year	8	10 - 20 days
Fourth Year	8	10 - 20 days

Fifth Year	8	10 - 20 days
Sixth Year	6	10 days
Seventh Year	6	10 days
Eighth Year	6	4 days
Ninth Year	5	4 days
Tenth Year	4	4 days

Unless otherwise agreed, each trip will involve only one individual. If more trips than mentioned above are requested in any particular year by the CHINESE PARTY, these will be at the expense of the CHINESE PARTY. For additional trips during the first year of this Agreement, the CHINESE PARTY shall pay INVESTOR (AMOUNT OF MONEY IN CASH — AUTHOR) per day per person for each day or part thereof during which any INVESTOR or INVESTOR'S designated personnel shall be reasonably required to be present in China _____ in order for INVESTOR to provide the information and assistance pursuant to this Agreement. For the second through Tenth years of this Agreement, said payment shall be increased as follows: second year, (AMOUNT OF MONEY IN CASH — AUTHOR); third year, (DITTO), fourth year, (DITTO), fifth year (DITTO), sixth year (DITTO), seventh year (DITTO), eighth year (DITTO), ninth year (DITTO), tenth year (DITTO). The CHINESE PARTY shall also reimburse INVESTOR for the first economy class round-trip airfare of any such personnel, together with their hotel accomodations and meals while in China _____ . The CHINESE PARTY shall also be responsible for the costs of a translator / interpreter, if required. Payments due under this Section shall be paid within ninety (90) days after INVESTOR submits a statement therefore to the CHINESE PARTY.

5.   The effective date of this Agreement shall be that date on which all necessary Chinese governmental approvals and / or registrations are obtained by the CHINESE PARTY in order to allow both the CHINESE PARTY and INVESTOR to perform their obligations under this Agreement. The term of this Agreement shall commence upon said effective date and shall continue until January _____ 19 _____ . If all such necessary governmental approvals have not been received by _____ , 19 _____ , INVESTOR, at its sole election, shall be excused from all obligations under this Agreement, effective immediately, without further obligation or responsibility of any kind whatsoever to the CHINESE PARTY.

6.   CHINESE PARTY acknowledges that the information supplied by INVESTOR hereunder is disclosed in confidence, and that CHINESE PARTY shall not in any way or manner whatsoever, make known, divulge or communicate to any person, firm or entity any of the information disclosed except for such _____ . Information that was already known to the CHINESE PARTY at the time of disclosure; was at the time of disclosure, or thereafter becomes or became, gererally available to the

public other than through an improper disclosure by CHINESE PARTY; or is received from a third party having no direct or indirect obligation of secrecy to INVESTOR.

7. If either of the parties hereto shall fail to comply substantially with the terms and provisions of this Agreement, except those terms and provisions relating to payment, for a period of sixty (60) days after the non-defaulting party has given written notice of the default to the defaulting party, then the non-defaulting party shall have the right to immediately terminate this Agreement by giving the defaulting party written notice to that effect.

8. It is understood that this technical assistance arrangement is intended only to be the beginning of a long-term association between the parties hereto. Thus, as the CHINESE PARTY develops or becomes aware of business opportunities in areas in which INVESTOR has expertise, the CHINESE PARTY shall offer INVESTOR first option to participate in such opportunities on mutually agreed terms and conditions.

9. Neither party hereto shall be liable to the other for any delay or failure in performing any of its obligations hereunder when any such delay or failure is occasioned, directly or indirectly, by Force Majeure or by other causes or contingencies beyond its control. Further, INVESTOR shall have no responsibility with respect to problems attributable to anything finalized prior to INVESTOR'S involvement in this project or anything done contrary to INVESTOR'S recommendations or advice.

10. All disputes in connection with this Agreement shall be settled by friendly consultations between both parties. In case no amicable agreement can be reached, the matter in dispute shall be finally decided by arbitration. The place of arbitration is _____ , _____ , and the arbitration shall be performed in accordance with the _____ arbitration procedure.

11. This Agreement contains all the understandings and representations between the parties relating to the matters referred to herein, and may be amended only by a fully executed written supplement.

12. This Agreement may not be assigned by either party hereto without the prior written consent of the other party.

THIS AGREEMENT is executed by the parties hereto as of this day and year first above written.

| Production Corporation of China | (INVESTOR) |
| (CHINESE PARTY) | |

BY _____   By _____

171

PROCESSING AND ASSEMBLY AGREEMENT OF ELECTRICAL ENGINEERING PRODUCTS

MEMORANDUM OF AGREEMENT made this _____ day of 19 _____
and entered by and between _____,
with principal offices in _____,
(hereinafter referred to as "Investor"), and _____,
_____ with its factory situated at _____,
China. (hereinafter referred to as the "Works"), and _____,
_____ with principal offices in _____,
China (hereinafter referred to as "Sino"). Works and Sino are referred to as "Chinese Organizations".

Article 1 : Objectives

1.1 Both parties agree to cooperate during the term of this Agreement by means of sub-contract arrangement (or assembly) of _____
_____ ,
(hereinafter referred to jointly and severally as the "Products"). Investor's contribution will consist of providing capital investment by way of consigned equipment, providing raw materials and semi-finished products, providing production technology and know-how and in purchasing and sales and marketing of the Products.

1.2 Works will be responsible for providing manpower, electricity, gas and water, the production in factory and the services necessary for production and assembly. The works will also be responsible for management. It will organize production in accordance with Investor's technical specifications. It will deliver all Products to Investor and calculate the processing fee in accordance with the established standard.

1.3 All Parties are willing to, and agree that they must render optimum support to each other to accomplish the above-stated goals and to insure the success of the venture which is the subject of the Agreement.

Article 2 : Variety of Products

2.1 The Products consist of _____ types of _____
_____ as described in
Investor's Engineering Bulletin No. _____
Such engineering bulletins describe the various case sizes, ratings and

172

configurations of the Products type to which they pertain.

2.2 Initially, the Products to be assembled by Works will consist of Type _____ of various ratings. Annex to the Agreement shows the initial percentage mix and case sizes of the initial Type _____ ratings and also the estimated weights of the assembly object to be used in the production of each of the various ratings. The percentage mix in will be subject to change during the term of the Agreement with advance notice (not less than four weeks before the change) by Investor to Works.

2.3 Unless otherwise noted, the use of the term Type __ as hereinafter used in the Agreement or in the Annex to the Agreement shall be deemed also to mean Type _____.

Article 3 : Consigned Equipment

3.1 Investor will consign all equipment (including spare parts) to be used by Works in manufacturing _____ units per week of the Products. Annex to this Agreement contains a listing and the current value of the equipment necessary for the manufacture by Works of _____ units of the Products per week. Investor will also supply consigned equipment for sample incoming inspection of Assembly object. Also shown on _____, for future information purposes only, are the current value costs of equipment necessary for the manufacture by Works of (location of the works — author), and units of the Products per week.

3.2 All the equipment belongs to Investor and, upon termination of the Agreement, it will be returned to Investor.

3.3 The equipment consigned by Investor will be.

3.4 Upon termination of this Agreement, the consigned equipment will be returned to Investor at (destination agreed by both parties.)

3.5 Investor guarantees that the consigned equipment is capable of producing good ____ units of the Products per week when operated _____ days on three normal shifts at _____ % yields.

3.6 Any non-metric tools for maintenance of the equipment will be consigned, free of charge, by Investor. Investor will supply for replacement, at its expense, any part of the consigned equipment which must be replaced due to ordinary wear and tear. Any worn out parts will be returned to Investor at (destination agreed by both parties.)

3.7 The electrical voltage supplied by Works will be (standard to be agreed by both parties) and will meet the requirements of the consigned equipment. If any equipment item requires better regulation than ____ %, Investor will supply regulation for such special equipment item.

3.8 Investor represents that the consigned equipment complies with the (relevant law of such juridication as agreed by both parties)

3.9 Investor will telex Works when consigned equipment is shipped to Works spare parts supplied by Investor after the shipment of the consigned equipment, Investor will pay freight, brokerage and insurance charges.

Article 4 : <u>Raw Materials</u>

4.1 Investor is responsible for supplying all raw materials necessary for the production of the Products. Included in such raw materials will be (detailed list of Catagory — author), expense materials and packing materials.

4.2 All raw materials and expense materials consigned to Works by Investor will be verified by Works that such materials conform to the accompanying packing list and will be presumed to have been received by Works in good usable condition unless, immediately upon discovery of any defect at any time. Works advises Investor by telex of any such defective or damaged materials, specifying the nature and extent of the defect or damage. Any materials verified by Investor to be defective or damaged will be replaced by Investor.

4.3 Investor will ship raw materials so that will arrive at Works _____ weeks, and other raw materials month prior to each scheduled weekly production.

Article 5 : Consigned Equipment and Supplied Materials <u>Supplemental Expenses</u>

5.1 Investor will pay freight, brokerage and insurance charges for shipment of the consigned equipment and accompanying spare parts consigned by Investor to (destination agreed by both parties) and for shipment of materials provided by Investor to the China Organization. For used only in the manufacture of Products ordered by Investor and will not be reproduced or used for any other purpose.

5.2 Investor will pay the cost of insurance coverage during the term of the Agreement.

5.3 Chinese Organization will pay for all costs (except for insurance) for shipment of consigned equipment and accompanying spare parts from (a location in China) to Work's premises in and for the return of all finished products, good and bad, and processed scrap from (a location in China) to a location in China.

5.4 Chinese Organization will pay for any customs duties, other taxes or any other charges required for entry or exit of consigned equipment and materials into and out of, and finished Product, goods or bad, and scrap out of, China, and for any taxes or other charges, (except for insurance) levied upon such equipment, materials, finished Products or scrap while within China.

5.5 Works will pay for installation and maintenance in good working condition of the consigned equipment, and, upon termination of this Agreement, the cost of returning the consigned equipment to (a place agreed by both parties).

Article 6 : Quality Control

6.1 All good units produced by Works will be returned with packing list of Investor.

6.2 It shall be a prime requirement of this Agreement that, of the Products started in a production cycle by Works, at least _____ % will meet Investor's Specification Number, outgoing visual inspection of Product, and Specification Number _____ processing production testing. Such two specifications are the same for Product and are set forth in Annex _____ to this Agreement.

6.3 All Products not meeting the two specifications set forth in Annex _____ and all scrap material shall be appropriately segregated by Works and returned to Investor, as instructed by Investor. A discrepancy of _____ % will be allowed in Product count.

6.4 Investor may, for good cause shown by Works, elect to waive the yield requirement set forth in Article 6.2 above, but any such waiver shall not constitute a waiver of future failures by Works to produce at such yield rate. In case of a failure to produce at such yield rate, Works and Investor shall immediately investigate and analyze the cause or causes of such failure, after which Investor and Works shall institute the necessary corrective measures, including, if necessary the suspension of operations by Works. It is agreed that continued failure, after the first _____ months of production, by Works to achieve the yield rate of at least _____ % or quality or production levels provided herein shall be cause for immediate termination of this Agreement by Investor without incurring obligation thereby.

Article 7 : Payment

7.1 For each good units of the Products shipped by Works during the term of the Agreement, Investor will pay Works Pound Sterling.

7.2 Investor shall open with bank, an Irrevocable Letter of Credit, allowing partial shipments and transsipments, in favour of Sino, payable at sight against first presentation of appropriate shipping documents to the Bank of China.

7.3 _____ years following start of production of the Products by Works, the parties will consider an adjustment in the price paid by Investor to Works for the Products. Any such price adjustment will not exceed the cost then available to Investor for the production of the Products in same quantity and with the same quality from third parties or from Investor's own facilities. For the remainder of the Agreement, Investor will pay Works the greater of Pound Sterling _____. (As specified in Article 7.1) or such adjusted price.

Article 8 : Technical Assistance

8.1 In order to put the consigned equipment in running order, Investor will send two engineers to Works for a period (estimated to be _____ weeks) to oversee the test running and use of the consigned equipment and the training or works personnel, reasonably following advice by Works that the equipment is installed and ready for operation.

8.2 After the start of production, Investor will cause periodic audits to be performed by its quality engineers. During the _____ year of production, such periodic audits will be performed and, thereafter, _____

8.3 In addition to such periodic audits, Investor, if it so desires, will be given the opportunity, at reasonable times during normal working hours, to visit Works and to review and inspect Work's production.

8.4 (a) Within _____ month after execution of the Agreement, Works will provide Investor with an original reproduceable drawing showing the space for production of the Product. Such drawing will identify physical features such as windows, doors partitions and all existing services such as exhausts, water pipes and main power sources, and the situation of adjacent buildings.

    (b) Within _____ months after receipt of Work's drawing, Investor will supply the following information to Works; a production layout showing the location of the equipment, power outlets and connections, exhausts, pipes and other required service facilities.

    (c) Within _____ months after the date of execution of the Agreement, Investor will supply Works with all information necessary for installation and operation of the consigned equipment, including general maintenance instruction, as well as production and inspection specifications.

    (d) When the consigned equipment is shipped by Works to Works, Investor will provide Works with detailed written instruction for operating and maintaining the equipment.

    (e) Approximately one month before shipment of the consigned equipment, Investor will notify Works and Works, after receiving notice from Investor, will begin preparation for installation of the consigned equipment.

8.5 Approximately ____ months after execution of the Agreement, investor will train personnel of Works in the production of the Products at Investor's plant in _____.
The training period will not exceed ____ weeks. The four personnel to be trained will include Work's Director, Equipment Engineer, Process Engineer and Quality Control/Production Manager. Investor will provide round trip air travel tickets for the Works personnel from _____ to _____, and pay for their lodging, meals and transportation during the training period and provide an interpreter.

8.6 The Chinese Organization will pay the costs of lodging (National Hotel or equivalent), meals and transportation expenses within _____, of Investor engineers visiting Works in accordance with Articles 8.1 and 8.2 but not exceeding costs paid by Investor under Article 8.5 and also provide such Investor engineers with an interpreter free of cost. Any excess costs for Sprague engineers will be paid by Investor.

Article 9 : Factory's Operations

9.1 Works will supply, at its cost, all necessary manufacturing space and services connected there with _____
to this Agreement sets forth the estimated electrical load and square footage requirements for production of the Products by _____ unit volume.

9.2 Works will supply and pay for all direct labour and supervisory personnel required for the manufacture of the Products. _____
to this Agreement sets forth the direct labour, support labour and quality control labour estimated to be needed by Works based upon weekly unit volume. _____
to this Agreement sets forth the estimated actual standard hours per _____ units for manufacture of the products by manufacturing and testing operations, broken down by the case size of the Products.

9.3 The work to be performed by Works in the production of the Products is described in general terms in _____
to this Agreement. Works will conduct operations in accordance with detailed processing specifications to be supplied by Investor, Investor will also supply incoming sample inspection specifications. It is understood that, during the period of the Agreement, technical improvements and changes may occur which may result in changes in Investor's processing and related specifications. Any such changes will be reported by Investor to Works. Investor will consign to Works any equipment required thereby. If any such changes increase Works's production costs, Investor will consult with Works.

9.4 In the process of production, the import and export of equipment, materials, finished Products, good or bad, and scrap, the Chinese Organization will obtain, at their cost, any and all licenses and permits which may be required by China or any governmental unit thereof.

9.5 All manufacturing by Works under this Agreement will be performed on the premises currently occupied by Works or at any such different location as may be agreed to in advance by Investor.

Article 10 : Purchases

10.1 After the beginning of production, at a mutually agreeable time in advance of each production quarter (not less than _____ months)

177

Investor will notify Works of the types and numbers of the Products which Investor will order for such production quarter and will provide Works with an appropriate shipping schedule. When Works is in full production, Investor's orders for the Products will average ____ units per week. In any given week during the production quarter, Investor may, upon appropriate advance notice (not less than _____ weeks) to Works, change the numbers and types of the Products it had previously ordered, but Investor will, over a period of time, place orders upon Works for a average of ____ units. The types and numbers of the Products to be ordered wihtin each production quarter shall be the subject of separate Releases by Investor to Works.

10.2 Works will deliver to Investor, during each production quarter, all good units of the types of the Products ordered by Investor during such production quarter.

Article 11 : Shipment

11.1 Works will make all shipments of the Products by air freight to ____ Investor in _____ on a weekly basis.

11.2 Works will, upon the occasion of each such shipment of the Products to Investor, immediately telex Investor advising Investor of the types and numbers of the Products in such shipment.

Article 12 : Volume

12.1 The equipment and materials for the start of Investor's production will be delivered to Works's premises by Investor within _____ months after the date of execution of this Agreement.

12.2 Works will install such equipment and begin initial production of the Products as soon as possible following the receipt of such equipment and materials by Works. It is expected that Works will achieve a production volume of ____ units of the Products per week within ____ months following the receipt of such equipment and materials.

12.3 Investor may, at its option, require Works to increase the number of the Products produced by Works from a rate of ____ units per week to successive weekly rates, at annual intervals, of ____, ____ and ____ units per week. If Investor introduces significant changes affecting costs at the time of any such __ unit increases, the parties will negotiate an appropriate price adjustment. Investor and Works will mutually work out a plan to achieve such increases as soon as possible.

12.4 For each such increase in the weekly volume of the Products, Investor will purchase and consign the necessary equipment to Works.

Article 13 : Confidentiality

13.1 Chinese Organization recognize that the information to be provided by Investor to Chinese Organization in respect to equipment, raw materials and production, processing and testing of the Products is proprietary to Investor and each of Chinese Organization agree to retain same in strict confidence and not to divulge same to any party not connected with the performance of this Agreement. The Chinese Organization will divulge to persons connected with the performance of this Agreement only the proprietary information, which they must know to perform this Agreement. The Chinese Organization further agree that they will not use any such proprietary information for the benefit of any persons or companies other than the parties in the execution of this Agreement now or at any time in the futrue. Finally, each of Chinese Organization will cause personnel having access to such proprietary information to retain same in confidence by drafting and enforcement of appropriate confidentiality rules or other meansures.

Article 14 : Effect of Agreement

14.1 The obligations and rights of the parties under this Agreement shall be governed solely by the written provisions of this Agreement. Such provisions supersede completely all prior agreements, conversations, negotiations, and communications among the parties, whether written or oral, all of which shall be of no effect once this Agreement has been signed by the parties.

Article 15 : Sino Obligations

15.1 SINO: is responsible for performing those import and export and other obligations under this Agreement which the Works can not perform.

15.2 In addition to the confidentiality obligations of SINO under Section 13.1, SINO agrees to take appropriate and timely action to prevent or stop any use of the information described in Section 13.1 by any other factory or unit under its administrative jurisdiction.

Article 16 : Force Majeure

16.1 If any of the parties to the Agreement is prevented from performing any of its obligations under the Agreement by force majeure, such as war, serious fire, flood, typhoon and earthquake or such other incident as may bc mutually agreed by the parties to be a force majeure, the time for performance of such obligation shall be extended for a period equal in length to the incident of force majeure.

16.2 The party prevented from performing by force majeure shall notify the

179

other party by telex or cable as soon as possible of the occurrence of the incident of force majeure and within thirty days thereafter send by registered airmail to the other party a certificate issued by the China Council for the Promotion of International Trade or the Chamber of Commerce of the site of such force majeure.

16.3 If the effect of the incident of force majeure continues for more than _____ days, the parties shall settle the question of further performance of the Agreement through friendly negotiations as soon as possible. If no settlement can be reached within sixty days each party shall have the right to terminate the Agreement without incurring obligations thereby.

Article 17 : Arbitration

17.1 All disputes relating to the Agreement or its performance shall be settled through friendly consultation among the parties. If no settlement can be reached, the dispute shall be submitted to arbitration.

17.2 Arbitration shall take place in _____, and be conducted by the Arbitration Institute of the _____, in accordance with the Statutes of the said Institute.

17.3 Each party shall appoint an arbitrator within thirty days after receipt of the notification from the opposite party and a third person shall be appointed as Chairman of the Arbitration Committee in accordance with the Statutes of the Arbitration Institute of the _____.
For purposes of appointing an arbitrator, the Chinese Organization shall be considered one party.

17.4 The arbitration award shall be final and binding on all parties and enforceable in the courts of law of competent jurisdiction.

17.5 The arbitration fee shall be borne by the losing party except as otherwise awarded by the Arbitration Institute.

17.6 During the course of arbitration, the Agreement shall be continuously performed by the parties except for the party which is the subject of arbitration.

Article 18 : Notices

18.1 All notices under this Agreement shall be in writing which may be by letter, telex, telefax or cable. The aprties will, from time to time, inform each other of changes of addresses or personnel to be contacted with. At present, the addresses of all parties are:
(a) Investor

Telephone
Telex
Cable

(b) Works

    Telephone
    Telex
    Cable

(c) Sino

    Telephone
    Telex
    Cable

Article 19 : <u>Export Control</u>

19.1 Investor's obligations under this Agreement are conditioned upon investor's obtaining relevant approval from the Government.

Article 20 : <u>Duration of Agreement</u>

20.1 This agreement shall take effect upon signature by all the parties and all terminate ____ years thereafter. All parties agree that the signatures of Chinese Organization must be notarized by the _____ of _____, China. If not so notarized within ____ days after signature by Investor, this Agreement will not become effective. This Agreement shall terminate ____ years after the date of notarization. The parties may renew this Agreement by mutual agreement in writing ____ months prior to the expiration of this Agreement.

Article 21 : <u>Execution</u>

21.1 This Agreement is done in duplicates, each of which shall be considered an original. This Agreement is written in Chinese and _____ languages, each of which shall be equally authentic.

(Signed)	(Signed)	(Signed)
For and on behalf of	For and on behalf of	For and on behalf of
Investor	Works	Sino
(_____)	(_____)	(_____)

AGREEMENT ON THE MUTUAL PROTECTION OF INVESTMENT

The government of the People's Republic of China and the government of, desiring to maintain fair and equitable treatment of investments by investors of one contracting state in the territory of the other contracting state, have agreed as follows:

Article 1

For the purpose of this agreement:

(1) The term "investment" shall comprise every kind of asset invested by investors of one contracting state in the territory of the other contracting state in accordance with the laws and regulations of that state, and more particularly, though not exclusively.

   (a) Movable and immovable property as well as any other rights in them, such as mortgage, lien, pledge, and similar rights;

   (b) Shares or other kinds of interest in companies;

   (c) Title to money or any performance having an economic value;

   (d) Copyrights, industrial property rights, technical processes, trade-names and good-will; and

   (e) Such business-concessions under public law or under contract, including concessions regarding the prospecting for, or the extraction or winning of natural resources, as give to their holder a legal position of some duration.

(2) The term "investor" shall mean:

   In respect of the People's Republic of China, any company, other legal person or citizen of China authorized by the Chinese Government to make an investment; in respect of Sweden, any individual who is a citizen of according to law as well as any legal person with its seat in Sweden or with a predominating interest.

Article 2

(1) Each contracting state shall at all times ensure fair and equitable treatment to investments by investors of the other contracting state.

(2) Investments by investors of either contracting state in the territory of the other contracting state shall not be subjected to a treatment less favourable than that accorded to investments by investors of third states.

(3) Notwithstanding the provisions of paragraph (2) of this Article, a contracting state, which has concluded with one or more other states an agreement regarding the formation of a customs union or a free-trade area, shall be free to grant a more favourable treatment to investments

182

by investors of the state or states, which are also parties to the said agreement, or by investors of some of these states. A contracting state shall also be free to grant a more favourable treatment to investments by investors of other states, if this is stipulated under bilateral agreements concluded with such states before the date of the signature of this agreement.

Article 3

(1) Neither contracting state shall expropriate or nationalize, or take any other similar measure in regard to, an investment made in its territory by an investor of the other contracting state, except in the public interest, under due process of law and against compensation, the purpose of which shall be to place the investor in the same financial position as that in which the investor would have been if the expropriation or nationalization had not taken place. The expropriation or nationalization shall not be discriminatory and the compensation shall be paid without unreasonable delay and shall be convertible and freely transferable between the territories of the contracting states.

(2) The provisions of paragraph (1) shall also apply to the current income from an investment as well as, in the event of liquidation, to the proceeds from the liquidation.

Article 4

Each contracting state shall, subject to its laws and regulations, allow without undue delay the transfer in any convertible currency of:

(a) The net profits, dividends, royalties, technical assistance and technical service fees, interest and other current income, accruing from any investment of the other contracting state;

(b) The proceeds of the total or partial liquidation of any investment by an investor of the other contracting state;

(c) Funds in repayment of borrowings which both contracting states have recognized as investment; and

(d) The earnings of nationals of the other contracting state who are allowed to work in connection with an investment in its territory.

Article 5

If a contracting state makes a payment to an investor under a guarantee it has granted in respect of an investment in the territory of the other contracting state, that contracting state shall, without prejudice to the rights of the former contracting state under Article 6, recognize the transfer of any right or title of such investor to the former contracting state and the subrogation of the former contracting state to any such right or title. The subrogation shall concern the claim of the investor from which shall be deducted any debts which the investor may have to the other contracting state.

Article 6

(1) Disputes between the contracting states concerning the interpretation or application of this agreement shall, if possible, be settled by negotiations between the governments of the two contracting states.

(2) If the dispute cannot thus be settled, it shall, upon the request of either contracting state, be submitted to an arbitral tribunal.

(3) Such arbitral tribunal shall be established in each individual case, each contracting state appointing one member, and those two members shall then agree upon a national of a third state as their chairman to be appointed by the governments of the two contracting state. Such members shall be appointed within two months, and such chairman within three months, after either contracting state has made known to the other contracting state that it wishes the dispute to be submitted to an arbitral tribunal.

(4) If the periods specified in paragraph (3) have not been observed, either contracting state may, in the absence of any other relevant arrangement, invite the Secretary-General of the United Nations to make the necessary appointments. If the Secretary-General is a national of either contracting state or if he is otherwise prevented from discharging the said function, the Under Secretary-General of Legal Affairs shall be invited to make the necessary appointments.

(5) The arbitral tribunal shall reach its decision by a majority of votes. Such decisions shall be binding. Each contracting state shall bear the cost of its own member and of its counsel in the arbitral proceedings; the cost of the chairman and the remaining costs shall be borne in equal parts by both contracting states. The arbitral tribunal may make a different regulation concerning costs. In all other respects, the arbitral tribunal shall determine its own procedure.

Article 7

Nothing in this agreement shall prejudice any rights or benefits accruing under national or international law to interests of a national or a company of one contracting state in the territory of the other contracting state.

Article 8

This agreement shall apply to all investments made after ____ , 19 _____ .

Article 9

(1) This agreement shall enter into force immdeiately upon signature.

(2) This agreement shall remain in force for a period of fifteen years and shall continue in force thereafter unless, after the expiry of the initial period of fourteen years, either contracting state notifies in writing the other contracting state of its intention to terminate this agreement. The notice

of termination shall become effective one year after it has been received by the other contracting state.

(3) In respect of investments made prior to the date when the notice of termination of this agreement becomes effective, the provisions of Articles 1 to 8 shall remain in force for a further period of fifteen years from that date. Done in Beijing on _____ , 19 _____ , in two originals in the Chinese, and languages, all texts being equally authentic.

(SIGNED)
Minister of Foreign Affairs
People's Republic of China

(SIGNED)
Ambassador
Embassy of _____

OFFSHORE JOINT VENTURE CONTRACT

MEMORANDUM OF AGREEMENT MADE THIS _____
Day of _____ 19 _____ between _____ of
(hereinafter referred to as "the Foreign Company", which expression shall, where the context admits, include the Foreign Company's associated companies, subsidaries, branch offices or nominees as the case may be) of the one part and _____ of _____
(hereinafter referred to as "the Chinese Organisation", which expression shall, where the context admits, include the Chinese Organisation's associated companies, subsidaries, branch offices or nominees as the case may be) of the other part.

Whereby it is mutually agreed as follows:

Objectives

1.   The Foreign Company and the Chinese Organisation agree to operate a joint venture to manufacture _____ .
The venture is to be named as _____
(hereinafter referred to as "The Company"). The Company shall be registered in the country. A factory wholly owned by The Company will produce at the first stage of operation and will expand its production capacity — insert stages of development —
             (author)

2.   The Company shall be governed by the laws of _____ .
By virture of — insert the specific provisions of the laws which protect the interest of foreign investors in that particular country — the Chinese Organisation's investment in The Company, its share of profits and its other rights and interests will be protected and be allowed to be remitted out of — that particular country —.
             (author)

Form of Co-operation

3.   The Company's total circulating funds set at _____ .
The Foreign Company is to invest _____ , or _____ % of the total, and the Chinese Organisation is to put in _____ , or _____ % of the total. The Foreign Company provides land, factory building _____ gratis for the joint venture.
The Chinese Organisation provides The Company gratis with technology and equipment. The Company shall be responsible for _____ raising

186

funds and for acquiring — insert equipment and other matters necessary for the venture —.   (author)

4. The period for the joint operation of the Company by the two parties is set at _____ years, beginning from the day when the company is formally put into operation. During this contracted period both parties shall be responsible for the management of the company and for its profits and losses. The Company's annual profits of losses should be shared by the two parties according to their respective equity shares as stipulated in the contract. Upon termination of the contract, The Company's fixed assets including land, factory buildings and equipment (with the exception of the circulating funds, the profits at the time and the newly acquired fixed assets) shall be turned over to the Foreign Company.

5. The company shall pay taxes in accordance with the tax laws of the government of the   —name of the country —
    (author)
    and, at the same time, enjoy the rights to tax exemptions and conveniences granted to investment projects as stipulated in —insert the specific provisions of the laws which protect the interest of foreign investors in that particular country — (author).

6. During the period of joint operation, the two parties shall form a board of directors which is to be The Company's highest organ of power. The scope of its powers and functions is stipulated in Articles 12 and 13 of this contract.

Use of Funds

7. The right to use all the funds invested by the two parties under Article 2 belongs to the board of directors after the contract comes into force.

8. An annual budget covering the use of funds shall be drafted by The Company's manager and deputy managers and submitted to the board of directors for examination and approval before it can be carried out.

9. During the period of joint operation, neither party shall have the right to transfer or appropriate any of The Company's property, including funds, assets, products, semi-finished products, and raw and auxiliary materials, nor transfer its funds and assets to a third party.

Responsibilities of the Two Contracting Parties.

10. The Foreign Company is responsible for:
    A. Providing the enterprise with land, factory buildings and other auxiliary facilities;
    B. Registering the enterprise with the_____ —name of the country —
        (author)
    C. Obtaining entry visas and residence and work permits for the Chinese personnel involved in the management, production and technical

187

work in the company and its factory;

D. Providing accomodation (including the necessary living and sanitation facilities) for the personnel of Party B;

E. Applying to the _____ —name of the Country— _____ for reductions
(author)

or exemptions and preferential treatment with regard to business and income taxes and customs duties on imports of raw materials and equipment and exports of products;

F. Employing and dismissing local workers in the company and its factory.

11. The Chinese Organisation is responsible for:

A. Providing technology needed by the enterprise;

B. Selecting and sending technical experts and giving technical guidance on the instalation of the equipment;

C. Selecting and sending the personnel of_____ —insert numbers— _____
(author)

including technical experts and executives as agreed upon by the two parties, who should arrive in groups at the worksite within ____ year in accordance with the agreed schedule.

The Board of Directors

12. The two parties agree that a board of directors shall be formed on the day when the contract comes into force. The board is to be made up of members, from Party A and from Party B. Its chairman shall come from Party A and the vice-chairman from Party B.

13. The board of directors is the highest organ of power in The Company. Important issues shall be decided by the two parties through friendly consultations on the principle of equality and mutual benefit. The board is responsible for discussing and deciding the company's development programme and scale of production and for examining and approving its production and business plans, budgets and final acounts, and employment and wage plans. It is also responsible for deciding The Company's size, organization and staff, appointing and removing the manager and deputy managers of The Company and the director and deputy directors of the factory as recommended by the two parties, as well as handling workers' welfare, reward and punishment and other important matters concerning the joint company.

Managers and Factory Directors

14. One manager and two deputy managers (concurrently director and deputy directors of the factory) shall be appointed under the board of directors to handle the company's day-to-day work. The manager shall come from The Chinese Organisation, and one deputy manager each from The Foreign Company and The Chinese Organisation.

15. Departments in charge of production and technology, financial affairs and supply and marketing shall be set up under the manager and deputy managers. Personnel from The Chinese Organisation shall take charge of the departments of production and technology and of financial affairs. Personnel from the Foreign Company shall take charge of the supply and marketing department. Drawing money from or making payments through banks must be countersigned by the two parties.

16. Personnel for the company's departments shall be recommended by the two parties respectively and be examined and appointed by the board of directors.

Management

17. The Company's accounting system shall be decided by the two parties through consultation. Profits or losses shall be computed on the basis of the Gregorian calendar year. A balance sheet shall be worked out within half a month following the end of the calendar year and cleared as soon as it is approved by the board of directors.

18. The Chinese Organisation shall apply to the X Country for preferential treatment in taxation on the products of the company, and be responsible for marketing them.

19. The Company shall sign long-term contracts with relevant foreign firms for the supply of raw and subsidiary materials the company needs for guaranteeing normal production in its factory.

20. The Company is scheduled to raise within year its production capacity to of and

21. The Company shall deduct % from the total value of production year for the renewal and overhaul of equipment. The balance after the expenses are defrayed shall be kept as profit to be distributed to the two parties according to the ratio of their investment upon the expiry of the term of joint operation.

22. To avoid losses, The Company shall reduce the number of non-productive personnel at the beginning of its inception. The two parties have agreed through consultation that the members of the board of directors shall draw no salaries, except for those holding concurrent posts who will receive salaries for the posts they hold concurrently.

23. The two parties have agreed that the technical experts from The Foreign Company who work in The Company's factory shall each receive a monthly pay of DOLLARS in the first three months after the founding of the company. If the enterprise runs at a profit, the said pay shall be DOLLARS in accordance with the minutes of the talks held in China between the two parties. The salaries for managerial personnel and wages of unskilled workers shall be decided by the board of directors. Salaries and wages shall be raised in line with the rise of the price index.

The personnel of the Foreign Company are entitled to a _____ month vacation (not including the time for the round trip) every two years for visiting their families at home and to full pay during the vacation. The air fares for the personnel of the Foreign Company, who are approved by the board of directors to work in the company or its factory, when travelling to the —name of the country—(author), and their round trip air fares when returning homes for vacation shall be defrayed out of The Company's administrative expenses. In accordance with the relevant provisions of the labour law of the —name of the country— (author), The Company shall pay attention to the medical and health care, labour protection and other welfare benefits for its staff and workers. The costs involved shall be covered by the company's administrative expenses.

24. All or part of the share of profits, wages and salaries for personnel and other legitimate proceeds of Party B may be remitted from the —name of the country— (author), through the Central Bank, to the People Manufacturing Company; China.

25. During its operation, the company shall insure its property with the Insurance Company of the —name of the country— (author). The insurance premium shall be paid from the total business income of the enterprise.

26. The personnel of Party B shall have their lives insured in the People's Insurance Company of China. The insurance premium shall also be paid from the company's total business income.

Enforcement of the Contract and Miscellaneous

27. All disputes between the Foreign Company and the Chinese Organisation in implementing this contract shall be settled through friendly consultations.

28. This contract has been submitted to the appropriate authorities of the government of the People's Republic of China and the government of the —name of country (author) for approval. The contract shall come into force on the date of its approval.

29. The term of joint operation stipulated in the contract is set at years, counting from the day when The Company begins to turn out its first batch of products. This contract shall cease to be effective after the accounts are cleared and all other matters stipulated in the contract are settled following the expiration of the term of joint operation.

30. Any revision, alteration and addition made to this contract shall be done with agreement reached by the two parties through consultation and a written document shall be signed by authorized representatives of the two parties as an inalienable part of this contract.

31. If one contracting party intends to continue the joint operation and has so proposed months prior to the expiration of the term of joint operation as

190

stipulated in this contract, the two parties, after reaching agreement through consultation, may go through the procedures related to the extension of the contract and make relevant revisions of the contract. If neither party proposes to extend the contract upon its expiry, the contract shall be regarded as terminated.

32. In case of calamities, war, turmoil and other force majeure events, which make it impossible for The Company to continue its business, the contract may be terminated ahead of schedule through consultation between the two parties.

    Except for the above-mentioned cases, the party which proposes unilaterally to terminate the contract shall compensate for the economic losses thus inflicted on the other party.

33. Upon the expiration of the contract, the two parties shall recover their own funds and receive their share of the profits according to their respect equity shares. The funds in kind recovered by the Chinese Organisation may be transferred or sold and all its monetary funds and proceeds may be remitted back to China.

(signed)
The Foreign Company

(singed)
The Chinese Organisation

Author's notes:

According to Mr. Guo Hanbin of the Department of Foreign Economic Co-operation of the Ministry of Foreign Economic Relations and Trade,

"China began to set up joint ventures abroad in 1979. By the end of 1983, some 100 such ventures had been established in more than 20 countries, and Hongkong and Macao. They included the United States, Japan, Federal Germany, France, Britain, Canada, Belgium, the Netherlands, Italy, Switzerland and Australia, as well as in some third world countries. The ventures covers industrial production, processing and assembling, building construction, transportation, designing, banking and insurance, restaurant services, product sales, labor service cooperation and technical consultancy services."

PART II:
STANDARD CONTRACTS PREPARED BY THE PRC GOVERNMENT

MACHINERY—INDIVIDUAL PURCHASE CONTRACT

A Chinese Machinery Import & Export Organization

Its address
Cables

Reference No.
Date:

Dear Sirs,
Re: _____

With reference to our cable number dated   19   and your cable number   dated 19   . we are sending you herewith two originals of Contract reference number for name of trade deal. Please sign and return us one original copy thereof after check-up.

This is the first business of our both parties and would be helpful for development in future transaction through this business.

Signed and sealed by the sender.

Encl: As above.

CONTRACT

No.
Peking,   19

THE BUYERS:
——Name of the Chinese
        Organization——
        (author)
CABLE ADDRESS:

THE SELLERS:

This Contract is made by and between the Buyers and the Sellers; whereby the Buyers agree to buy and the Sellers agree to sell the under-mentioned commodity according to the terms and conditions stipulated below:-

1. Commodity, Specifications, Quantity and Unit Price:

Price:	Each	Total
—Name of the items—		
(author)		
packing charges ....$		

2. Total Value: U.S.Dollars   C & F, _____ China
    including sea worthy packing charges.

3. Country of Origin and Manufacturer:
                                Name of the Foreign Country
                                (author)

MACHINERY—INDIVIDUAL PURCHASE CONTRACT

4. Packing: To be packed in new strong wooden cases suitable for long distance ocean transportation and well protected against dampness, moisture, shock, rust and rough handling. The Sellers shall be liable for any damage of the commodity and expenses incurred therefrom on account of improper packing and for any rust damage attributable to inadequate or improper protective measures taken by the Sellers in regard to the packing.

5. Shipping Mark: On the surface of each package, the package number, measurement, gross weight, net weight and the wordings "DO NOT

STACK UP SIDE DOWN", "HANDLE WITH CARE", "KEEP AWAY FROM MOISTURE", the lifting position and the following shipping mark shall be stencilled legibly with fadeless paint:

90ABC-1997HK

KOWLOON, CHINA

6. Time of Shipment: August, 19   in one consignment.

7. Port of Shipment: U.S. Sea Port.

8. Port of Destination: China.

9. Insurance: To be covered by the Buyers after shipment.

10. Payment: The Buyers, upon receipt from the Sellers of the delivery advice specified in Article 13 hereof, shall,   days prior to the date of delivery, open an irrevocable Letter of Credit with the Bank of China, Peking, through a British Bank, in favour of the Sellers, for an amount equivalent to the total value of the shippment. The Credit shall be payable against the presentation of the draft drawn on the opening bank and the shipping documents specified in Article 11 hereof. The Letter of Credit shall be valid until the   th day after the shipment is effected.

11. Documents: The Sellers shall present to the paying bank the following documents for negotiation:

    1. One full set of Clean "On Board" ocean Bills of Lading marked "Freight Prepaid" and made out to order, blank endorsed, and notifying the China National Foreign Trade Transportation Corporation at the port of destination.
    2. Five copies of Invoice, indicating contract number and shipping mark.
    3. Two copies of Packing List with indication of shipping weight, number and date of corresponding invoice.
    4. Two copies of Certificate of Quality and Quantity issued by the Manufacturers as specified in Item 1 of Article 16 hereof.
    5. Certified copy of cable to the Buyers, advising shipment immediately after the shipment has been made.

    The Sellers shall within 10 days after the shipment is effected, send by airmail one copy each of the above-mentioned documents with the exception of Item 5; one set to the Buyers and the other set to the China National Foreign Trade Transportation Corporation at the port of destination.

12. Terms of Shipment: The Sellers shall ship the goods within the shipment time from the port of shipment to the port of destination. Trans-shipment is not allowed. The carrying vessel shall not call en route at any port in the vicinity of Taiwan. If the carrying vessel is not a regular liner scheduled for transporting freight to China, the Sellers shall, not less than 30 days before the anticipated date of shipment, inform the Buyers by cable of the name of vessel, names of the ship's owner and the shiping company for the Buyer's confirmation before effecting shipment.

13. Delivery Advice: The Sellers shall, immediately upon completion of the loading of the goods, advise by cable the Buyers of the Contract number, commodity, quantity, invoiced value, gross weight, name of vessel, number of Bill of Lading and date of sailing. In case the Buyers fail to arrange insurance in time due to the Sellers not having cabled in time, all losses shall be borne by the Sellers.

14. Technical Documents: One (1) copy each of the operation, service and repair instruction books shall be packed and despatched together with each Machine.

15. Guarantee of Quality: The Sellers shall guarantee that the commodity contracted herein is made of the best materials, with first class workmanship, brand new, unused and complies in all respects with the quality, specifications and performance as stipulated in this Contract. The Sellers shall guarantee that the goods, when correctly mounted and properly operated and maintained, shall give satisfactory performance for a period of 18 months counting from the date on which the commodity arrives at the port of destination.

16. Inspection:

    1. The Manufacturer shall before making delivery, make a precise and comprehensive inspection of the goods as regards quality, specifications, performance, and quantity, and issue a Quality and Quantity certificate certifying that the goods are in conformity with the stipulations of this Contract. The said certificate shall form an integral part of the documents to be presented to the paying bank for negotiation of payment but shall not be considered as final in respect of quality, specifications, performance and quantity. Particulars and results of the test carried out by the manufacturer must be shown in a statement which has to be attached to the Quality and Quantity Certificate.

    2. After arrival of the goods at the port of destination the Buyers shall apply to the China Commodity Inspection Bureau (hereinafter called the Bureau) for a preliminary inspection in respect of the quality, specifications and quantity of the goods and a Survey Report shall be issued therefore. If any discrepancies are found by the Bureau regarding specifications or the quantity or both, except when the responsibilities lie with insurance company, the Buyers shall within sixty (60) days after arrival of the goods at the port of destination, have the right to reject the goods or to claim against the Sellers.

    3. Should the quality and specifications of the goods be found not in conformity with the Contract, or should the goods prove defective within the guarantee period stipulated in Article 15 for any reason, including latent defect or the use of unsuitable materials, the Buyers shall arrange for a survey to be carried out by the Bureau, and have the right to claim against the Sellers on the strength of the Survey Report.

17. Claims:
    1. In case that the Sellers are liable for the discrepancies and a claim is made by the Buyers within the time-limit of inspection and guarantee period as stipulated in Article 15 and 16 hereof, the Sellers shall settle the claim upon the agreement of the Buyers in one or the combination of the following ways:
        a/ Agree to the rejection of the goods and refund to the Buyers the value of the goods so rejected in the same currency as contracted herein, and to bear all direct losses and expenses in connection therewith including interest accrued, banking charges, freight, insurance premium, inspection charges, storage, stevedore charges and all other necessary expenses required for the custody and protection of the rejected goods.
        b/ Devalue the goods according to the degree of inferiority, extent of damage and amount of losses suffered by the Buyers.
        c/ Replace new parts which conform to the specifications, quality, and performance as stipulated in this Contract, and bear all the expenses and direct losses sustained by the Buyers. The Sellers shall, at the same time, guarantee the quality of replaced parts for a further period according to Article 15 hereof.
    2. The claims mentioned above shall be regarded as being accepted if the Sellers fail to reply within thirty (30) days after the Sellers receive the Buyers' claim.

18. Force Majeure: The Sellers shall not be held responsible for the delay in shipment or non-delivery of the goods due to Force Majeure, which might occur during the process of manufacturing or in the course of loading or transit. The Sellers shall advise the Buyers immediately of the occurrence mentioned above and within fourteen (14) days thereafter, the Sellers shall send by airmail to the Buyers for their acceptance a certificate of the accident issued by the competent organisation where the accident occurs as evidence thereof. Under such circumstances the Sellers, however, are still under the obligation to take all necessary measures to hasten the delivery of the goods. In case the accident lasts for more than ten (10) weeks the Buyers shall have the right to cancel the Contract.

19. Late Delivery: Should the Sellers fail to make delivery on time as stipulated in the Contract, with exception of Force Majeure causes specified in Article 18 of this Contract, the Buyers shall agree to postpone the delivery on condition that the Sellers agree to pay a penalty which shall be deducted by the paying bank from the payment under negotiation. The penalty, however, shall not exceed 5% of the total value of the goods involved in the late delivery. The rate of penalty is charged at 0.5% for every seven (7) days, odd days less than seven (7) days shall be counted as seven (7) days. In case the Sellers fail to make delivery ten (10) weeks later than the time of shipment stipulated in this Contract, the Buyers shall

have the right to cancel the contract and the Sellers, in spite of the cancellation, shall still pay the aforesaid penalty to the Buyers without delay.

20. Arbitration: All disputes in connection with this Contract or the execution thereof shall be settled friendly through negotiations. In case no settlement can be reached, the case may then be submitted for arbitration to the Arbitration Committee of the China Council for the Promotion of International Trade in accordance with the Provisional Rules of Procedures promulgated by the said Arbitration Committee. The Arbitration shall take place in Peking and the decision of the Arbitration Committee shall be final and binding upon both parties; neither party shall seek recourse to a law court or other authorities to appeal for revision of the decision. Arbitration fee shall be borne by the losing party.

IN WITNESS THEREOF, this Contract is signed by both parties on the date as first above mentioned in two original copies; each party hold one copy.

THE BUYERS: THE SELLERS:

_____   _____

Another form of purchase contract, used as an alternative to the one printed above:

CONTRACT

No._____

Beijing Date:_____

The Buyers: CHINA NATIONAL CORPORATION, BEIJING BRANCH, People's Republic of China._____

Cable Address:_____   TELEX:_____

The Sellers:_____

Cable Address: TELEX:

1. This contract is made by and between the Buyers and the Sellers; whereby the Buyers agree to buy and the Sellers agree to sell the undermentioned commodity according to the terms and conditions stipulated below:

Item No.	Commodity Sepcifications	Unit	Quan.	Unit Price	Total Amount
Total Value:					

2. COUNTRY OF ORIGIN AND MANUFACTURERS:
3. PACKING: To be packed in strong wooden case(s) or in carton(s), suitable for long distance ocean/parcel post/air freight transportation and to change of climate, well protected against moisture and shocks.
    The Sellers shall be liable for any damage of the commodity and expenses incurred on account of improper packing and for any rust attributable to inadequate or improper protective measures taken by the Sellers in regard to the packing.

4. SHIPPING MARK: The Sellers shall mark on each package with fadeless paint the package number, gross weight, net weight, measurement and the wordings: "KEEP AWAY FROM MOISTURE" "HANDLE WITH CARE", "THIS SIDE UP" etc. and the shipping mark:

5. TIME OF SHIPMENT:

6. PORT OF SHIPMENT:

7. PORT OF DESTINATION: CHINA

8. INSURANCE: To be covered by the Buyers after shipment.

9. PAYMENT: Under (A) (B) (C) below:

    (1) Under Letter of Credit: The Buyers, upon receipt from the Sellers of the delivery advice specified in Clause 11 (1)a hereof, shall 15 - 20 days prior to the date of delivery, open an irrevocable letter of credit with Bank of China, Beijing, in favour of the Sellers, for the total value of shipment. The credit shall be available against Sellers' draft(s) drawn at sight on the opening bank for 100% invoice value accompanied by the shipping documents specified in Clause 10 hereof. Payment shall be effected (by the opening bank, for telegraphic transfer/airmail transfer) against presentation to them of the aforesaid draft(s) and documents. The Letter of Credit shall be valid until the 15th day after the shipment is effected.

    (2) On Collection: After shipment, the Sellers may draw on the Buyers at sight and send the draft(s) together with the shipping documents specified in Clause 10 hereof, to the Buyers through the Sellers' bankers and Bank of China, Beijing for collection.

    (3) By direct Remittance: Payment shall be effected by the Buyers, by telegraphic transfer/airmail transfer, within seven days after receipt from the Sellers of shipping documents specified in Clause 10 hereof.

10. DOCUMENTS:

    (1) In case of seafreight:
    Full set of clean on board ocean bills of lading marked "Freight to Collect"/"Freight Prepaid" made out to order blank endorsed notifying China National Foreign Trade Transportation Corporation at the port of destination.
    In case of airfreight:
    One copy of airway bill marked "Freight to Collect"/"Freight Prepaid" and consigned to the Buyers.
    In case of air parcel post:
    One copy of air parcel post receipt addressed to the Buyers.

    (2) Invoice in 5 copies indicating contract number and shipping mark (in case of more than one shipping mark, the invoice shall be issued separately), made out in details as per the relative contract.

    (3) Packing list in 2 copies issued by the Manufacturers.

(4) Certificate of Quality and Quantity issued by the Manufacturers.

(5) Copy of cable/letter to the Buyers advising particulars of shipment immediately after shipment is made.

In addition, the Sellers shall, within 10 days after shipment, send by airmail two extra sets of the aforesaid documents (except item 5) one set directly to the Buyers and one set directly to the China National Foreign Trade Transportation Corporation at the port of destination.

11. SHIPMENT:

(1) In case of FOB Terms:

a. The Sellers shall, 40 days before the date of shipment stipulated in the Contract, advise the Buyers by cable/letter of the Contract No., commodity, quantity, value, number of package, gross weight, measurement and date of readiness at the port of shipment for the buyers to book shipping space.

b. Booking of shipping space shall be attended to by the Buyers' Shipping Agents Messrs. China National Chartering Corporation, Beijing, China. (Cable address:).

c. China National Chartering Corporation, Beijing, China, or it's Port Agents, (or Lines' Agents) shall send to the Sellers 10 days before the estimate date of arrival of the vessel at the port of shipment, a preliminary notice indicating the name of vessel, estimated date of loading, Contract No. for the Sellers to arrange shipment. The Sellers are requested to get in close contact with the shipping agents. When it becomes necessary to change the carrying vessel or in the event of her arrival having to be advanced or delayed the Buyers or the Shipping Agent shall advise the Sellers in time.

Should the vessel fail to arrive at the port of loading within 30 days after the arrival date advised by the Buyers, the Buyers shall bear the storage and insurance expenses incurred from the 31st day.

d. The Sellers shall be liable for any dead freight or demurrage, should it happen that they have failed to have the commodity ready for loading after the carrying vessel has arrived at the port of shipment on time.

e. The Sellers shall bear all expenses, risks of the commodity before it passes over the vessel's rail and been released from the tackle, all expenses of the commodity shall be for the Buyers' account.

(2) In case of C & F Terms:

a. The Sellers shall ship the goods within the shipment time from the port of shipment to the port of destination. Transhipment is not allowed. The contracted goods shall not be carried by a vessel flying the flag of the country which the Buyers can not accept.

  b. In case the goods are to be despatched by parcel post/air-freight, the Sellers shall, 30 days before the time of delivery, as stipulated in Clause 5, inform the Buyers by cable/letter of the estimated date of delivery, Contract No., commodity, invoiced value, etc. The Sellers shall, immediately after despatch of the goods, advise the Buyers by cable/letter of the Contract No., commodity, invoiced value and date of despatch for the Buyers to arrange insurance in time.

12. SHIPING ADVICE:

The Sellers shall, immediately upon the completion of the loading of the goods, advise by cable/letter the Buyers of the Contract No., commodity, quantity, invoiced value, gross weight, name of vesel and date of sailing etc. In case the Buyers fail to arrange insurance in time due to the Sellers not having cabled in time, all losses shall be borne by the Sellers.

13. TECHNICAL DOCUMENTS:

(1) One complete set of the following technical documents written in English, shall be packed and despatched together with each consignment.

  a) Wiring instructions, diagrams of electrical connections and/or pneumatic hydraulic connections.
  b) Manufacturing drawings of easily worn parts and instructions.
  c) Spare parts catalogues.
  d) Erection, operation, service and repair instruction books.

(2) The Sellers shall in addition send to the Buyers by airmail the respective technical documents as stipulated in paragraphs a), b), c) and d) of Item (1) of this Clasue within_____months, after the signing of this Contract.

14. GUARANTEE OF QUALITY:

The Sellers guarantee that the commodity hereof is made of the best materials with fist class workmanship, brand new and unused, and complies in all respects with the quality and specification stipulated in this Contract. The guarantee period shall be 12 months counting from the date on which the commodity arrives at the port of destination.

15. CLAIMS:

Within 90 days after the arrival of the goods at destination, should the quality, specification, or quantity be found not in conformity with the stipulations of the Contract except those claims for which the insurance company or the owners of the vessel are liable, the Buyers shall, on the strength of the Inspection Certificate issued by the China Commodity Inspection Bureau, have the right to claim for replacement with new goods, or for compensation, and all the expenses (such as inspection chargos, froight for roturning tho goods and for sonding tho roplacomont, insurance premium, storage and loading and unloading charges etc.) shall be borne by the Sellers. As regards quality, the Sellers shall guarantee that if, within 12 months from the date of arrival of the goods at destination, damages occur in the course of operation by reason of inferior quality, bad workmanship or the use of inferior materials, the Buyers shall immediately notify the Sellers in writing and put forward a claim supported by Inspection Certificate issued by the China Commodity Inspection Bureau. The Certificate so issued shall be accepted as the base of a claim. The Sellers, in accordance with the Buyers' claim shall be responsible for the immediate elimination of the defect(s), complete or partial replacement of the commodity or shall devaluate commodity according to the state of defect(s). Where necessary, the Buyers shall be at liberty to eliminate the defect(s) themselves at the Sellers' expenses. If the Sellers fail to answer the Buyers within one month after receipt of the aforesaid claim, the claim shall be reckoned as having been accepted by the Sellers.

16. FORCE MAJEURE:
The Sellers shall not be held responsible for the delay in shipment or non-delivery of the goods due to Force Majeure, which might occur during the process of manufacturing or in the course of loading or transit. The Sellers shall advise the Buyers immediately of the occurrence mentioned above and within fourteen days thereafter, the Sellers shall send by airmail to the Buyers for their aceptance a certificate of the accident issued by the Competent Government Authorities where the accident occurs as evidence thereof.
Under such circumstances the Sellers, however, are still under the obligation to take all necessary measures to hasten the delivery of the goods. In case the accident lasts for more than 10 weeks, the Buyers shall have the right to cancel the Contract.

17. LATE DELIVERY AND PENALTY:
Should the Sellers fail to make delivery on time as stipulated in the Contract, with exception of Force Majeure causes specified in Clause 16 of this Contract, the Buyers shall agree to postpone the delivery on condition that the Sellers agree to pay a penalty which shall be deducted by the paying bank from the payment under negotiation. The penalty, however, shall not exceed 5% of the total value of the goods involved in the late delivery. The rate of penalty is charged at 0.5% for every seven days, odd days less than seven days should be counted as seven days. In case the Sellers fail to make delivery ten weeks later than the time of shipment stipulated in the Contract, the Buyers shall have the right to cancel the contract and the Sellers, in spite of the cancellation, shall still pay the aforesaid penalty to the Buyers without delay.

18. ARBITRATION:
All disputes in connection with this contract or the execution thereof shall be settled friendly through negotiations. In case no settlement can be

reached, the case may than be submitted for arbitration to the Arbitration Committee of the China Council for the Promotion of International Trade in accordance with the Provisional Rules of Procedures promulgated by the said Arbitration Committee. The Arbitration shall take place in Beijing and the decision of the Arbitration Committee shall be final and binding upon both parties; neither party shall seek recourse to a law court of other authorities to appeal for revision of the decision. Arbitration fee shall be borne by the losing party. Or the Arbitration may be settled in the third country mutually agreed upon by both parties.

IN WITNESS THEREOF, this Contract is signed by both parties in two original copies; each party holds one copy.

THE BUYERS: THE SELLERS:
CHINA CORPORATION BRANCH

_____   _____

MACHINERY—PURCHASE CONTRACT

CONTRACT

No. _____

Peking. Date: _____

The Buyers: _____

— Name of the Chinese Organization —
(author)
(Cable Address:)

The Sellers: _____

This Contract is made by and between the Buyers and the Sellers; whereby the Buyers agree to' buy and the Sellers agree to sell the under-mentioned commodity according to the terms and conditions stipulated below:

1. COMMODITY, SPECIFICATIONS, QUANTITY AND UNIT PRICE:

2. TOTAL VALUE:

3. COUNTRY OF ORIGIN AND MANUFACTURERS:

4. PACKING:
   To be packed in new strong wooden case(s) suitable for long distance ocean transportation and well protected against dampness, moisture, shock, rust and rough handling. The Sellers shall be liable for any damage to the commodity and expenses incurred thereof on account of improper packing and for any rust damage attributable to inadequate or improper protective measures taken by the Sellers in regard to the packing.

5. SHIPPING MARK:
   On the surface of each package, the package number, measurements, gross weight, net weight, the lifting positions, such cautions as "DO NOT STACK UP SIDE DOWN". "HANDLE WITH CARE", "KEEP AWAY FROM MOISTURE" and the following shipping marks shall be stencilled legibly in fadeless paint:

6. TIME OF SHIPMENT:

7. PORT OF SHIPMENT

8. PORT OF DESTINATION

9. INSURANCE: To be covered by the Buyers after shipment.

10. PAYMENT: for / by
    (1) In case of payment by L / C: The Buyers, upon receipt from the Sellers of the delivery advice specified in clause 12 (1) hereof, shall, 15 20 days prior to the date of delivery, open an irrevocable Letter of Credit with the Bank of China, Peking, in favour of the Sellers, for an amount equivalent to the total value of the shipment. The Credit shall be payable against the presentation of the draft drawn on the opening bank together with the shipping documents specified in clause 11 hereof. The Letter of Credit shall be valad until the 15th day after the shipment.
    (2) In case of payment by Collefction: After delivery is made, the Sellers shall send through the Sellers's bank the draft drawn on the buyers together with the shipping documents specified in clause 11 hereof, to the Buyers through the Buyers' bank, the Bank of China, Peking, for collection.
    (3) In case of payment by M / T or T / T: Payment to be effected by the buyers not later than seven days after receipt of the shipping documents specified under clause 11 hereof.
11. DOCUMENTS:
    (1) The Sellers shall present the following documents to the paying bank for negotiation (or collection):
        a) One full set of Clean On Board Ocean Bills of Lading marked "FREIGHT TO COLLECT" and made out to order, blank endorsed, and notifying the China National Foreign Trade Transportation Corporation at the port of destination.
        b) Five copies of Invoice, indicating contract number and shipping mark (in case of more than one shipping mark, the invoice shall be issued separately).
        c) Two copies of Packing List with Indication of shipping weight, number and date of corresponding invoice.
        d) Two copies of Certificate of Quality and Quantity issued by the manufacturers as specified in Item (1) of Clause 16 hereof.
        e) Certified copy of cable to the Buyers advising shipment immediately after the shipment has been made, as specified in clause 13 hereof.
    (2) The Sellers shall within 10 days after the shipment is effected, send by airmail another two sets of one copy each of the above-mentioned documents with the exception of Item (e) of this Clause; one set to the Buyers and the other set to the China National Foreign Trade Transportation Corporation at the port of destination.
12. TERMS OF SHIPMENT:
    (1) The Sellers shall, _____ days before the date of shipment stipulated in clause 6 hereof, advise the Buyers by Cable / letter of the Contract number, commodity, quantity, value, number of packages, gross

weight and measurement and date of readiness at the port of shipment in order for the Buyers to book shipping space. Should any package reach or exceed 20 tons in weight, 10 meters in length, 3.4 meters in width or 3 meters in height, the Sellers shall provide the Buyers with 5 copies of drawing delineating the shape of the external packing with indication of the detailed measurement and weight, 50 days before dispatch of the goods in order to enable the Buyers to arrange transportation.

(2) Booking of shipping space shall be attended to by the Buyers' Shipping Agents Messrs. China National Chartering Corporation, Peking, China. (Cable address: Zhongzu Peking), with whom the Buyers are requested to keep in close contact in the matter of shipment.

(3) China National Chartering Corporation, Peking, China, or their Port Agents, shall send the Sellers, 10 days before the estimated date of arrival of the vessel at the port of shipment, a preliminary notice indicating the name of vessel, estimated date of loading, contract number in order for the Sellers to arrange shipment. When it becomes necessary to change the carrying vessel or in the event of her arrival having to be advanced or delayed, the Buyers or the Shipping Agents shall advise the Sellers in time. Should the vessel fail to arrive at the port of loading within 30 days after the arrival date advised by the Buyers, the Buyers shall bear the storage and insurance expenses incurred from the 31st day.

(4) The Sellers shall be liable for any dead freight or demurrage, should it happen that they have failed to have the commodity ready for loading after the carrying vessel has arrived at the port of shipment on time.

(5) The Sellers shall bear all expenses and risks (involved in the handling) of the commodity before it passes over the vesel's rail and is released from the tackle, whereas after it has passed over the vessel's rail and has been released from the tackle, all expenses (involved in the handling) of the commodity shall be for the Buyer's account.

13. SHIPPING ADVICE:

The Sellers, immediately upon the completion of the loading of the commodity, shall notify by cable the Buyers of the contract number, name of commodity, quantity, gross weight, invoiced value, name of carrying vessel and date of sailing. If any package of which the weight is above 9 metric tons, width over 3400 m.m. or height on both sides over 2350 m.m., the Sellers shall advise the Buyers of the weight and measurements of each such package. In case the Buyers fail to arrange insurance in due time owing to the Sellers not having thus cabled in time, all losses shall be borne by the Sellers.

14. TECHNICAL DOCUMENTS:

(1) One complete set of the following technical documents written in English, shall be packed and despatched together with each

consignment.

a) Foundation drawings.

b) Wiring instructions, diagrams of electrical connections and / or pneumatic hydraulic connections.

c) Manufacturing drawings of easily worn parts and instructions.

d) Spare parts catalogues.

e) Certificate of quality as stipulated in item 1 of Clause 16 hereof.

f) Erection, operation, service and repair instruction books.

(2) The Sellers shall in addition send to the Buyers by airmail the respective technical documents as stipulated in paragraphs a), b), c), d) and f) of Item (1) of this Clasue within _____ months, after the signing of this Contract.

15. GUARANTEE OF QUALITY:

The Sellers shall guarantee that the commodity is made of the best materials, with first class workmanship, brand new, unused and complies in all respects with the quality, specifications and performance as stipulated in this Contract. The Sellers shall also guarantee that the goods, when correctly mounted and properly operated and maintained, will give satisfactory performance for a period of 18 months counting from the date date on which the commodity arrives at the port of destination.

16. INSPECTION AND CLAIMS:

(1) The manufacturers shall before making delivery, make a precise and comprehensive inspection of the goods as regards the quality, specifications, performance, and quantity / weight, and issue certificates certifying that the goods are in conformity with the stipulations of this Contract. The certificate shall form an integral part of the documents to be presented to the paying bank for negotiation (or collection) of payment but shall not be considered as final in respect of quality, specifications, performance and quantity / weight. Particulars and results of the test carried out by the manufacturers must be shown in a statement to be attached to the said Quality Certificates.

(2) After arrival of the goods at the port of destination the Buyers shall apply to the China Commodity Inspection Bureau (hereinafter called the Bureau) for a preliminary inspection in respect of the quality, specifications and quantity / weight of the goods and a Survey Report shall be issued therefor by the Bureau. If any discrepancies are found by the Bureau regarding the specifications or the quantity or both, except when the responsibilities lie with the insurance company or shipping company, the Buyers shall within _____ days after arrival of the goods at the port of destinations, have the right to reject the or to claim against the Sellers.

(3) Should the quality and specifications of the goods be not in conformity with the contract, or should the goods prove defective within the guarantee period stipulated in Clause 15 hereof for any

reason, including latent defect or the use of unsuitable materials, the Buyers shall arrange for a survey to be carried out by the Bureau, and have the right to claim against the Sellers on the strength of the Survey Report issued therefor by the Bureau.

(4)   The claims mentioned above shall be regarded as being accepted if the Sellers fail to reply within 30 days after receipt of the Buyers' claim.

17. SETTLEMENT OF CLAIMS:

In case that the Sellers are liable for the discrepancies and a claim is made by the Buyers within the time-limit of inspection and quality guarantee period as stipulated in Clause 15 and 16 of this Contract, the Sellers shall settle the claim upon the agreement of the Buyers in one or the combination of the following ways:

(1)   Agree to the rejection of the goods and refund to the Buyers the value of the goods so rejected in the same currency as contracted herein, and to bear all direct losses and expenses in connection therewith including interest accrued, banking charges, freight, insurance premium, inspection charges, storage, stevedore charges and all other necessary expenses required for the custody and protection of the rejected goods.

(2)   Devaluate the goods according to the degree of inferiority, extent of damage and amount of losses suffered by the Buyers.

(3)   Replace new parts which conform to the specifications, quality, and performance as stipulated in this Contract, and bear all the expenses incurred to and direct loses sustained by the Buyers. The Sellers shall, at the same time guarantee the quality of the parts thus replaced for a further period as specified in Clause 15 of this Contract.

18. FORCE MAJEURE:

The Sellers shall not be held responsible for the delay in shipment or non-delivery of the goods due to Force Majeure, which might occur during the process of manufacturing or in the course of loading or transit. The Sellers shall advise the Buyers immediately of such occurrence and within fourteen days thereafter, the Sellers shall send by airmail to the Buyers for their acceptance a certificate issued by the competent Government Authorities where the accident occurs as evidence thereof. Under such circumstances the Sellers, however, are still under the obligation to take all necessary measures to hasten the delivery of the goods. In case the accident lasts for more than ten weeks the Buyers shall have the right to cancel the Contract.

19. LATE DELIVERY AND PENALTY:

Should the Sellers fail to make delivery on time as stipulated in the Contract, with exception of Force Majeure causes specified in Clause 18 of this Contract, the Buyers shall agree to postpone the delivery on condition that the Sellers agree to pay a penalty which shall be deducted by the paying bank from the payment under negotiation (or collection). The penalty is charged at a rate of 0.5% for every seven days, odd days less than seven days counting as seven days. The total penalty, however, shall not exceed 5% of the total value of the goods involved in the late delivery. In case the Sellers fail to make delivery ten weeks later than the time of shipment stipulated in this Contract, the Buyers shall have the right to cancel the contract and the Sellers, in spite of the cancellation,shall still pay the aforesaid penalty to the Buyers without delay.

20. ARBITRATION:

All disputes in connection with this Contract or the execution thereof shall be settled friendly through negotiations. In case no settlement can be reached through negotiations, the case (unless otherwise stipulated in clause 21 that it should be referred to arbitration in a third country agreed upon by both parties,) should then be submitted for arbitration to the Arbitration Commission of the China Council for the Promotion of International Trade in accordance with the Provisional Rules of Procedures promulgated by the said Arbitration Commission. The Arbitration shall take place in Peking and the decision of the Arbitration Commission shall be final and binding upon both parties; neither party shall seek recourse to a law court or other authorities to appeal for revision of the decision. Arbitration fee shall be borne by the losing party.

21. SUPPLEMENTARY CONDITION:

This Contract is made in two original copies, one copy to be held by each Party in witness thereof.

The Buyers:	The Sellers:
—Name of Chinese Organization—	
(author)	

MACHINERY SALES CONTRACT

Contract No._____

Date: _____

Sellers: _____

      name of the Chinese Organization
      (author)

Buyers: _____

This Contract is made by and between the Buyers and the Sellers; whereby the Buyers agree to buy and the Sellers agree to sell the under-mentioned commodity according to the terms and conditions stipulated below:

1.   Commodity, Specification, Quantity, Unit Price & Total Value:

2.   Total Value of Contract:
3.   Packing:
4.   Insurance
5.   Shipping Marks

6.   Port of Shipment:
7.   Port of Destination :
8.   Time of Shipment:
9.   Terms of Payment:

10. Shipping Documents: The sellers shall present the following documents:
11. Claims.

     Should the quality, quantity and/or specification of the goods be found not in conformity with the stipulations of the contract, the Sellers agree to examine any claim, which shall be supported by a report issued by a reputable surveyor approved by the Sellers. The Sellers are not responsible for claims arising out of incorrect installation or wrong operation. The Sellers are only responsible for claims against badworkmanship or faulty materials. Claims concerning quality shall be made within_____months after the arrival of the goods at destination. Claims concerning quantity and / or specification shall be made within_____days after the arrival of the goods at destination.

12. Force Majeure:

     The Sellers shall not be held responsible for late delivery or non-delivery of the goods due to Force Majeure. However, in such case, the Sellers shall submit to the Buyers a certificate issued by the China Council for the Promotion of International Trade or competent organiza-

tions as evidence thereof.
13. Arbitration:

All disputes in connection with the execution of this Contract shall be settled through friendly negotiations. Should an arbitration be necessary, either party shall appoint one arbitrator, and the arbitrators thus appointed shall nominate a third person as umpire, to form an arbitration committee. Arbitration shall take place at _____ The award of the Arbitration Committee shall be accepted as final by both Parties. Arbitration fee, unless otherwise awarded, shall be borne by the losing party. The Arbitrators and the umpire shall be confined to persons of Chinese or_____Nationality.

In case the Arbitration is to be held in Peking, the case in dispute shall then be submitted for arbitration to the Foreign Trade Arbitration Commission of the China Council for the Promotion of International Trade, Peking, in accordance with the "Provisional Rules of Procedure of the Foreign Trade Arbitration Commission of the China Council for the Promotion of International Trade.". The decision of the Commission shall be accepted as final and binding upon both parties.

14 Other Conditions:

Any alterations and additions to this Contract shall be valid only if made out in writing and duly signed by both parties. Neither party is entitled to transfer its right and obligations under this Contract to a third party without a written consent thereto being obtained from the other party.

After the signing of this Contract all preceding negotiations and correspondence pertaining to same shall become null and void.

15. Done and signed in _____ on this _____ day _____ of _____ 19_____.
16. Remarks:

Sellers: _____   Buyers: _____

Address: _____   Address: _____

Cable Address: _____   Cable Address: _____

中国粮油食品进出口公司上海市粮油分公司

CHINA NATIONAL CEREALS, OIL & FOODSTUFFS IMPORT AND EXPORT CORP.

SHANGHAI CEREALS & OILS BRANCH

Cable Address:
"CHINAFAT" SHANGHAI.

售方名称及地址：
Messrs.

CONFIRMATION OF ORDER

合同编号
Order No.

成交日期
Date

根据你方和我方函电交换结果，兹特确认我方向你方订购下列货物，各项条款载明於下：
In accordance with the exchange of your telegrams/letters dated.
and our dated
we hereby confirm having purchased from you the following goods under the terms and conditions stated herein:

(1) 货 名 及 规 格 COMMODITY AND SPECIFICATIONS	(2) 数 量 QUANTITY	(3) 单 价 UNIT PRICE	(4) 总 值 TOTAL AMOUNT

(5) 制造厂商／生产国别：
MANUFACTURERS / COUNTRY OF ORIGIN:

(6) 到货口岸：
PORT OF DESTINATION:

(7) 保 险：
INSURANCE:

(8) 唛 头：
SHIPPING MARKS:

(9) 包 装：
PACKING:

(10) 装运期限及装货口岸：
TIME OF SHIPMENT & LOADING PORT:

(11) 付 款 条 件：
TERMS OF PAYMENT:

付款由中国银行开立不可撤销的按合同货款96%信用证，在上海见单据议付，余额4％在货到达后——天内经复验合格后付。
Payment against irrevocable, 96% L/C of contract value, established through Bank of China, payable upon presentation of documents, 4 % balance to be paid within —— days after discharge of goods if results of reinspection are in conformity with the stipulations of the order.

(12) 单 据：
DOCUMENTS REQUIRED (according to F.O.B., C & F, or C.I.F. terms):
(A) 缴 给 银 行 For presentation to Bank.
(B) 航寄我公司 Copies to be airmailed to us·within 7 days after shipment has been made.

214

		A	B	
1	洁净无此装船提单，证明运费到付／已付及运费金额。 Full set of Negotiable clean on board ocean Bills of Lading Marked "Freight payable of destination" / "Freight Pre-paid" and indicating freight amounts.	Full set	2	
2	发票注明确认书号码。 Signed invoice indicating order number.	3	7	
3	重量单。 Weight Memo.	2	4	
4	原厂或公认公证行品质证明书及重量证明书。 Quality Certificate & Weight Certificate issued by Manufacturers or Public-recognized Surveyors.	1		
5	发票通知电报副本。 Copy of cable advice of shipment/despatch.	1		
6	船公司航程表说明在抵达到货口岸前不靠美国口岸及台湾地区。 Steamship Company's scheduled itinerary evidencing that the carrying vessel, prior to her arrival at the port of destination, shall not call at U.S.A. ports and Taiwan area.	1		
7	发货人寄出副本单据证明函。 A letter certifying that all the copies of the required documents have been sent to us by airmail.	1		
8	保险单或保险证明书。 Insurance Policy or Certificate.			
9	船公司出具之"不中途转船"证明函。 Steamship Co.'s letter undertaking shipment to the destination without any transhipment.			
10				

(13) 装运条件(离岸条款)：

1. 货物由买方自行租船运输。售方按合同交装期30天前，将预计装船日期、合同号码、商品名称、数量以电报通知买方，以便安排舱位。

2. 买方应在船只受期前10天前，将船名、预计受做日期、装做量、台约号码、船舶代理人以电报通知售方。售方将联系船舶代理人配台船备妥货物和装船。如买方因故需要变更船只，或遇与船只提前或延迟情况发生，买方或船舶代理人应及时通知售方。

3. 买方所租船只按期到达装运口岸后，如售方不能按时备货装船，因而发生空舱费或延期费，概由售方负担。如船只不能于受做期满后20天内到达，自第21天起发生的仓库租费和保险费，由买方负担。双方凭原始单据核实支付。

(14) 发货通知(离岸加运费条款)：

1. 售方应于货物起运后，在48小时内以电报将台约号码、发票金额、船名、装运口岸及日期通知买方；如系分批装运，并预告明货物名称及实装数量。

2. 倘由于售方不依时将装船通知电告买方致使买方未能及时投保各险，买方因而遭受之任何损失均由售方负担。

(15) 到岸品质重量检验及索赔：

1. 本合同内货物系列岸重量以中国商品检验局检验结果为最后依据。

(13) TERMS OF SHIPMENT (FOB) :

1. The vessel shall be booked/chartered by the Buyers. The Sellers shall, 30 days before the contracted delivery date, advise the Buyers by cable of the contract number, commodity, quantity and the expected date of arrival of the goods at the loading-port, for arranging shipping space.

2. 10 days before the laydays the Buyers shall advise the Sellers telegraphically of the contract number, name of vessel, laydays, quantity to be loaded and the name of the shipping agents, and then the Sellers shall come into contact with the shipping agents and arrange for the goods to be ready for loading. If it becomes neccessary for the Buyers to book/charter a substitute for the original vessel, or in the event of the vessel having to arrive at the loading port earlier or later than scheduled, the Buyers or the shipping agents shall advise the Sellers to the effect in due time.

3. In the event of the Sellers' failure to make delivery for loading when the vessel arrives duly at the loading port, the dead freight and/or demurrade thus incurred shall be for Sellers' account. If the vessel fails, however, to arrive at the loading port 20 days after the laydays as previously advised, the storage and the insurance from the 21st day shall be borne by the Buyers. The payments for these charges and expenses either by the Sellers to the Buyers or by the Buyers to the Sellers shall be effected against original bills or invoices.

(14) SHIPPING ADVICE (C & F)

1. The Sellers are requested to send the Buyers Cable advice of shipment/despatch indicating order number, invoice value, vessel's name, loading port and shipping date within 48 hours after loading of the goods; for partial shipment, pleses also indicate goods name and quantity.

2. Should the Buyers be unable to arrange insurance in time owing to the Seller's failure to give advice of shipment by Cable, the Sellers shall be held responsible for any and all damage and/or loss attributable to such failure.

(15) INSPECTION AND CLAIMS ON BASIS OF LANDED QUALITY AND LANDED WEIGHT

1. Goods under this order are contracted on basis of landed quality and landed weight, with certificates issued by the China Commodity Inspection Bureau as final.

2. 所订货物应经到货口岸之中国商品检验局检验。如发现品质、规格、数量及／或重量与合同规定不符，除属于保险公司或船公司负责者外，买方根据中国商品检验局之鉴定证明书有权拒绝收货，和／或向售方提出索赔，检验费用由售方负担。检验索赔规定为卸货后　　　　天之内。	2. The goods purchased under this order shall be subject to the inspection by the China Commodity Inspection Bureau at the port of destination. Should the quality, specifications, quantity and/or weight be found not in conformity with the stipulations of the order, due to causes other than those for which the Insurance Company or Shipping Company are liable, the Buyers shall on the strength of the Survey Report issued by the afore-said Bureau have the right to reject the goods delivered and/or to file claim against the Sellers, with the survey fees for the Sellers' account. The time for inspection and claim should be within　　days after discharge of the goods.
3. 如复验不符合合同规定，买方有权在 4 % 余额内扣除应赔款项，如应赔款项超过 4 % 余额，差额应由卖方另行汇付。	3. If results of reinspection are not in conformity with the stipulations of the order, the buyers have the right to deduct their claim from 4% balance. In case amount claimed exceeds 4% balance, then the difference is to be remitted by the sellers.
4. 所有货物如在限期内不能装运，除因下述不可抗力事故外，买方有权取销合约兹撤回信用证，售方凭负责赔偿买方因此而所受之全部直接损失。	4. In the event of the Sellers' failing to make delivery/effect shipment within the stipulated time, unless caused by Force Majeure as specified below, the Buyers shall have the right to cancel the Order and withdraw the Letter of Credit, if opened, and in such case the Sellers shall reimburse the Buyers for all the losses and expenses incurred directly attributable to the non-delivery/non-shipment.
5. 由于不可抗力事故如战争、严重之水、火、霜冻、冰等自然灾害而不能如期交货，售方必须立即将情况以电报通知买方并于发电后十五日内以航函提供实灾害属实之证明文件，送买方审核认可。但售方仍须采取必要措施设法尽速装运，如灾害拖延八个星期以上买方有权取消合约。	5. In case of delayed delivery/shipment due to Force Majeure such as war, serious flood, fire, frost, ice or other natural calamities, the Sellers shall immediately advise the Buyers by cable of the occourrence, and within 15 days thereafter airmail to the Buyers a certificate evidencing such accident/incident to be approved by the Buyers. Under such circumstances, the Sellers, however, are still under obligation to take all necessary measures to hasten the delivery of the goods so delayed; in case the accident/incident lasts for more than eight weeks, the Buyers shall have the right to cancel the Order.
(16) 仲裁： 有关本合同可能发生的一切争执，双方应以友好态度协商解决，如双方不能达成协议时，可提交北京中国国际贸易促进委员会所设对外贸易仲裁委员会按该会现行仲裁程序仲裁，以裁决为终局裁决，双方均应接受并受其约束，仲裁费用除另有裁决外，应由败诉一方负担。	(16) ARBITRATION: All disputes and differences in connection with this contract or execution thereof shall be settled amicably by negotiation. In case of failure to reach an agreement through negotiation, the case shall be refer red to the Foreign Trade Arbitration Committee of the China Council for the Promotion of International Trade in Peking for arbitration according to the provisional rules of procedure of the Council. The award made by the Arbitration Committee shall be accepted as final and binding upon both parties. The arbitration expenses unless otherwise awarded shall be borne by the losing party.
(17) 附加条件： 本合同上列各条款如与下述附加条款有抵触时，以附加条款为准。	(17) SUPPLEMENTARY CONDITION(S): Should any of the clauses stipulated in this order be in conflict with the following Supplementary Condition(s), the Supplementary Condition(s) shall be taken as valid and binding.

请 于 收 到 后 五 天 内 将 本 合 同 正 本 一 份 签 字 航 空 寄 回。
Please return by airmail a duplicate copy of this Confirmation of Order duly signed within five days after receipt.

售 方 确 认 签 字　　　　　　　　　　中國糧油食品進出口公司上海市糧油分公司
Confirmed by the Sellers:　　　　　　CHINA NATIONAL CEREALS, OILS & FOODSTUFFS IMPORT & EXPORT CORP.
　　　　　　　　　　　　　　　　SHANGHAI CEREALS & OILS BRANCH

CHINA NATIONAL CEREALS, OILS & FOODSTUFFS
IMPORT AND EXPORT CORPORATION

ORIGINAL
正　本

SALES CONTRACT

No. _____

Date. _____

The China National Cereals, Oils & Foodstuffs Import and Export Corporation, hereinafter called the Sellers, agree to sell and Messrs. _____

hereinafter called the Buyers, agreee to buy the undermentioned goods subject to the terms and conditions stipulated below:

1. Name of Commodity & Specifications	2. Quantity	3. Unit Price	4. Amount

With _____ % more or less both in amount and quantity allowed at the Sellers' option.

5.   Time of Shipment:

6.   Packing:

7.   Loading Port and Destination:

8.   Insurance

9.   Terms of Payment: To be made against sight draft drawn under an irrevocable, transferable, divisible Letter of Credit, without recourse, for the total value of the goods in _____ , allowing 5% more or less both in amount and quantity at Sellers' option in favour of the —name of the Chinese Organization— (Author) , _____ Branch, established through _____

_____

The Letter of Credit in due form must reach the Sellers at least 30 days before shipment and remain valid for at least 15 days in China after the last day of shipment.

10.   The General Terms and Conditions on the back page consitute an inseparable part of this Contract and shall be equally binding upon both parties.

THE SELLERS   THE BUYERS

Address: _____

Cable Address: _____

Telex: _____

GENERAL TERMS AND CONDITIONS

1. Documents to be submitted by the Sellers to the Bank for negotiation:
   (a) Full set clean-on-board shipped Bill of Lading.
   (b) Invoice.
   (c) Inspection Certificate on Quality and Inspection Certificate on weight issued by the China Commodity Inspection Bureau at the port of shipment.
   (d) Insurance Policy.

2. Quality and Weight:
   Quality and Weight certified by the China Commodity Inspection Bureau at the port of shipment as per their respective certificates are to be taken as final.

3. Shipping Advice:
   Immediately after loading is completed, the Sellers shall notify by cable the number of credit, quantity and name of vessel to the Buyers.

4. Amendments of Letter of Credit:
   The Buyers shall open Letter of Credit in accordance with the terms of this Contract. If any discrepancy is found, amendments of Letter of Credit should be made immediately by the Buyers upon receipt of the Sellers' advice, failing which the Buyers shall be held responsible for any losses thus incurred as well as for late shipment thus caused.

5. Force Majeure:
   Should the Sellers fail to deliver the contracted goods or effect the shipment in time by reason of war, flood, fire, storm, heavy snow or any other causes beyond their control, the time of shipment might be duly extended, or alternatively a part or whole of the Contract might be cancelled without any liability attached to the Sellers, but the Sellers have to furnish the buyers with a certificate attesting such event or events.

6. Arbitration:
   Should there be any disputes between the contracting parties, they shall be settled through negotiation In case no settlement can be reached, the case under dispute may then be referred to arbitration.

7. Claims:
   Should the Quality, quantity and/or weight be found not in conformity with those stipulated in this Contract, aside from those usual natural changes of quality and weight in transit and losses within the responsibility of the shipping company and/or insurance company, the Buyers shall have the right within 30 days after the arrival of the goods at the port of destination, to lodge claims concerning the quality, quantity or weight of the goods. (Claims for perishable goods are to be put forward immediately after arrival of the goods at destination), but the Buyers should provide the Sellers with the Certificates issued by the concerned Inspection Organization.

《中国粮油食品进出口公司粮油分公司销售合同》
CHINA NATIONAL CEREALS, OILS & FOODSTUFFS IMPORT AND EXPORT CORPORATION, CEREALS AND OILS BRANCH

SALES CONTRACT

No. _____

Shanghai, _____

The China National Cereals, Oils & Foodstuffs Import and Export Corporation, Shanghai Cereals and Oils Branch, hereinafter called the Sellers, agree to sell the Messrs. _____

hereinafter called the Buyers, agree to buy the undermentioned goods subjects to the terms and conditions stipulated below:

1. Commodity: Chinese White Rice, Long-shaped

2. Specifications:

	Broken Grains	Moisture	Admixture
(1)	35% max.	15% max.	1% max.
(2)	25% max.	15% max.	0.25% max.

3. Quantity:
   (1) 735,000 metric tons
   (2) 125,000 metric tons
   (Buyers have the option to take 10% more or less of the quantity contracted, such excess or deficiency to be settled at the contracted price)

4. Unit Prices
   (1) US$ _____ per metric ton FOBS GUANGZHOU, gross for net
   (2) US$ _____ per metric ton FOBS GUANGZHOU, gross for net
   Destination: Abidjan (excluding Madagascar and Mauritius)

5. Total Value:

6. Time of Shipments:
   (1) During Feb./Mar./Apr. in monthly shipments of about _____ metric tons each
   (2) During Mar./Apr. in monthly shipments of about _____

7. Packing:
   (1) (2) Both in new single gunny bags of about _____ metric tons each 50 kgs each

8. Insurance: To be arranged and covered by the Buyers.

9. Payment: The Buyers shall establish through a bank acceptable to the Sellers a Confirmed Irrevocable Sight Credit with T/T Reimbursement allowing 10% more or less both in amount and quantity, in favor of China National Cereals, Oils & Foodstuffs Import and Export Corp., Cereals and Oils Branch. The Credit must reach the Bank of China, 15 days before the month of shipment and remain valid for negotiation in China until the 15th day after the month of shipment.

10. Remarks: This Contract is made as per Buyers' Telex of _____ and Sellers' of _____ in two originals in English. Each party keeps one original.
    The Gereral Terms and Conditions on the back page constitute an inseparable part of this Contract and shall be equally binding upon both parties.

SELLERS:
CHINA NATIONAL CEREALS, OILS & FOOD-
STUFFS
IMPORT AND EXPORT CORPORATION,
CEREALS AND OILS BRANCH.

BUYERS:

_____
(SIGNED)

_____
(SIGNED)

Address: _____

Address: _____

Cable Address: _____

219

中 国 化 工 进 出 口 总 公 司
CHINA NATIONAL CHEMICALS IMPORT & EXPORT CORPORATION

订 购 合 同
PURCHASE CONTRACT

台同号码：
CONTRACT NO.: _____

广　州
KWANGCHOW _____

买　方： 中国化工进出口总公司　　北京二里沟　　电报挂号：''SINOCHEM'' PEKING
The Buyers: CHINA NATIONAL CHEMICALS IMPORT & EXPORT CORPORATION. Erh Li Kou, Peking. Cable Address: ''SINOCHEM'' PEKING

卖　方：
The Sellers:

兹经买卖双方同意按照以下条款由买方购进卖方售出以下商品：
This Contract is made by and between the Buyers and the Sellers; whereby the Buyers agree to buy and the Sellers agree to sell the under-mentioned goods subject to the terms and conditions as stipulated hereinafter:

(1)　商品名称及规格：
　　　Name of Commodity and Specification:

(2)　数　　量：
　　　Quantity:
(3)　单　　价：
　　　Unit Price:
(4)　总　　值：
　　　Total Value:
(5)　包　　装：
　　　Packing:
(6)　生产国别及制造厂商：
　　　Country of Origin & Manufacturer:
(7)　付款条件：　买方于成交后送运　　中国银行开出以卖方为抬头的不可撤销的信用证，卖方在货物装船启运后凭本合同交货条款3(A)所列单据在开证银行议付货款。信用证有效期为装船后15天止。
　　　Terms of Payment: After conclusion of business the Buyers shall open with the Bank of China, an irrevocable letter of credit in favour of the Sellers payable at the issuing Bank against presentation of the shipping doucments as stipulated under Clause 3 (A) of the Terms of Delivery of this Contract after departure of the carrying vessel. The said letter of credit shall remain in force till the 15th day after shipment.
(8)　保　　险：　由买方负责。
　　　Insurance: To be covered by the Buyers..
(9)　装运时间：
　　　Time of Shipment:
(10) 装运口岸：
　　　Port of Loading:
(11) 目的口岸：
　　　Port of Destination:
(12) 装运唛头：
　　　Shipping Mark(s):
　　　每种货物上应刷明到货口岸、件号、每件毛重及净重、尺码及右列唛头（如系危险及／或有毒货物，应按惯例在每件货物上明显刷出有关标记及性质说明）。
　　　On each package shall be stencilled conspicuously: port of destination, package number, gross and nett weights, measurement and the shipping mark shown on the right side. (For dangerours and/or poisonous cargo, the nature and the generally adopted symbol shall be marked conspicuously on each package)
(13) 其他条款：(a)本台同其他有关事项均按交货条款(详见背面)之规定办理，诚交货条款为本台同之不可分割部分。(b)本台同以中文及英文两种文字书就，两种文字的条款具有同等效力。
　　　Other terms: (a) Other matters relating to this Contract shall be dealt with in accordance with the Terms of Delivery as specified overleaf, which shall form an integral part of this Contract. (b) This Contract is made out in Chinese and English, both versions being equally authentic.
(14) 附加条款(本台同其他任何条款如与本附加条款有抵触时，以本附加条款为准。)：
　　　Supplementary Condition(s) (Should any other clause in this Contract be in conflict with the following Supplementary Condition(s), the Supplementary Condition(s) should be taken as final and binding.):
　　　1. 本台同于　　　年　　　广州交易会成交。
　　　　 This Contract is concluded at the Kwangchow Fair.

　　　2. 本台同签订后，有关台同执行事宜，卖方直接与买方　　　分公司联系。
　　　　 For all the matters in connection with the execution of this Contract after signing, the Sellers shall approach direct the Buyers' Branch.

　　　　　　买　方　　　　　　　　　　　　　　　　　　　买　方
　　　　　 THE SELLERS　　　　　　　　　　　　　　　　THE BUYERS

CHINA IMPORT & EXPORT CORPORATION
BRANCH
SALES CONTRACT

CONTRACT No. __

DATE: _____

The Sellers : CHINA NATIONAL CORPORATION BRANCH.
ADDRESS : China.
Cable Adress:

The Buyers :

Address :
Cable Address:

    This Sales Contract is made by and between the Sellers and the Buyers whereby the Sellers agree to sell and the Buyers agree to buy the under-mentioned goods according to the terms and conditions stipulated below:

1. Name of Commodity, Specification & Packing	2. Quantity	3. Unit Price	4. Total Amount

(The Sellers are allowed to load the quantity with 3% more or less. The price shall be calculated according to the unit price stipulated in this Contract.)

5.   Shipping Mark: To be designed by the Sellers. In case the Buyers desire to designate their own shipping mark, the Buyers shall advise the Sellers __ ____ days before loading and the Sellers' consent must be obtained.

6.   Insurance: To be covered by the Buyers / Sellers for ____ % of the total

invoice value against _____ risk. Should the Buyers desire to cover for other risks besides the afore-mentioned or for an amount exceeding the afore-mentioned limit, the Sellers' approval must be obtained first, and all additional premium charge incurred therewith shall be for the Buyers' account.

7. Port of Shipment:

8. Port of Destination:

9. Time of Shipment:

10. Terms of Payment: The Buyers shall establish a Confirmed, Irrevocable, Without Recourse, Transferable and Divisible Letter of Credit in favour of the Sellers covering the total value of the contracted goods plus 3% in HK$ _____ payable at sight against presentation of the shipping documents, to the negotiating Bank in China. The Letter of Credit must reach the Sellers before _____ 198 ____ and remain valid for negotiation in China till the 15th day after the aforesaid time of Shipment.. The content of the covering Letter of Credit shall be in strict accordance with the stipulations of the Sales Contract. In case of any variation thereof necessitating amendment to the L / C, the Buyers shall bear the expenses incurred in such amendment, and the Sellers shall not be held responsible for possible delay of shipment resulting from this necessity of amending the L / C.

11. Shipping Documents: The Sellers shall present the following documents to the negotiating bank for payment:
    (1) Full set clean on board of shipped Bills of Lading made out to order and blank endorsed, marked "Freight Prepaid"
    (2) _____ copies of invoice
    (3) _____ copies of the packing list(s) or weight memos.
    (4) One original and _____ duplicate copies of the Transferable Insurance Policy or Insurance Certificate.
    (5) One original and _____ duplicate copies of the Inspection Certificate of Quality, Quantity/Weight issued by

12. Inspection: The Inspection Certificate of Quality, Quantity / Weight issued by _____ shall be taken as the basis of delivery.

13. Force Majeure: The Sellers shall not be held responsible if they, owing to Force Majeure cause or causes, fail to make delivery within the time stipulated in the Contract or cannot deliver the goods. However, in such a case, the Sellers shall inform the Buyers immediately by cable and if it is requested by the Buyers, shall also deliver to the Buyers by registered letter a certificate attesting the existence of such a cause or causes.

14. Discrepancy and Claim: In case the Sellers fail to ship the whole lot or part of the goods within the time stipulated in this Contract, the Buyers shall have the right to cancel the part of the Contract which has not been performed 30 days following the expiry of the stipulated time of shipment,

unless there exists a Force Majeure cause or the contract stipulation has been modified with the Buyers' consent.

In case discrepancy on the quality of the goods is found by the Buyers after arrival of the goods at the port of destination, the Buyers may, within 30 days after arrival of the goods at the port of destination, lodge with the Sellers a claim which should be supported by an Inspection Certificate issued by a public surveyer approved by the Sellers. The Sellers shall, on the merits of the claim, either make good the loss sustained by the Buyers or reject their claim, it being agreed that the Sellers shall not be held responsible for any loss or losses due to natural causes or causes falling within the responsibility of Shipowners or the Underwriters. In case the Letter of Credit does not reach the Sellers within the time stipulated in the Contract, or if the Letter of Credit opened by the Buyers does not correspond to the Contract terms and that the Buyers fail to amend thereafter its terms in time, after receipt of notification by the Sellers, the Sellers shall have the right to cancel the contract or to delay the delivery of the goods and shall have also the right to claim, for compensation of losses against the Buyers.

15. Arbitration: Any dispute arising from the execution of, or in connection with this Contract should be settled through negotiation. In case no settlement can be reached, the case shall then be submitted to the Foreign Trade Arbitration Commission of the China Council for the Promotion of International Trade, Peking, for settlement by arbitration in accordance with the Commission's Provisional Rules of Procedure. The award rendered by the Commission's Provisional Rules of Procedure shall be final and binding on both parties.

16. Obligations: Both the Signers of this Contract, ie the Sellers and the Buyers as referred to above, shall assume full responsibilities in fulfilling their obligations as per the terms and conditions herein stipulated. Any dispute arising from the execution of, or in connection with this Contract shall be settled in accordance with terms stipulated above between the Signers of this Contract only, without involving any third party.

The Sellers: The Buyers:

_____   _____

CHINA _____ CORPORATION
_____ BRANCH.

223

CHEMICALS—SALES CONTRACT

CHINA NATIONAL CHEMICALS IMPORT AND EXPORT CORPORATION
CABLE ADDRESS: "SINOCHEM PEKING"

No. _____

SALES CONTRACT

The China National Chemicals Import and Export Corporation,
Peking, China (herein-after called the Sellers) and _____
(herein-after called the Buyers) agree to sign this Contract according to the terms and conditions stipulated below:

1. Name of Commodity	Specifications and Packing	Quantity	Unit Price	Total Value

2. Shipping Mark: At the Seller's option

3. Terms of Payment: To be made against sight draft drawn under a Confirmed, Irrevocable, Divisible assignable and transferable Letter of Credit with Telegraphic Transfer Reimbursement Clause without Recourse, Transshipment and Partial shipment allowed, in favour of the Tientsin Branch of the Sellers, established through a bank of a third country acceptable to both parties. The Letter of Credit with Telegraphic Transfer Reimbursement Clause without Recourse, Transshipment and Partial shipment allowed, in favour of the Tientsin Branch of the Sellers, established through a bank of a third country acceptable to both parties. The Letter of Credit in due form must reach the Sellers' Branch 30 days before shipment and remain valid for at least 15 days in China after the last day of shipment and the amount of the credit shall allow plus or minus 5%.

4. Terms of Shipment:
   (1) Port of Shipment: China Port
   (2) Port of Destination* SEATTLE
   (3) Time of Shipment: In Jan. / Feb., 19_____, _____ M / T, Feb. / March, _____ M / T.

and techniques for _____
and techniques to improve performance and product quality, and, _____

5. Advices and consulting services concerning other communications and matters as may be required from time to time.

Responsibility for the above effort will be with:
and coordination in the South East Asia and the Middle East will be with:

Dated this _____ day of _____ , 19 _____
in _____ , China.

_____   _____

(Signed)   (Signed)
For and on behalf of   For and on behalf of

225

合　同

CONTRACT

No.:

Date:

卖　方　　中　国　五　金　矿　产　进　出　口　总　公　司　　　北京二里沟　　电报挂号：
The Sellers: CHINA NATIONAL METALS & MINERALS IMPORT & EXPORT CORPORATION, Erh Li Kou, Peking. Cable Address: MINMETALS PEKING

买　方
The Buyers:

Cable Address:

双　方　同　意　按　下　列　条　款　由　卖　方　出　售，买　方　购　进　下　列　货　物：
The Sellers agree to sell and the Buyers agree to buy the undermentioned goods on the terms and conditions stated below:

(1) 货物名称、规格、包装及唛头 Name of Commodity, Specifications, Packing term and Shipping Marks	(2) 数　量 Quantity	(3) 单　价 Unit Price	(4) 总　值 Total Amount
包　装： 小捆 70—120 公斤 及／或 大捆 500—1000 公斤。 Packing: In bundles of 70—120 kilos each and/or in lift bundles of about 1000 kilos.	卖方有权在 3 % 以内多装或少装 Shipment 3% more or less at Sellers' option	上述价格内包括给买方佣金　%按FOB计算。 The above price includes a Buyers' commission of　% to be calculated on FOB value.	

(5) 装运期限
　　Time of Shipment:

(6) 装运口岸：
　　Port of Loading: China Ports.

(7) 目的口岸：
　　Port of Destination:

(8) 保　　险： 由卖方按发票金额 110% 投保
　　Insurance: To be effected by the Sellers for 110% of invoice value covering.

(9) 付款条件： 买方应通过买卖双方同意的银行，开立以卖方为受益人的、不可撤销的、可转让和可分割的、允许分批装运和转船的信用证。该信用证凭装运单据在中国的中国银行见单即付。
　　Terms of Payment: The Buyers shall open, with a bank to be accepted by both the Buyers and the Sellers, an Irrevocable, Transferable and Divisible Letter of Credit, allowing partial shipments and transhipment, in favour of the Sellers, payable at sight against first presentation of the shipping documents to the Bank of China in China.

该信用证必须在　　　　　　　　前开出。信用证有效期为装船后十五天在中国到期。
The covering Letter of Credit must be opened before　　　　　　　　　　　　　　　　　　　　　　　　and to remain valid in China until the
　　15th day (inclusive) from the day of shipment.

(10) 单据： 卖方应向议付银行提供已装船清洁提单、发票、装箱单／重量单；如果本合同按 CIF 条件，应再提供可转让的保险单或保险凭证。

Documents: The Sellers shall present to the negotiations bank, Clean On Board Bill of Lading, Invoice, Packing List/Weight Memo, and Transferable Insurance Policy or Insurance Certicate when this Contract is made on CIF basis.

(11) 装运条件：

Terms of Shipment:

1. 载运船只由卖方安排，允许分批装运并允许转船。

   The carrying vessel shall be provided by the Sellers. Partial shipments and transhipment are allowed.

2. 卖方于货物装船后，应将合同号码、品名、数量、船名、装船、日期以电报通知买方。

   After loading is completed, the Sellers shall notify the Buyers by cable of the contract number, name of the commodity, quantity, name of the carrying vessel and date of shipment.

(12) 品质和数量／重量的异议与索赔： 货到目的口岸后，买方如发现货物品质及／或数量／重量与合同规定不符，除属于保险公司及／或船公司的责任外，买方可以凭双方同意的检验机构出具的检验证明向卖方提出异议。品质异议须于货到目的口岸之日起30天内提出，数量／重量异议须于货到目的口岸之日起15天内提出。卖方应于收到异议后30天内答复买方。

Quality/Qantity Discrepancy and Claim:
In case the quanlity and/or quantity/weight are found by the Buyers to be not in conformity with the Contract after arrival of the goods at the port of destination, the Buyers may lodge claim with the Sellers supported by survey report issued by an inspection organization agreed upon by both parties, with the exception, however of those claims for which the insurance company and/or the shipping company are to be held responsible. Claim for quality discrepancy should be filed by the Buyers within 30 days after arrival of the goods at the port of destination, while for quantity/weight discrepancy claim should be filed by the Buyers within 15 days after arrival of the goods at the port of destination. The Sellers shall, within 30 days after receipt of the notification of the claim, send reply to the Buyers.

(13) 人力不可抗拒： 由于人力不可抗拒事故，使卖方不能在本合同规定期限内交货或者不能交货，卖方不负责任。但卖方必须立即以电报通知买方。如买方提出要求，卖方应以挂号函向买方提供中国国际贸易促进委员会或有关机构出具的发生事故的证明文件。

Force Majeure: In case of Force Majeure, the Sellers shall not be held responsible for late delivery or non-delivery of the goods but shall notify the Buyers by cable. The Sellrs shall deliver fo the Buyers by registered mail, if so requested by the Buyers, a certificate issued by the China Council for the Promotion of International Trade or any competent authorities.

(14) 仲裁： 凡因执行本合同与本合同有关事项所发生的一切争执，应由双方通过友好方式协商解决。如果不能取得协议时，则在被告国家根据被告国家仲裁机构的仲裁程序规则进行仲裁。仲裁决定是终局的，对双方具有同等的约束力。仲裁费用除非仲裁机构另有决定外，均由败诉一方负担。

Arbitration: All disputes in connection with this Contract or the execution thereof shall be settled by negotiation between two parties. If no settlement can be reached, the case in dispute shall then be submitted for arbitration in the country of defendant in accordance with the arbitration regulations of the arbitration organization of the defendant country. The decision made by the arbitration organization shall be taken as final and binding upon both parties. The arbitration expenses shall be borne by the losing party unless otherwise awarded by the arbitration organization.

15 备 注：
Remarks:

卖 方　　　　　　　　　　　　　　　　买 方
Sellers:　　　　　　　　　　　　　　　Buyers:
中 国 五 金 矿 产 进 出 口 总 公 司
CHINA NATIONAL METALS & MINERALS
IMPORT & EXPORT CORPORATION

成交确认书
SALES CONFIRMATION

字第　　　　　　号
No. --

日期
Date: --

卖　方
Sellers: --

签约地点：
Signed At: --

地　址
Address: --

电报挂号
Cable Address: --

买　方
Buyers: --

地　址
Address: --

电报挂号
Cable Address: --

兹 经 卖 买 双 方 同 意 成 交 下 列 商 品 订 立 条 款 如 下：
The undersigned Sellers and Buyers have agreed to close the following transactions according to the terms and conditions stipulated below:

1. 商　　品
   Name of Commodity:

2. 规　　格
   Specification:

3. 数　　量
   Quantity:

   数量及总值均得有　　　%的增减，由卖方决定。
   with 　　% more or less both in amount and quantity allowed at the Sellers' option.

4. 单　价
   Unit Price:

5. 总　　值
   Total Value:

6. 包　　装
   Packing:

7. 装　运　期
   Time of Shipment:

8. 装运口岸和目的地
   Loading Port & Destination:

9. 保　　险
   Insurance:

10. 付 款 条 件
    Terms of Payment: 买方须于19　　　年　　　月　　　日前将保兑的、不可撤销的、可转让可分割的即期信用证开到卖方，信用证议付有效期延至上列装运期后　　　天在　　　　　　到期。
    By Confirmed, Irrevocable, Transferable and Divisible Letter of Credit to be available by sight draft, to reach the Sellers before　　　　　　　　　　19　　　　　and to remain valid for negotiation 　　　　　　　　　　until the　　　　　day after the aforesaid Time of Shipment.

11. 装 船 标 记
    Shipping Mark:

12. 品质、数量、重量，以中国商品检验局检验证或卖方所出之证明书为最后依据。
    Quality, quantity and weight certified by the China Commodity Inspection Bureau or the Sellers, as per the former's Inspection Certificate or the latter's certificate, are to be taken as final.

13.

卖　方
(The Sellers)

买　方
(The Buyers)

中国纺织品进出口总公司
CHINA NATIONAL TEXTILES IMPORT AND EXPORT CORPORATION

中国北京东安门大街82号
82, Tung An Men Street, Peking China

号数
No.......................................

To Messrs.

售货确认书
SALES CONFIRMATION

日期
Date-----------------------19

你方函电
Your Reference:

我方函电
Our Reference:

敬启者：兹确认于　　年　月　日
售予你方下列货品，其成交条款如下：
We hereby confirm having sold to you on ....19.....,
the following goods on terms and conditions as set forth
hereunder:

实际买户名称及地址：
For Account of Messrs:

货 名 ARTICLE No.	品 名 及 规 格 COMMDODITY AND SPECIFICATION	数 量 QUANTITY	金 额 AMOUNT

总 金 额
TOTAL AMOUNT

总　值
TOTAL VALUE:

装运期限：
SHIPMENT:

目 的 地
DESTINATION:

付款方式：
PAYMENT:

In Renminbi Yuan (Chinese Currency). To be made against sight draft drawn under a Confirmed, Irrevocable, Divisible and Assignable Letter of Credit without recourse, with transhipment & partial shipment allowed, in favour of the　　　　　　　　　of the Sellers, established through the branch office in U.S.A. of a bank of a third country acceptable to both parties.

特约条款：
SPECIAL CLAUSE:

The Letter of Credit, which should be in every respect in conformity with the terms of this
Sales confirmation, must reach the Sellers 30-days before the month of Shipment and remain
valid for at least 15 days in China for negotiation after the last day of shipment and the amount,
quantity of the credit shall allow plus or minus 5%.

229

电报挂号 Cable Address:
"CHINATEX" Peking

中国纺织品进出口公司总公司
CHINA NATIONAL TEXTILES IMPORT AND EXPORT CORPORATION

中国北京东安门大街82号
82, Tung An Men Street, Peking China

号数
No.------------------------------------

To Messrs.

售货确认书
SALES CONFIRMATION

日期
Date----------------------19

你方函电
Your Reference:

我方函电
Our Reference:

兹经卖买双方同意成交下列商品订立条款如下：
The undersigned Sellers and Buyers have agreed to close the following transactions according to the terms and conditions stipulated below:

实际买户名称及地址：
For Account of Messrs:

(1) 品 名 Quality No.	(2) 商品名称，规格 Name of Commodity and Specification	(3) 数 量 Quantity	(4) 单价 Unit Price	(5) 金 额 Amount	(6) 装运期 Time of Shipment

(数量与金额允许增或减 _____ %
  Amount and Quantity _____ % More or less Allowed)

总 值
Total Amount

(7) 装运口岸和目的地：
Loading Port and Destination:

(8) 付款条件：
Terms of Payment: (See Remarks in reverse side)

(9) 保 险： 由买方／卖方办理
Insurance: To be effected by the Buyers/Sellers.

注 意： 开立信用证时，请在证内注明本售货确认书号码
IMPORTANT: When establishing L/C, please indicate the number of this Sales Confirmation in the L/C.

中国纺织品进出口总公司
China National Textiles Import and Export Corporation

....
买 方 (The Buyers)

....
卖 方 (The Sellers)

一　般　条　款　（见 本 台 同 反 面）
GENERAL TERMS & CONDITIONS: (PLEASE SEE OVERLEAF)

注　　意：　　开立信用证时，请在证内注明本售货确认书号码
IMPORTANT:　　When establishing L/C, please indicate the number of this Sales Confirmation in the L/C.

中 国 纺 织 品 进 出 口 总 公 司
CHINA NATIONAL TEXTILES IMPORT AND EXPORT
CORPORATION

买　方　*(The Buyers)*

卖 方 *(The Sellers)*

请 在 本 确 认 书 上 签 字 后 退 回 一 份 给 卖 方
Please sign and return one copy to the Sellers.

补上面表

单价及价格条款
UNIT PRICE
& TERMS
单价及价格条款
UNIT PRICE
& TERMS

本确认书有关内容，除双方另有协议或经卖方同意接受者外，应适用下列条款，买方任何其他合约或定单与本确认书内容如有不符，应以本确认书规定为准。买方如转售或代理第三者时买方仍应对本确认书负完全履行责任。

(1) 本确认书所确定的数量，卖方可有 5 %的增减。分批出运者，每批装运数量，必要时卖方亦得在买方规定范围内增减 5 %。

(2) 商品得在中国任何口岸装出，提单日期作为装运日期，变更目的地，应事先经卖方同意，因此增加的运保费，应由买方负担。

(3) 如因人力不可抗拒的事故而致延期交货或无法交货时，卖方不负任何责任。

(4) 除另有规定者外，买方应通过为卖方所接受的第一流银行，开具全部货款即期保兑，可分割、可转让、不可撤回及无追索权的信用证。买方应保证信用证最迟在确认书规定装运月份前30天前送达卖方，否则因此不能按期装运者，卖方不负责任。如超过装运期仍未开来者，卖方有权取消确认书并向买方提出索赔。

(5) 买方信用证内，一般请勿指定航线、船名、及承保保险公司名称。信用证有效期应规定在最后装运日期后至少10天，在中国到期，信用证金额、数量应允许增减 5 %，证在信用证内应允许转船及分批装运。请在信用证内应允许转船及分批装运。

(6) ( )本确认书所载坯布纱支数系指织制时所用纱支数，每方时经纬密度，经向纬向均可有 1 %上下。(二漂布、色布、印花布、色织布之纱支数及经纬密度，系指未经加工整理时之纱支数及经纬密度。

(7) 花布、色布及色织布必要时可有10%的二段拆匹，其短的一段应不低于10码，（拆匹免费另加半码）此外，每一配色，在数量上可有10%上下差额。

(8) 花布、色布、漂布及色织布的花样、色样，如系按买方指定者或在卖方花色样中选定者，均应在确认书规定装运月份前45天以前（色织布应在90天以前）寄达卖方，并应经厂方最后同意为准，否则卖方取消交易或延迟交货，买方不得藉故不同意，如因此造成买方损失时，买方应负责赔偿。

(9) 买方所指定或选定之花色样，卖方有权根据厂方意见稍予修改，对花布、色布、及色织布并应容许合理的色差。

(10) 花布超过确认书规定的套色，色织布中的特殊花样，色织布、花布及色布中需用成本较高的染料，其增加之成本，均应另行加价，幅度另议。

(11) 买方应接受卖方之折法、包装及商标，买方不得藉故不同意，如因此造成损失，卖方并得保留索赔权利。

(12) "到岸交货"者概由卖方发票金额的110%投保，如来证规定货物需转运内陆或其他口岸者，由卖方代保至内陆或其他港口，但此项额外保费应由买方负担。

(13) 索赔应在货到目的地后30天内提出，并须由买方提出充分证明供买方参考，以便通过友好协商解决。

(14) 请买方在收到本确认书后即行签署，并将正本一份寄回卖方存查，如本确认书到达买方处所后10天内买方尚未签回者，应视为买方已接受本确认书所规定之全部条款。

GENERAL TERMS AND CONDITIONS

The sale specified in this Sales Confirmation shall be subject to the following terms and conditions unless otherwise agreed upon between the Buyers and the Sellers. In case of any inconsistency of the terms and conditions between this Sales Confirmation and any form of contract or order or indent sent by the Buyers to the Sellers (irrespective of its date), the provisions of this Sales Confirmation shall prevail. If the Buyers resell the goods to, or conclude the transaction as representative of a third party, the Buyers shall still be responsible for the complete performance of all the obligations stipulated in this Sales Confirmation.

1. A usual trade margin of 5% plus or minus of the quantities confirmed shall be allowed. Where shipment is spread over two or more periods, the abovementioned trade margin of plus or minus 5% shall, when neccessary, be applicable to the quantity designated by the Buyers to be shipped each period.

2. Shipment may be made from any Chinese port, the date of Bill of Lading shall be taken as the date of shipment. Any change of destination should be agreed to by the Sellers beforehand. Extra freight and/or insurance premium thus incurred are to be borne by the Buyers.

3. In the event of force majeure or any other contingencies beyond the Sellers' control, the Sellers shall not be held responsible for late delivery or nondelivery of the goods.

4. Unless otherwise agreed to by the Sellers, payment is to be made against sight draft drawn under a Confirmed, Irrevocable, Divisible & Assignable Letter of Credit, Without Recourse for the full amount, established through a first class bank acceptable to the Sellers. The Letter of Credit in due form must reach the Sellers at least 30 days before the month of shipment stipulated in this Sales Confirmation, failing which the Sellers shall not be responsible for shipment as stipulated; in case the Buyers' credit still fails to reach the Sellers after the expiry of the shipping period, the Sellers shall have the right to cancel this Sales Confirmation and claim for damage against the Buyers.

5. The Buyers are requested to refrain from SPECIFYING ANY PARTICULAR SHIPPING LINE, NAME OF STEAMER, or INSURANCE COMPANY in the Letter of Credit. To facilitate negotiation of the credit by the Sellers, the validity the Letter of Credit shall be so stipulated as to remain valid for at least 10 days (expiring in China) after the last day of shipment and the amount, quantity of the credit shall allow plus or minus 5%. The Buyers are requested always to stipulate in the Letter of Credit that TRANSHIPMENT AND PARTIAL SHIPMENT ARE ALLOWED.

6. a. For grey goods, the counts of yarn indicated in this Sales Confirmation are those which were used in weaving, and the numbers of ends and picks per square inch shall allow plus or minus one percent (1 %) in wrap and/or weft way.

   b. For bleached, dyed, printed and yarn-dyed goods, the counts of yarn and the numbers of ends and picks indicated are those which were in loom-state.

7. For printed, dyed, and yarn-dyed goods, a maximum of 10% of two-part pieces with the short part not less than 10 yds. is permissible if necessary and for each two-part piece an additional length of 1/2 yd. (half yard) will be supplied free. Also a tolerance of plus or minus 10% in quantity for each colourway (for each shade in case of dyed goods) shall be permitted.

8. Designs, Colourways and Colour Shades for printed, dyed, bleached and yarn-dyed goods designated by the Buyers or chosen by the Buyers from the Sellers designs, colourways and colour shades must be sent to reach or made known to the Sellers at least 45 days (for yarn-dyed goods 90 days) before the month of shipment stipulated in this Sales Confirmation and subject to final acceptance by the mills. Otherwise the Sellers will have the option either to cancel the transaction or to postpone the time of shipment which the Buyers should not refuse to accept on any excues and the Buyers shall held responsible for compensation of whatever losses thus incurred to the Sellers.

9. Acting upon the request of the mills, the Sellers shall have the right to make minor alterations to the designs designated or chosen by the Buyers. For printed, dyed and yarn-dyed goods, resonable tolerance in colour shades must be allowed.

10. For colours of the prints designated exceeding those confirmed, special designs for producing yarn-dyed goods, and colour shades requiring more expensive dyes prices should be adequately adjusted through negotiation.

11. Sellers' trade mark, stamping and mode of folding and packing will be accepted by the Buyers. The Buyers should not refuse to accept on any excuses, and in case of any damage thus incurred to the Sellers, the Sellers shall reserve the right to claim against the Buyers for damage.

12. The sellers are to cover insurance at invoice value plus 10% thereof of the goods sold on CIF basis. If the Letter of Credit stipulates that the goods after arrival at the port of destination are to be transported to an inland city or some other ports, the Sellers will cover insurance up to that city or ports, and the Buyers are to be responsible for payment of this additional premium.

13. Claims for damage should be filed by the Buyers with the Sellers within 30 days after arrival of the goods at destination and supported by sufficient evidence for Sellers reference so that claims can be settle through friendly negotiation.

14. The Buyers are requested sign and return one orignal copy to the Sellers for file immediately upon receipt of this Sales Confirmation. Should the Buyers fail to do so within 10 days after arrival of this Sales Confirmation at the Buyers' end, it shall be considered that the Buyers have accepted all the terms and conditions set forth in this Sales Confirmation.

《中国纺织品进出口公司分公司售货确认书》

中国纺织品进出口公司分公司
CHINA NATIONAL TEXTILES IMPORT AND EXPORT CORPORATION BRANCH

电报挂号 CABLE ADDRESS: 　　　　中山东一路×号　　　　号数
电　码 CODES USED:　　　　CHUNGSHAN ROAD E.1., CHINA　　No.

售 货 确 认 书
SALES CONFIRMATION

日期：
Date

To Messrs.

你方函电
Your Reference:

我方函电
Our Reference:

敬启者兹确认于19XX年12月13日
售予你方下列货品，其成交条款如下：
We hereby confirm having sold to you on _____,
19 ____ , the following goods on terms and conditions as set forth
hereunder:

实际买户名称及地址：
For Account of Messrs:

数量 QUANTITY	货号 ARTICLE No.	品名及规格 COMMODITY AND SPECIFICATION	单价及价格条款 UNIT PRICE & TERMS	金额 AMOUNT

总金额

总　值
TOTAL VALUE:

装运期限
SHIPMENT:

目的地
DESTINATION:

付款方式
PAYMENT:　　凭不可撤销信用证见票后30天付款
　　　　　　　By Irrevocable Credit at 30 days after sight

特约条款
SPECIAL CLAUSE:

备　注
REMARKS:

保　险：　由卖方投保一切险和战争险
INSURANCE:　To be covered by the Sellers against All Risks and War Risk.

一般条款　（见本合同后面）：
GENERAL TERMS & CONDITIONS: (PLEASE SEE OVERLEAF)

注　意：　开立信用证时，请在证内注明本售货确认书号码
IMPORTANT:　When establishing L／C, please indicate the number of this Sales Confirmation in the L／C.

中国纺织品进出口公司分公司
China National Textiles Import and Export Corporation Branch

买　方 (The Buyers) Manager　　　　　卖　方 (The Sellers) Manager

请在本确认书上签字后退回一份给卖方。
Please sign and return one copy to the Sellers.

233

PART III:
CONTRACTS AND RELATED DOCUMENTS EXECUTED IN 1987

JOINT VENTURE CONTRACT

ON

SETTING UP AN ANIMAL HUSBANDRY CENTRE
======================================

Chinese Party :

Address :

Legal Representative :

Title :

Address :

Foreign Party :

Address :

Legal Representative :

Title :

Address :

Date of Signing :

Date of Enforcement :

Duration :

Expiration Date :

Date of Renewal :

Language :

Laws of Interpretation :

PREMIER

By reference to the Seventh five-year Plan of the People's Republic of China for Economic and Social Development 1986-1990, it is learnt that China is going to promote the all-round development of the rural economy. In Chapter 7, Agriculture, the Plan states that :

"The following changes in the structure of rural production are anticipated by 1990 :-

- - - of total agricultural output value (not counting products of village industries), the proportion contributed by crop farming will drop from 66 per cent in 1985 to 62 per cent, while that contributed by forestry, animal husbandry, aquatic and sideline production will rise from 34 per cent to 38 per cent. . ''

Moreover, in the same Chapter, Clause 3 Animal Husbandry stipulates that :

"In 1990 target for the output of major animal products are as follows:-
meat: 22.75 million tons, and increase of 19.7 per cent over 1985.

236

milk: 6.25 million tons, a 2.1-fold increase over 1985.

eggs: 8.75 million tons, an increase of 65 per cent over 1985.

In developing animal husbandry, we shall place equal emphasis on farming and pastoral areas and encourage peasants and specialized households to breed livestock supplemented by the state and collectives in the endeavour as animal husbandry increases, we shall focus on improving breeds to increase their marketability. An animal husbandry network will be gradually established on the outskirts of large and medium-sized cities, combining stock breeding, fodder production, livestock raising, processing of animal products and consultant services. We shall promote the development of pastures and make better use of the grassy hills and slopes in south China.

In view of the systematic planning of the Chinese Government in husbandry as stated above, both parties have negotiated with each other on the possibility of setting up an Animal Husbandry Centre in China since 1984. After more than a year of negotiation, both parties have agreed to co-operate with each other as follows :-

Chapter 1 :   Definitions

1.1   Chinese Party means :

1.2   Foreign Party means :

1.3   The Joint Venture proposed is :
(hereinafter referred to as ''the JV'')

1.4   The JV is located in :

1.5   Husbandry means :

1.6   China means the Mainland China excluding Hong Kong, Macau and Taiwan.

(Remarks: It depends on the intention of both parties as it is a very sensitive issue).

Chapter 2 :   Background Data of Both Parties

2.1   Chinese Party :

(1) Date of Formation : _____

(2) Brief history of development :
a/.
b/.
c/.

(3) Nature of business : _____
a/.
b/.
c /.

(4) Products (this list should be exhaustive - - - Author):

a/.
b/.
c/.
d/.
e/.
(5) Production capacity (supported by Auditor's report - - Author):
    a/. per day _____
    b/. per month _____
    c/. per year _____
    d/. forecast (supported by a feasibility report - - - Author)
      (Remark : the feasibility report may be included as part of this
                contract as Annex 1 - - Author)
(6) Addresses of Chinese Party's other operations :
    a/.
    b/.
    c/.
    d/.
    e/.
(7) The province where JV is located :

    a/. General investment atmosphere of this province :
        (i)
        (ii)
        (iii)
        (iv)
        (v)
        (vi)

    b/. Rules and regulation where are related to the operation of JV in
       the province :
        (i)
        (ii)
        (iii)
        (iv)
        (v)
        (vi)
        (vii)

    (Remarks : Details of each rule and regulation should be included
              as part of this contract as Annex 2 - - - Author)
(8) Parent company of Chinese Party :
    a/.
(9) Address of parent company :
    a/.
(10) Administrative headquarters of Chinese Party are
    a/.

2.2 Foreign Party :
    (1) Date of Formation : _____
    (2) Brief history of development :
        a/.
        b/
        c/.
    (3) Nature of business :
        a/.
        b/.
        c/.
        d/.
        e/.
    (4) Products :
        a/.
        b/.
        c/.
        d/.
        e/.
        f/.
        g/.
        h/.
    (5) Production capacity (supported by Auditor's report - - Author) :
        a/. per day _____
        b/. per month _____
        c/. per year _____
        d/. forecast (support by a feasibility report - Author)
            (i)
            (ii)
            (iii)
            (iv)
            (v)
            (vi)
            (vii)
      (Remark : The feasibility report may be included as part of this
                contract as Annex 1 - - Author)
    (6) Address of Foreign Party's Other operations :
        a/.
        b/.
        c/.
        d/.
        e/.
        f/.
    (7) Foreign Party's Executive Offices are at :
        a/.

b/.

c/.

(8) Foreign Party's Administrative Offices are at :

a/.

b/.

c/.

Chapter 3 : Joint Venture

3.1 Form of the Joint Venture (JV)

The proposed JV is an equity Joint Venture with limited liability. The JV bears no liability for obligations of the JV beyond its obligations to contribute to registered capital pursuant to the contract.

3.2 Term of the Joint Venture

The term of the JV is 30 years investments. However, since this JV will be up to the required standard of :

"large amounts of investment, long construction period and low interest rates on funds"

as stipulated in :

"Amendment to Article 100 of the Regulations for the Implementation of the Law of the PRC on Joint Ventures Using Chinese and Foreign Investment" issued by the State Council on January 15, 1986.

The JV may, prior to the expiration of the term, be extended to another 20 years upon the special approval of the State Council.

(Remarks : This Amendment may be attached as Annex 3 of this contract - - - Author)

3.3 Estimate of Total Investment

The total amount of investment of the JV is RMB _____ yuen, or other currency equivalent to the same amount of RMB yuen.

(1) Chinese Party's portion

a/. in kind in the following manners :

(i) Site for the JV which is equivalent to the value of RMB _____ yuen.

(ii) Building for the JV which is equivalent to the value of RMB _____ yuen.

(iii) Supply of facilities which is equivalent to the value of RMB _____ yuen.

(iv) Amount of stock which will be used solely by the JV.

b/. in cash, which will be remaining amount of Chinese Party's investment portion after deduction of its contribution in kind as stipulated in (i) to (iv) above.

(2) Foreign Party's portion:

a/. in kind in the following manners :

(i) new imported equipment which is equivalent to the value of

RMB _____ yuen.

(ii) know-how which is equivalent to the value of RMB ____ yuen.

(iii) installation and supervision which are equivalent to the value of RMB _____ yuen.

(iv) training which is equivalent to the value of RMB _____ yuen.

b/. in cash, which will be the remaining amount of Foreign Party's investment portion after deduction of its contribution in kind as stipulated in (i) to (iv) above.

Chapter 4 : Constitution and Payment of Share Capital

4.1 Number of shares

As contemplated under the Letter of Intent signed between the Chinese Party and the Foreign Party on December 31, 1984, the shareholding in the JV shall remain on a 50% Chinese Party / 50% Foreign Party contribution basis.

In this aspect, shares allotted and subscribed for are as follows :-

(1) Chinese Party
   Number of Shares : _____
(2) Foreign Party
   Number of Shares : _____

4.2 Chinese Party's Allotment

Chinese Party shall receive its allotment of capital in the JV fully paid up in return for its contribution to the JV comprising its commitment to supply things in kind as stipulated in Clause 3.3 (1) (a) (i) to (v) above.

4.3 Foreign Party's Allotment

Foreign Party shall receive its allotment of capital in the JV fully paid up in return for its contribution to the JV comprising its commitment to supply things in kind as stipulated in Clause 3.3 (2) (a) (i) to (v) above.

4.4 Share Certificate

A share certificate evidencing that the shares have been allotted fully paid shall be issued immediately upon allotment of each party.

Chapter 5 : Market for the JV Products

5.1 Population in China

It is necessary to make a detailed research on the population of China in each province, especially, when the products are permitted to sell in the domestic market - - - Author).

5.2 Breakdown of population in those provinces where the products are permitted to sell there .

This breakdown will include age group, sex, occupation - - - Author.

5.3   Consumption of the proposed JV products in China

Again, the clause is only relevant for those products which are permitted for domestic sale. The study of consumption will be more accurate if it can be sub-divided into :

(1)   Age group

(2)   Sex

(3)   Seasonal (if applicable - - Author)

5.4   Existing Domestic Market for Products Similar to the JV Product

The General Statistical Bureau of China has a detailed record of products sold each month in China, it is very useful for preparing the analysis - - - Author.

5.5   Estimate of Demand in the Domestic Market

For most of the Joint Venture signed in China since 1979, it is the foreign investors' practice to forecast production and demand at least for the first 5 years. However, some objective factors may happen and interrupt the production rate or market demand. It is, therefore, advisable to make an annual adjustment after the operation of the JV - - - Author.

5.6   Overseas Market

The Clauses and contents there in will be similar to those mentioned in Clause 5.1 to 5.5 above. Moreover, it is very common for the foreign investors to take care of the overseas markets - - - Author.

5.7   Competitors

Competitors can be classified as local and overseas competitors, a detailed list of these competitors including their production capacity and marketing strategy - - - Author.

5.8   Marketing Strategy

Marketing Strategy can be divided into domestic market and that of the overseas, in which, a feasibility study of the JV's production capacity as well as sales and distribution should be dealt with jointly - - - Author.

Chapter 6 :   Technical Analysis of the J.V.

6.1   Scope

The following technical analysis is made to show how the JV envisages to operate efficiently with automation and know-how imported by the Foreign Party.

6.2   Presentation

The presentation of this project report covers the supply of all machinery technical installations of the collecting stations and the factory, including detailed design and planning, supervision of installation and the final operations of the J.V.

6.3 Categories of Products

The JV is design to produce

(1)

(2)

(3)

(Remarks : Exhaustive list of products to be produced by the JV - - - Author)

6.4 Capacities of the J.V.

The main capacities of the J.V. are

(1)

(2)

(3)

(Remarks : Exhaustive list of JV's capacities should be stipulated in this Clause - - - Author)

6.5 Farm workers related to the J.V.

In order to assist the farmers in animal husbandry and farm hygiene the JV recommends that four to five field officers be employed to establish a program and speak with the farmers to help them as assess and select superior animals from which to breed the next generation, and improve in :-

(1) Comfort and health of the animal.

(2) Hygienic conditions of the production.

(3) Cleanliness of the animal.

(4) Cleanliness of the farmer himself in relation to his work.

(5) Efficient cleaning of equipment and other utensils.

6.6 Meat Collecting Stations

The proposed equipment in each meat collecting station is selected and arranged so as to reduce the manual task and improve the sanitary practice of meat handling as well as the efficiency of meat receiving and meat despatch.

(1) The incoming meat is tested and weighed.

(2) The meat is cleaned with ground water.

(3) The meat is dispatched for storage.

6.7 Building of Meat Processing Stations

The JV recommends that each collecting station building is being upgraded from the standpoint of compliance with Good Manufacturing Practices.

(1) Floors and Drains - The floors are to be re-surfaced where concrete is damaged or slope to the external drainage is not properly pitched or non-existing. All drainage must lead to a septic tank.

(2) Walls and Ceilings - smooth, inpermeable light coloured interior surfaces which can be readily cleaned is

essential. All ceilings must be lined.

(3) Windows - Windows must be re-constructed so that they are tight fitting, and flyscreens over openings of windows will be necessary.

(4) Doors - The doors must be re-constructed if necessary to give a tight fit and be properly screened.

(5) Lighting & Ventilation - Sufficient natural and/or artificial light must be provided. Ventilation must be provided to prevent undue condensation.

(6) Personal Hygiene - Toilets and hand washing facilities must be installed in all stations. Clean uniforms and shoes are essential.

6.8 Meat Collecting Truck

The JV proposal is to import 20 trucks with build-in stainless steel tanks for collecting meat.

(1) The collecting tanks are to be insulated (80mm) stainless steel with a capacity of 2 metric tons each.

6.9 Transport Frequency and Route

(1) It is estimated that 16 road trucks will be required to collect the meat based on a mounted truck capacity of 2 metric tons each and two collection per day to start with.

(2) 4 trucks will be used for stand-by and/or alternative when one of the 16 tankers are under general maintenance.

6.10 Meat Collection Schedule

(1) Route

(2) Collection Stations

(3) Maximum loading per day each truck

(4) Maximum traffic time per trip

Chapter 7 : Responsibilities of both parties to the JV

7.1 Responsibilities of Party A

"In this Clause, it is necessary to put down details concerning setting up of the JV, its operation and matters related to the operation. e.g.

(1) Registration of business licence

(2) Application for use of site

(3) Construction of factory

(4) Setting up infrastructure

(5) Import duties

(6) Manpower recruitment

(7) Procedures for expatriates coming to China

- - - Author."

7.2   Responsibilities of Party B
''Party B's responsibilities will usually include :
(1) Provision of equipment
(2) Provision know-how (a separate Chapter should be devoted to discussion of know-how and technology-transfer)
(3) Provision of training programmes
(may set up a Chapter for separate discussion)
- - - Author.''

Chapter 8 and the remaining Chapters may be arranged as follows :
Chapter 8 : Know-how and Technology Transfer
Chapter 9 : Patent Protection
Chapter 10 : Training Programme
Chapter 11 : Administration of the JV and Labour Policies
Chapter 12 : Procurement of Equipment
Chapter 13 : Transition Period Prior to the Operation of JV
Chapter 14 : Financial Arrangement
Chapter 15 : Taxation and Customs Duties
Chapter 16 : Auditing of Accounts
Chapter 17 : Duration of the JV
Chapter 18 : Disposal of Assets after Expiration
Chapter 19 : Bankruptcy Provision
Chapter 20 : Insurance
Chapter 21 : Amendment of the JV and Related matters
Chapter 22 : Liabilities for Breach of Contract
Chapter 23 : Force Majeure
Chapter 24 : Miscellaneous

(Details of the above Chapters can be found from other similar clauses in the other parts of this books. In drafting the details of the clauses, special attention should be paid to the available laws governing the particular topic. e.g. in drafter Clauses of Technology Transfer, readers are advised to refer to the   :
*   ''Interim Provisions of the State Council on Technology Transfer, promulgated by the State Council on January 10, 1985.
and
*   ''Regulations of the People's Republic of China on Technology Import Contract Administration'', promulgated by the State Council on May 24, 1985.
- - - - - - Author'')

Joint Venture Agreement by using

Chinese and Foreign Investments

on

setting up ABC Textile Production Plant
=========================

Agreement Code : _____

Date of Signing :

Date of Execution :

Parties to this Agreement

Party A :

_____

_____

Party B :

_____

_____

Registered Office :

_____

Place of Operation :

_____

Expiry Date : _____

Date for discussing renewal of this Agreement

_____

Renewal Date (if applicable) : _____

Name of Chinese Party
Address
(hereinafter referred to as ''Party A'')
and
Name of Foreign Party
Address
(hereinafter referred to as ''Party B'')

have discussed with each other on several official occasions and have reached
mutual understanding to sign this agreement on co-operation for the establishment of a Joint Venture Corporation registered in the People's Republic of

China (PRC) with limited liability called :
Name of the Plant
(hereinafter referred to as the ''Plant'')

Temporary office of the Plant in the PRC
Proposed site of the Plant in the PRC

Article 1 : Interpretations of Terms

1.1 Profit shall mean : _____
1.2 Revenue shall mean : _____
1.3 Consulting fee shall mean : _____
1.4 Expenses shall mean : _____
1.5 Documentation shall mean : _____
1.6 China shall mean : _____
1.7 Installation shall mean : _____
1.8 Personnel shall mean : _____
  * (Remarks: it is advisable to have a comprehensive list of terms used
       in the agreement - - - Author)

Article 2 : Objectives

2.1 The Plant shall combine the laser beam drawing technology and devices provided by Party B and supportive technique and craftsmanship of Party A in order to do further researches and develop different technique of dyeing methods, laser weaving skill and related technology needed in domestic and overseas markets. With the findings of these researches and/or studies, we can prove to the majority users in Chinese textile industry that the Plant is the model of its kind for China's Four Modernizations.

2.2 Have the maximum number of textile mill operational personnel in China to realize the benefits of following the combine devices currently in use by our Plant. Subsequently, they can take advantage of sharing the achievements of our Plant.

2.3 Display and present the up-to-date weaving technology and products of Party B to Chinese end users and textile mills, and provide laser printing services on garments to end users, for a fee, with a view of promoting the development of laser weaving and knitting technology in China. Provide maximum exposure of the products of the Plant to textile mills in China who are potential users of the products and services of the Plant and of Party B's products.

2.4 Provide installation, maintenance and other technical services for the equipment of the Plant.

2.5 Provide consultation and technical training to users and potential users of the equipment and other services at the Plant.

2.6 Establish a Plant that will be a leader in the practice of laser weaving and knitting technology in China with a research laboratory.

2.7 Provide a device to gather and analyze data regarding needs of the China market and applications requirements of textile industry in China.

Article 3 : Size of the Plant

3.1 The Plant shall have a permanent premises granted by the Chinese Government with a long term leasehold of not less than Thirty (30) years.

3.2 The Plant shall have an office immediately next to the factory and research laboratory. The floor areas of them are as follows:

Office ; _____

Factory ; _____

Research laboratory ; _____

Article 4 : Employees

4.1 The Plant shall have One Thousand (1000) staff of which Eight Hundred (800) full-time staff.

4.2 Among these 800 full time staff, there will be

300 technicians
300 workers
100 data analysts and researchers
 50 clerical staff
 30 scientists
 20 managerial staff

4.3 Most of the employees shall be recruited in China, however the managerial level shall maintain a ratio of 1 local employee to 1 expatriate.

Article 5 : Equipment of the Plant

5.1 The Plant shall have the equipment necessary to meet the objectives as stipulated in Article 2 above including but not limited to :

a : _____

b : _____

c : _____

d : _____

e : _____

f : _____

g : _____

h : _____

i : _____
j : _____
k : _____
l : _____
m : _____
n : _____
o : _____
p : _____
q : _____
r : _____
s : _____
t : _____

Article 6 : Present Targets

6.1 The development of advanced weaving technology in order to meet current international standard like :
    a. _____
    b. _____

6.2 Carrying out the studies of laser weaving technology by merging it with traditional Chinese craftsmanship like :
    a. _____
    b. _____
    c. _____

6.3 Development of the Chinese knitting and engraving technique and application technology for :
    a. _____
    b. _____

6.4 Laboratory analyst services for other textile mills.

6.5 Conduct or participate in exhibitions, conference, and seminars on new textile products and new technology.

6.6 Rendering equiry, repair, maintenance and training services.

6.7 Entering into separate agreements with textile mills on the economic terms of maintenance, installation and training programme.

Article 7 : Intermediate Developments

7.1 Production of a set of software and hardware which will fulfill a very broad range of textile weaving mechanism and system.

7.2 Application of high speed laser weaving technique which will include the following technique currently used by Party B :
    a. _____

b. _____

c. _____

7.3 Redevelopment of the existing machinery currently used by Party A and upgrade them to reach the following standard :

    a. _____

    b. _____

    c. _____

7.4 Party A will provide a team of designers who are experts in traditional Chinese handicrafts to satisfy the requirements for superb garment products. The categories are as follows :-

    a. _____

    b. _____

    c. _____

    d. _____

    e. _____

7.5 The finished products as stipulated in clause 7.4 above will be sold in China and to other overseas markets like, U.S.A., U.K., France, Federal Republic of Germany, Italy, Spain, Switzerland and Japan.

7.6 Analysis of the present marketing strategy by carrying out several feasibility studies both in China and the overseas. As a result, the findings of the said studies will be used as reference in promoting the products.

7.7 Party B may from time to time, consult Party A about the feedback of customers in China, so as to adjust the manufacturing and promoting programme.

7.8 Party A may, with the consent of Party B, invite experts from other textile mills in China, to give second opinion on the finished products made by the Plant.

7.9 Both Parties have to share opinions on the progress of these intermediate developments and put these opinions in writing.

Article 8 : <u>Long Term Developments</u>

8.1 The development of China's first complete automatic laser weaving and knitting system with support of Party B's software and hardware.

8.2 Joint Venture production of a new textile products to meet the need of international markets in the 90's. These products will include :

    a. JV code   101 : _____

    b. JV code   201 : _____

    c. JV code   301 : _____

    d. JV code   717 : _____

    e. JV code 8621 : _____

    f. JV code 8622 : _____

    g. JV code   901 : _____

h. JV code   9011 : _____

8.3 A textile product quality control centre with laboratory not only serving the Joint Venture but other textile mills in China.

8.4 Running exhibitions of the products made by the Joint Venture in the overseas markets like ;
                    a. Paris
                    b. New York
                    c. Tokyo
                    d. Milano

8.5 Holding scheduled seminars for the heads of other textile mills in China.

8.6 Holding irregular seminars for personnel of the textile industry all over the world. These seminars will be held at :
                    a. Paris
                    b. Milano
                    c. Geneve
                    d. Madrid
                    e. New York
                    f. Tokyo

8.7 Expansion of the Joint Venture by setting up a branch manufacturing plant in the north-western part of China, where the supply of raw materials for textile industry is plentiful.

8.8 Setting up overseas representative offices in the following cities :

                    a. London
                    b. Paris
                    c. Milano
                    d. New York
                    e. Tokyo
                    f. Sidney   Sydney
                    g. Hong Kong

Article 9 : Contributions of Both Parties

9.1 The Plant shall carry out operatons on a self-supporting basis. Any profit from the operation of the Plant will be used to support the said developments.

9.2 Party A shall provide without compensation to the Plant air-conditioned premises, reasonable facilities, water supply, electricity, furnishings and all other necessary infrastructure.

9.3 Party A shall provide without compensation, to the Plant salary for all full-time staff members employed locally.

9.4 Party A shall provide without compensation to the Plant the existing Chinese handicraft technology needed for the development work mentioned in above Clauses.

9.5 Before setting up and at the initial stage of operation Party A shall provide in cash the amount which the Plant is short of due to insufficient bussiness up to a maximum amount of 11,800,000 (RMB) yuan. If at any time during its operatons the Plant requires additional funds, the Plant will obtain a loan from Party A or its banker to provide all necessary funds.

9.6 Party B shall provide without compensation to the Plant all the equipment, software and documents mentioned in above Clauses. Party B shall provide furnishing of the Plant that are not available in China and are determined by both Party A and Party B to be required.

9.7 Party B shall provide without compensation training programmes for Party A's personnel.

9.8 The equipment to be provided by Party B without compensation shall include all components of the machines and spare parts and consumables to ensure that the equipment of the Plant becomes operational.

9.9 The Plant shall be responsible to purchase all spare parts, consumable and supplies in accordance with instructions given by Party A and Party B.

Article 10 : Organizational Structure of the Plant

10.1 Parties A and B shall form a Eight (8) member Board of Directors, of which Four (4) members shall be appointed by Party A and Four (4) members shall be appointed by Party B. The Chairman of the Board of Directors shall be nominated by Party A, and its Vice-Chairman shall be nominated by Party B.

10.2 The Board of Directors shall make decisions on the management of business co-operation and other important issue of the Plant. The Board of Directors shall meet at least once every six (6) months. The time and place of the meetings shall be decided through exchange of telexes. The Board of Directors will attempt to reach consensus and at least a two-thirds majority will be required for all decisions.

10.3 The Board of Directors shall discuss and appoint the Executive Director of the Plant. The Executive Director shall be a representative of both parties. The Executive Director shall take up overall responsibility for the research and development and other work of the Plant, and shall regularly report his work to the Board of Directors in writing.

10.4 The role and duties of each staff are as follows :
    a. _____
    b. _____
    c. _____
    d. _____
    *(Remarks: an organization chart shall be provided for easy reference, Author)

10.5 A Supervisory Council shall be established to provide advice and overall direction to the research and development activities of the Plant and any additional research and development activities that may be supported through profits of the Plant. The Supervisory Council should consist of technical experts from Chinese institutions related for textile industry and laser physics and laser experts from Party B and should be responsible for their own expenses.

The number of members, mode of operation and other details of the Supervisory Council, will be decided later based upon friendly discussions between the Parties.

10.6 The Chinese Institutions represented could include but not necessarily be limited to :
(a)   Chinese Academy of Science
(b)   Textile Research Institute, China.
(c)   Department of Laser Physics, Gilin University.
(d)   Chinese University of Technology
(e)   Beijing University
(f)   Dr. Sun Yet Sun University
(g)   Ministry of Textile Industry
(h)   Computer System Engineering Research Institute
(i)   All China Computer Center

Laser experts from Party B will be invited by Party B from various overseas institutions like :
(a)   Cambridge University
(b)   University of Manchester
(c)   London University
(d)   Yale University
(e)   Stanford University
(f)   Oxford University
(g)   Princeton University
(h)   University of British Columbia
(i)   Tokyo University

Article 11 :   Interests and Rights

11.1 Each Party shall retain its legal title to all the assets it provides to the Plant.

11.2 All results in the form of laser weaving products developed with the support of the Plant shall be jointly owned by Party A and Party B. Party A shall take all necessary action to record and protect joint ownership rights in China in accordance with applicable trademark and patent laws of China (also copyrights laws when they are promulgated). Party B shall protect ownership outside China by appropriate action when deem commercially prudent. The Parties agree to co-operate to prosecute and stop infringement of Products by third Parties. When

253

Products or modified Products belonging to either Party A or Party B is used by the other Party or third parties, standard Products License Agreements will be executed to protect this Products. Such license agreement shall in no way restrict the use of Products belonging to Party A or Party B by the Plant for development purposes.

11.3 Party A grants to Party B the exclusive right to commercial marketing throughout the world for laser weaving products and other products that may be result of research and development tasks of the Plant. In compensation for the granting of this right, Party B will pay to Party A a license fee equal to three (3) percent of its gross revenue attributable to sale of such product or other products. In addition, Party B will pay a fee of one (1) percent on the same basis to the Plant.

11.4 Additional rights for marketing products of the Plant may be granted by the Board of Directors with terms and conditions to be determined by the Board of Directors. Provided however, the commercial marketing by the Plant shall be for use on Party B's equipment and any commercial marketing for use on Party B's equipment shall be made only with the written consent of Party B.

11.5 The rights to commercial marketing granted by the Party A to Party B in no way restricts the access or use of the products by the Plant or Party A. Party A agrees that such use is to be internal to Party A's activities for research and development purposes. Party B shall provide to Party A the calculation of the license fee and Party A shall have the right to examine the evidence of such calculation.

11.6 In view of the fact that co-operative technical development is the main purpose of the Plant, profits generated form the operation of the Plant, after payment of taxes in accordance with the applicable laws of the People's Republic of China, shall be allocated to the development and operation funds.

11.7 Party A shall provide quarterly financial information relating to the operations of the Plant to Party B on a timely basis and Party B shall have the right to perform or appoint its agents or representatives who are qualified accountants with international recognition to perform audits of the books and records of the Plant.

Article 12 : Selection and Training of Personnel

12.1 Party A shall select and provide competent research and management personnel to the Plant. Party A shall assure that Plant personnel selected for training by Party B shall remain assigned to the Plant. Party A shall use its best efforts to ensure that the personnel sent by him shall be competent and helpful with all the necessary knowledge and experience related to the responsibilities undertaken. Only personnel formally assigned to full time, long term employment at the Plant for the task subject to the training shall be selected and sent by Party A and Party A and B shall use their best efforts to keep turnover of trained personnel to an absolute minimum within a reasonable period of time.

12.2 The Plant shall send a total of twelve (12) persons to Party B to receive technical training program, these persons shall consist of the following :
- One (1) Operation Manager Director
- Five (5) System Analysts
- Four (4) Laser Engineers
- One (1) Customer Services Engineer
- One (1) Field Engineer

12.3 Party B shall provided training free of charge for Twelve (12) Plant staff described above. A fee may be charged for other training as may requested by the Plant. Party A shall bear living and transportation costs associated with the said training.

12.4 The training programme shall begin as soon as possible upon the execution of the this Agreement, and shall completed before the start-up of operation of the Plant, the total training period is not expected to exceed Twelve (12) months.

12.5 Before the personnel of the Plant leave for the place of Party B for the training programme, Party B shall group together such personnel and give them an English language proficiency course to satisfy the needs of the work of the Plant.

12.6 The Parties shall determine the contents of the training programme.

12.7 Party B shall assist Party A's personnel in obtaining entry visas from relevant government authorities.

12.8 Training of the users of Party B's products shall be provided by the Plant and conducted by the personnel of the Plant.

12.9 The requirements and responsibilities of the staff of the Plant shall be clearly defined in accordance with their rank as stipulated in Article 13.

12.1 Party A shall be responsible for translation into Chinese all training and other documents required for effective operation of the Plant and the Plant shall be responsible for the cost of translation.

Article 13 :   Ranking and Duties of the Staff

13.1 (1) Executive Director
Duties : a. _____
b. _____
(Remarks : to be specified and tailor-made at your own demand - - - - Author)

(2) Operation Manager
Duties : (Ditto)

(3) System Analysts
Duties : (Ditto)

(4) Laser Engineers
Duties : (Ditto)
(5) System Design Engineers
Duties : (Ditto)
(6) Customer Services Engineers
Duties : (Ditto)
(7) Field Engineers
Duties : (Ditto)
(8) Technicians (system)
Duties : (Ditto)
(9) Technicians (operation)
Duties : (Ditto)
(10)Technicians (field)
Duties : (Ditto)

13.2 (1) Administrative Office
Duties : (Ditto)
(2) Clerical Officer
Duties : (Ditto)
(3) Laser Engineers
Duties : (Ditto)
(4) System Design Engineers
Duties : (Ditto)
(5) Customer Services Engineers
Duties : (Ditto)
(6) Technicians (system)
Duties : (Ditto)
(7) Technicians (operation)
Duties : (Ditto)

13.3 Field Staff
(1) Plant Supervisors
Duties : (Ditto)
(2) Field Engineers
Duties : (Ditto)
(3) Technicians (field)
Duties : (Ditto)
(4) Plant Worker
Duties : (Ditto)
(5) Minor Staff
(Ranks and duties, to be decided in accordance with the needs of
the Plant - - - - Author)

13.4 Marketing Staff
(1) Marketing Executive
Duties : (Ditto)

13.5 Administrative Office

(1) Administrative Officer
    Duties : (Ditto)
(2) Clerical Officer
    Duties : (Ditto)

Article 14 : Shipping

14.1 Documentation
Party B shall prepare and provide a list of the documentation delivered by courier to Party A. Party B shall also send by courier to Party A an airway bill in triplicate giving details of the documents and marked with the Agreement number, flight number, flight date, number of cases, gross weights and dimension.

14.2 Equipment
Party B shall prepare a detailed list of equipment before shipping all the equipment to be provided by Party B. Within thirty-six (36) hours of loading the systems, equipment on vessel or airplane. Party B shall give notice to Party A by Fax or telex on the description and quantities of the goods to be delivered, the numbers of packages, value, flight no./ship's name and date of shipment.
After the shipment of the above-mentioned goods, Party B shall hand over three copies of clear and accurate delivery invoice and packing list to Party A, and send another three copies by airmail within three (3) working days of the shipment of the goods, one (1) of the copies to be mailed to Party A and the other two (2) copies airmailed to China National Foreign Trade Transportation Corporation (CCTCE) at the port of destination. The date of shipment must be the same as the date of the delivery order.

14.3 Supportive equipment
Party B shall deliver the supportive equipment and a list and description of the supportive equipment to Party A.

14.4 Import License
Party A shall be responsible for all import licenses and related documentation.

Article 15 : Packing and Marking

15.1 All equipment shipped by Party B shall be properly packed in strong cases, suitable for long-distance land, air and sea transportation and multiple handling and loading/unloading operations, and shall be protected with measures against shock, moisture, rust, rain and corrosion, to ensure that all goods shall safely arrive at the place of installation.

15.2 On the four sides of each packing case, Party B shall mark the following items using indelible paint:-

Agreement No.:
Shipping Marks:
Case No./No. of units contained within:
Code of Consignee: Name of Party A
Port of Destination: Airport (by air), Whampoa (by ship), Shanghai
Railway Station (by train) Shanghai, People's
Republic of China.
Gross Weight: KG

Party B shall mark in English words like "Fragile", "Handle with Care", "Right Side Up" and "Protect from Moisture", and the packing cases shall have prominently displayed international transportation symbols such as point of hooking. Party A shall provide a template to Party B in Chinese writing which states the same warnings and precautions. Pieces of equipment disassemmbled for shipment shall be marked with symbols in accordance with the assembly drawings inserted into the cases.

15.3 All packs of documentation delivered by Party B shall be fit for long-distance air transportation and multiple handling and loading/unloading operations, and shall be moisture-proof measures. On all four sides of the cases, the following items shall be marked with indelible paint:-
Agreement No.:
Shipping Marks:
Case No./No. of units contained within:
Code of Consignee: Name of Party A
Port of Destination: Airport (by air), Whampoa (by ship), Shanghai
Railway Station (by train) Shanghai, People's
Republic of China.
Gross Weight: KG

Enclosed in each case shall be three (3) copies of packing list giving the contents and number of copies of the documents and there will be one (1) copy of airway bill and one copy of invoice.

All documents and letters sent by airmail shall be marked with the words "Commercial Documents" and shall be addressed to Party A.

Article 16 : Guarantee

16.1 Each Party guarantees that it shall not use the other Party's technology in co-operation with any third party that could compete with the said other Party.

16.2 Party A guarantees that it shall not enter into co-operation with other parties in the field of electronic printing without obtaining the consent of Party B.

16.3 Party B guarantees that it shall not enter into co-operation with other Chinese entities in China without obtaining the consent of Party A.

Article 17 : Installation

17.1 Party B will install and test all equipment and systems it supplies to assure normal operation.

17.2 Party B undertakes to replace those defective equipment and systems in all time.

Article 18 : Taxation

18.1 All taxes, duties and charges related to the implementation of this Agreement after the Plant starts operation, imposed on the Plant by the Government of the People's Republic of China in accordance with current tax laws, shall be paid by the Plant.

18.2 All taxes, duties and charges related to the implementation of this Agreement before the Plant starts business and imposed on the Plant by the Government of the People's Republic of China in accordance with applicable current laws shall be paid by Party A. Since the equipment is being provided to the Plant by Party B, without compensation, and is to be used to develop technique to enable progress of laser weaving applications in China, Party A will endeavour to find means to enter the equipment into China duty and tax free. Party A will be responsible to pay any taxes or duties that cannot be relieved and they will deem to be the cost of the Plant.

18.3 All taxes, duties and charges related to the implementation of this Agreement and imposed outside the People's Republic of China shall be paid by Party B and they will deem to be the cost of the Plant.

Article 19 : Confidentiality

19.1 The Parties will periodically communicate to each other business and technical information including but not limited to craftsmanship and designs. All such information shall be kept strictly confidential, whether or not so identified, and each agrees not to disclose any part thereof to anyone outside of the Plant without the prior written consent of the other and shall limit its disclosure within the Plant to those persons having a need to know for the purpose of performing this Agreement. These obligations shall not apply to such information where it was in the public domain at the time of disclosure, or entered the public domain subsequently. The foregoing obligations of confidentiality shall continue in full force and effect notwithstanding the termination of this Agreement. The Parties agree that this obligation shall be binding upon the Plant and its employees as well as upon the Parties.

Article 20 : Insurance

20.1 Insurance of all equipment and properties of the Plant shall be taken out with a related insurance company in the People's Republic of China, the premiums to be paid for by the Plant. Insurance will be kept in force at all times during the terms of this Agreement and all extensions thereof. At the end of this Agreement, insurance will be kept in effect during shipment to a Port of Exit from China.

20.2 If Party B requests the subscription of a foreign currency insurance policy, the amount of foreign currency required to pay for the premiums shall be paid by Party B and such payment will deem to be the cost of the Plant.

20.3 Party B will be responsible for insurance of equipment during shipment to a Port of Entry into China.

Article 21 : Force Majeure

21.1 If either Party shall be unable to discharge its obligations hereunder because of war, severe natural calamities such as flooding, fire, snow, earthquake or any other force majeure event to be agreed upon by both Parties, the affected Party shall immediately inform the other Party by fax, telex or cable of the situation of the event which is affecting the implementation of this Agreement, and shall send by registered airmail within seven (7) days a detailed description of the event and a document certifying the degree to which the implementation of this Agreement is affected. The above-mentioned certifying document shall be issued by the Ministry of Textile Industry of the People's Republic of China, if it is sent by Party A, or issued by the appropriate legal authority of Party B's Government, if it is sent by Party B.

21.2 If the force majeure event continues to exert influence for a period shorter than ninety (90) days, the duration of this Agreement shall be extended for a period equivalent to duration of influence of event, and neither Party shall seek damage claims for any losses incurred on it in relation to the event during the said period. If the influence of the force majeure event continues for a period longer than ninety (90) days, the Parties shall as soon as possible consult amicably on matters concerning the implementation of this Agreement in order to resolve the problems.

Article 22 : Arbitration

22.1 The Parties shall try to resolve any dispute arising from the implementation of this Agreement through friendly consultation of the Board of Directors. In case that no settlement can be reached, such disputes shall be submitted to the Arbitration Institute in Stockholm, Sweden, for arbitration in accordance the Arbitration Rules of the Institute. The award of the Arbitration Institute shall be final and be obeyed by both Parties.

All arbitration costs shall be borne by the losing Party.

(Remarks : Chinese Party usually favours arbitration executed by China Council for the Promotion of International Trade - - - Author).

22.2 During the period of arbitration, each Party shall continue to fulfil its obligations hereunder with the exception of the obligation provided for in the clause related to the arbitration.

22.3 Both parties agree not to bring the case to court if they first decided it to be done by Arbitration.

Article 23 : Validation of this Agreement

23.1 This Agreement shall become effective upon signing by the representatives of both Parties and approval by the Bank of China for release of Foreign currency and the Government of the People's Republic of China.

Article 24 : Language

24.1 This Agreement is written in Chinese and English. Both versions shall be signed and shall have equal legal validity.

Article 25 : Duration

25.1 This Agreement shall continue in force for a duration of ten (10) years. Although it is the intent of both Parties that this Agreement should lead to long term co-operation of mutual benefit, it is recognized that unforeseen circumstances may change the mutual benefit. Therefore, either Party may terminate this Agreement upon six (6) months prior notification in writing and serve onto the attention of other party by registered mail to the other party's latest known address. If either Party wishes to extend the Agreement, a proposal for such extensiion shall be submitted to the Board of Directors, and after approval by the Board of Directors shall be submitted for approval to the appropriate authorities of the People's Republic of China at least six (6) months prior the expiration of the current Agreement.

25.2 Upon the signing of this Agreement, all correspondence, fax and telex messages, cables, oral or written agreements and other documents inconsistent with this Agreement between the parties shall be void.

25.3 The Parties agree that each party shall refrain from incriminating the other Party for the death, injury or crippling of any of its personnel during his stay at the place of the other Party. However, each Party shall take appropriate precautionary measures to prevent any injury, crippling or death or any loss of money or belongings to the personnel of the other Party.

25.4 Although the Parties do not wish the occurence of any of the above-mentioned accidents, neither party shall be liable to the other Party for any consequences related to this Agreement or resulting from a civil infringement act including a negligence act. The Plant shall be a limited liability co-operative Joint Venture and neither Party shall be liable to the Center or Third Party for damages.

Article 26 : Termination

26.1 At the termination of this Agreement for whatever reason, the assets contributed to the Plant shall be returned to the respective Parties. Profit gained by the Plant after initial operation shall be divided between Party A and Party B as mutually agreed, but the profit can be paid only in RMB Yuan, if the Plant has not any foreign exchange. Other assets acquired by the Plant incidental to the operation of the Plant, such as supplies, or equipment and tools, shall be given to Party A, and Party A shall be responsible for the financial loss of the Plant in case it happens.

Article 27 : Supplementary Clauses

27.1 Export Controls. The Parties acknowledge that the export of component parts and equipment to the People's Republic of China and the transfer of technical information by Party B pursuant to this Agreement can be accomplished only in accordance with United States export administration regulations and this Agreement is hereby made expressly subject to such regulations as such may be amended or interpreted from time to time. Party B shall review with Party A any such amendments or interpretations that bear on this Agreement and use their best efforts to reduce any adverse impact that result from the changes.

A B C Textile Production Plant
Articles of Association

Chapter 1 : Legal References

1.1 By virtue of :

   (a) The Laws of the People's Republic of China on Joint Ventures Using Chinese and Foreign Investment (July 1, 1979)

   (b) Implementation Procedures of the Laws of the People's Republic of China on Joint Ventures Using Chinese and Foreign Investment (September 20, 1983)

   (c) Income Tax Laws of the People's Republic of China on Joint Ventures Using Chinese and Foreign Investment (September 10, 1980) and its Amendments (September 2, 1983)

   (d) Implementation Procedures of Income Tax Laws of the People's Republic of China on Joint Ventures Using Chinese and Foreign Investment (December 10, 1980)

   (e) Provisions of the General Customs Office, the Ministry of Finance and the Ministry of Foreign Economics & Trade for the Supervision, Collection or Remission of Customs Duties on Imports and Exports for Joint Ventures Using Chinese and Foreign Investment (April 30, 1984)

   (f) Provisional Regulations of the People's Republic of China on Foreign Exchange Control. (December 18, 1980)

   (g) Implemention Procedures on Foreign Exchange Control concerning Enterprises Using Overseas Chinese Investment, Foreign Investment and Joint Ventures Using Chinese Foreign Investment (August 1, 1983)

   (h) Regulations on the Balance of Income and Expenditure concerning Joint Ventures Using Chinese and Foreign Investment (January 15, 1986)

   (i) Regulatins on Management of Labour Concerning Joint Ventures Using Chinese and Foreign Investment (July 26, 1980)

   (j) Implementation Procedures on Management of Labour Concerning Joint Ventures Using Chinese and Foreign Investment (January 19, 1984)

1.2 Any forthcoming legislation concerning joint ventures promulgated by the Government of the People's Republic of China.

1.3 Pursant to the above clauses, the joint venture shall be governed by the Laws of the People's Republic of China.

Chapter 2 : Name of the Joint Venture

2.1 The name of the Joint Venture shall be presented in both Chinese and English versions,

2.2 Name of the Joint Venture in Chinese :

_____

2.3 Name of the Joint Venture in English :

_____

Chapter 3 : Address of the Joint Venture

3.1 Address in Chinese :

_____

3.2 Address in English :

_____

Chapter 4 : Official Communication of the Joint Venture

4.1 Telephone Number : _____
4.2 Fax Line   : _____
4.3 Telex Number   : _____
4.4 Cable   : _____

Chapter 5 : Name and Legal address of Parties to the Joint Venture

5.1 Party A

    Name of the Party : _____

    Country of Registration : _____

    Legal Address : _____

    Legal Representative (First)

    Name : _____

    Title : _____

    Nationality : _____

    Second Legal Representative (when the first legal representative is absence)

    Name : _____

    Title : _____

    Nationality : _____

5.2 Party B

    Name of the Party : _____

_____

    Country of Registration : _____

    Legal Address : _____

    Legal Representative (First)

    Name : _____

    Title : _____

Nationality : _____
Second Legal Representative (when the first legal representative
is absence)
Name : _____
Title : _____
Nationality : _____

Chapter 6 : <u>Aims of Business</u>

6.1 The aims of the Joint Venture by both Party A and Party B are to combine the pioneering laser weaving technology and equipment provided by party B with Party A's traditional technology, develop textile traditional products suited to China's domestic market and needed by international markets, and show Party B's latest laser and products, so as to accelerate the reform of China's traditional textile industry. These products are competitive in the international market in terms of quality, pricing and other aspects.

Chapter 7 : <u>Scope of Business</u>

7.1 Research and develop various textile spinning technologies needed by domestic and overseas markets, laser system technology, system analysis technology, textile automation technology and the technologies needed for the reform of the traditional textile industry. Sell technology and products developed by the Plant.

7.2 Show and introduce the latest laser weaving technologies and the latest electronic spinning products of Party B to end-users and to overseas textile industry.

7.3 Offer paid services of research and analysis to customers.

7.4 Offer consulting and technical training to textile mills users who ask for the Plant's service.

7.5 Determine users' opinions and demands, conduct marketing analysis, so as to constantly improve and renew products and satisfy market demands.

Chapter 8 : <u>Saleable Products of the Plant</u>

8.1 Products offered for sale in China
(1). Model CN 101 : _____
(2). Model CN 102 : _____
(3). Model CN 103 : _____
(4). Model CN 104 : _____
(5). Model CN 105 : _____
(6). Model CN 106 : _____
(7). Model CN 107 : _____

(8). Model CN 108 : _____
(9). Model CN 109 : _____
(10). Model CN 110 : _____

8.2 Products offered for sale to the overseas.

(1). Model F201 : _____
(2). Model F202 : _____
(3). Model F203 : _____
(4). Model F204 : _____
(5). Model F205 : _____
(6). Model F206 : _____
(7). Model F207 : _____
(8). Model F208 : _____
(9). Model F209 : _____
(10). Model F 210 : _____
(11). Model F 310 : _____
(12). Model F 311 : _____
(13). Model F412 : _____
(14). Model F512 : _____
(15). Model F612 : _____
(16). Model F712 : _____
(17). Model F812 : _____
(18). Model F912 : _____

8.3 Proposed new products

1. JV Code 101 : _____
2. JV Code 201 : _____
3. JV Code 301 : _____
4. JV Code 717 : _____
5. JV Code 8621 : _____
6. JV Code 8622 : _____
7. JV Code 901 : _____
8. JV Code 9011 : _____

Chapter 9 : Product Selling Channels

9.1 Domestic Market
1. Promotion Centers in each province run by the Ministry of Textile with the assistance of the China Council for the Promotion of International Trade.
2. Official publications of the Ministry of Textile.

9.2 Overseas Market
1. Branch offices of Party B in Seven (7) cities all over the world.
2. International Exhibitions.
3. Seminars and Conferences run by the Plant.

Chapter 10 : Registered Capital

10.1 The Total investment to be subscribed by various Parties which is the registered capital of the Plant is :

U.S. Dollars Ten Million   (US$10,000,000.00)

10.2 Party A and Party B shall regard the following as subscribed capital :

Party A:

Cash in the amount of 500,000.00 RMB Yuan, plus contributions of site.

Party B:

Cash in the amount of US Dollars 300,000.00 plus contributions of equipment.

Chapter 11 : Additional Equipment

11.1 Party B may provide additional equipment to the Plant as the needs of the change and as new equipment becomes available. Any such additions to the equipment provided by Party B will be agreed to by the Board of the Directors.

11.2 Neither Party is liable to assign to a third party or to dispose of, by other means, its prescribed capital or property in part or in whole without a decision unanimously passed by the Board of Directors.

11.3 Decisions on the increase and assignment of the Center's Registered capital, or disposal of it by other means shall be passed by the Board of Directors unanimously, and shall be submitted to the original examination and approval organization for approval.

Chapter 12 : Board of Directors

12.1 The Board of Directors of the Plant is to be set up within one month upon registration of the Plant.

12.2 The Board of Directors is composed of Eight (8) members, with Party A designating four (4) members and Party B designating four (4) members. The Chairman of the Board of Directors is to be designated by Party A, and the Vice-Chairman of the Directors is to be designated by Party B. The term of office of the Directors and the Chairman and Vice-Chairman of the Board of Directors is Five (5) years. However, their term of office may be renewed if they are re-designated by their respective Parties. Designation is to be conducted by the respective Parties in writting.

12.3 The Board of Directors is the highest organization of power of the Plant which decides all major matters of the Plant. With regard to issues of major importance, decisions shall be passed unanimously through friendly consultation on the basis of the principle of equality and mutual benefit.

With regard to other issue, decisions must be passed by a two-thirds majority of all members of the Board of Directors.

12.4 Issues of major importance discussed by the Board of Directors including but not limited to :

(1) Amendment of the Article of Association of the Plant

(2) Alternation of the registered capital of the Plant

(3) Extenson of the Agreement of the Plant

(4) Merger of the Plant with other organization

(5) The development policy and business orientation of the Plant

(6) The drawing proportion of the Plant's reserve fund, development fund and award fund.

12.5 The Chairman of the Board of Directors is the representative of the legal entity which is the Plant. In case the Chairman of the Board of Directors is unable to perform his duties for some reason, the Vice-Chairman or in his absence other Director may be temporarily empowered to act on his behalf. At least two members from each Party are required to form a quorum for a Board of Directors meeting.

12.6 The Board of Directors meeting is to be held at least once a year, to be called and presided over by the Chairman of the Board of Directors. Where a proposal is put forward by more than one-third of the Directors, the Chairman of the Board of Directors may call a Board of Directors meeting after giving reasonable notice to all members. [notice will be treated as unreasonable if it is less than Twenty-Four (24) hours] Minutes of the Meeting shall be placed on file for safe-keeping. The time and place for the Board of Directors meeting is to be decided by both Parties through consultation; the travel and living expenses of the participants are to be borne by the respective Parties.

Chapter 13 : Administration of The Plant

13.1 The specific business operation of the Plant is entirely to be administered by the personnel designated by Party A.

13.2 In the initial stage of business operation of the Plant, a administrative department is established for day to day operation work.

13.3 In the initial stage, the Plant has the following full-time working personnel recommended by Party A and approved and appointed by the Board of Directors.

Chapter 14 : Executive Director and Vice Director

14.1 The Executive Director and Vice-Director of the Plant are to be appointed by the Board of Directors for a term of Five (5) years, and their term of office may be renewed if the Board of Directors reappoints them. The Executive director of the Plant is directly responsible to the Board of

Directors, carries out the decisions made by the Board of Directors and organizes and takes full charge of the Plant's day-to-day business operation and administrative work.

14.2 The Executive Director of the Plant is not allowed to concurrently assume the post of director or vice-director of other economic entity, and is not allowed to be involved in commercial entity competitive with the Plant.

14.3 In case the Executive Director asks for resignation, he should submit a written report to the Board of Directors in advance.

14.4 Should the Executive Director and Vice Director ends or seriously neglect their duties, they may be discharged at any time upon the Board of Director's decision. Should their conduct violate the criminal law, legal responsibility shall be investigated and affixed.

Chapter 15 : Other staff members

15.1 The full-name personnel of the Plant shall be relatively stable. If they are required to be transferred outside the Plant by Party A for other work needs, this must be approved by the Board of Directors.

15.2 Party A is responsible for the employment of staff members and workers of the Plant, and the work is to be handled in accordance with the legal references stipulated in Chapter 1 above.

15.3 The Plant has the right to punish the staff members and workers who violate the Plant's rules and regulations and labour discipline by giving them warning, demerit record and reduction of wages. If the case is serious, the violator will be discharge from his duties.

15.4 Matters such as wages, welfare, bonus, labour protection and insurance are to be handled in accordance with the legal references as stipulated in Chapter 1 above. The Plant will formulate these stipulations into various rules and regulations in order to ensure the staff members and workers to carry out production and work under normal conditions.

15.5 The working personnel to be employed by the Plant shall execute Labour Contracts with the Plant individually. The duties, term of office and welfare treatment are to be stipulated in these Contracts.

Chapter 16 : Finance, Accounting Auditing

16.1 Financial accounting of the Plant shall be handled in accordance with the legal reference as stipulated in Chapter 1 above Financial Accounting System for Joint Ventures Using Chinese and Foreign Investment stipulated by the Ministry of Finance of the People's Republic of China.

16.2 Financial year of the Plant will be that of financial year, commencing from January 1 to December 31.

16.3 All certificates, accounts and ledgers of the Plant will be written in Chinese. English may be added upon Party B's request.

16.4 The Plant will use RMB Yuan as accounting currency. The exchange rate of RMB Yuan with other currency will be calculated upon the rate announced by the Foreign Exchange Control Bureau of the People's Republic of China on the date when the transaction actually incurred.

16.5 The Plant will open RMB Yuan and foreign currency accounts at the Bank of China or at other banks approved by the Bank of China.

16.6 The Plant will use the liability incurrance system and debit and credit accounting method which are commonly used worldwide for its account.

16.7 The management department of the Plant shall prepare, during the first three months of every financial year, a balance sheet and a profit and loss account of the last financial year for auditor's audit and signature, thereafter, submitting them to the Board of Directors for approval.

16.8 Either party of the joint venture is entitled to appoint, at its cost, an auditor to examine the account of the Plant. The Plant shall provide facilities during such examinatiion.

16.9 All matters related to the foreign exchange of the Plant shall be handled in accordance with the legal references as stipulated in Chapter 1 above.

Chapter 17 : Distribution of Profits

17.1 During each financial year, the Plant shall draw reserve funds in accordance with the regulation, enterprise development fund and staff award and welfare fund. The above fund shall be drawn by the Plant from the profit amount after tax. The proportion of such amount shall be decided by the Board of Directors.

17.2 The profit of the Plant after tax and apportioned for the fund shall not be drawn by either Party before the termination of the agreement. It shall be used as the development fund of the enterprise and for development of the Plant's laser weaving and knitting system.

Chapter 18 : Duration of the Joint Venture

18.1 The duration of the joint venture is (ten) 10 years, commencing from the date of receiving the business licence.

18.2 If both Parties agree to extend the term of operation of the joint venture, after a formal decision by the Board of Directors, application shall be made in writing to the Ministry of Textile Industry of the People's Republic of China (six) 6 months prior to the expiration of the joint venture. The extension can only be valid after the Ministry's approval and procedures for registration of alteration have been done at the State Administration Bureau for Industry and Commerce.

Chapter 19 : Termination of the Joint Venture

19.1 Either Party may terminate this agreement upon six (6) months prior notification in writing to the other Party, should any of the following situations occur:

1.   Expiration of the joint venture duration of the Plant.

2.   The Plant incurs severe loss and deficit and cannot continue to operate its business.

3.   Either Party to the joint venture cannot execute the duties as stipulated in the agreement and Articles of Association of the Plant so that the ''Plant'' is unable to continue its business.

4.   Due to Force Majeure, like natural disaster which causes severe loss and deficit and continuation of business is impossible.

5.   The Plant cannot achieve its business objective and at the same time has no prospect for development.

6.   Should unforeseen circumstances create a situation in which in the view of either party continued functioning of the Joint Venture is detrimental to the interests of either party.

19.2 Should joint venture of the Plant terminate prematurely, it should have the decision made at a meeting of the Board of Directors and report of which shall be submitted to the Ministry of Textile Industry of the People's Republic of China for approval.

Chapter 20 : Liquidation

20.1 Upon expiration or premature termination of the joint ventre, the Board of Directors shall propose a liquidation procedure, its principle and nominees for the Liquidation Committee. These nominees will form a Liquidation Committee and commence liquidation work of the Plant.

20.2 The duties of the Liquidation Committee are to carry out an examination and liquidation of the Plant's property, credits and debts, thereafter, to make a Capital and Asset Balance and a Property List. A liquidation plan will then be made and submitted to the Board of Directors for approval before execution.

20.3 During liquidation period, the Liquidation Committee will be the representative for initiating and attending legal proceedings.

20.4 The liquidation fee and remuneration of the members of the Liquidation Committee shall be paid in priority over others from the assets of the Plant.

20.5 The principals for liquidation shall be as follows:-

1.   The equipment and software provided by Party B shall be returned to Party B.

2.   All other assets of the Plant, except software or technology developed by the Plant and jointly owned by Parties A and B, shall be given to Party A, however, if the Plant has any profits in its final year before liquidation, these profits shall be prudently invested in Plant activities.

20.6 After completion of liquidation, the Plant shall submit a report to the Ministry of Textile Industry, execute the procedures of canceling the registration with the State Administration Bureau for Industry and Commerce, surrender its business licence and announce it to the general public.

20.7 After termination of the joint venture of the Plant, all kinds of accounts and ledgers will be retained by Party A.

20.8 All the above clauses stipulated in this Chapter shall be executed by reference to any forthcoming legislation concerning liquidation and/or bankruptcy for example, ''The Provisional Bankruptcy Laws of the People's Republic of China.'' which will come into force shortly.

Chapter 21 :   Language

21.1 These Articles of Association are written in Chinese and English, both language shall have equal legal effect.

Chapter 22 :   Approval

22.1 These Articles of Association shall only be effective upon the approval of the Ministry of Textile Industry and the Bank of China (in the aspect of using foreign currency) the same will be applied to amendment.

Chapter 23 :   Amendment and Wordings

23.1 Amendment of these Articles of Association shall have the unanimous decision passed at the meeting of the Board of Directors and have it approved by the original examination and approval organ.

23.2 Should any ambiguity arise between the wording of these Articles of Association and the underlying Agreement establishing a Joint Venture called the ''ABC Textile Production Plant'' dated _____ and signed by Parties A and B hereto, the wording of the underlying agreement shall be followed.

Party A :   Party B :

(Name in Full)   (Name in Full)

Registered Office :

Representative signing

_____

Name : (Printed)

Title : _____

Date : _____

Registered Office :

Representative signing

_____

Name : (Printed)

Title : _____

Date : _____

APPLICATION FOR EXEMPTION FROM TAX

To   : CHINESE AUTHORITY
From : APPLICANT
         (NAME OF COMPANY)
         (ADDRESS)
Date : _____

Re: Concerning the exemption from income tax on income received by the
      applicant from sources within the People's Republic of China, pursuant
      to the Contract (cite the name of the Contract) _____
      _____ .
      _____

We take pleasure in referring to the Contract for _____
_____ between
_____
_____ of
_____
China (hereinafter collectively referred to as the Buyer) and _____
_____ of _____
(hereinafter referred to as the Applicant) signed on _____
_____ at _____, China (hereinafter referred to as the
Contract).
Under the Contract the Applicant will sell high technology machinery,
materials, equipment, process engineering, spare parts and related items
for _____ (hereinafter referred to as the Plant) to the Buyer.
Further, in connection with this sale the Applicant will provide the Buyer with
technical documentation, technical services and training to facilitate the
installation and operation of the equipment.
As mentioned above the Plant will have a capacity of _____
_____ per day, making it one of the _____
in China. As China is implementing the Four Modernizations, the construction
of roads, ports, airports and other infrastructural works, as well as the construction of hospitals, residental apartments, office buildings and factories,
is vital, all topics that the Seventh Five-Year Plan also gives top priority. Since
the capability of producing large quantities of high quality Product is vital for
the construction of these facilities the Plant will play a useful role in the
implementation of the Four Modernizations. We therefore consider that the
Applicant should benefit from all the preferential tax treatment available under
the laws of the PRC.
The Contract is a trade contract, consisting of a number of various income
items, among which the supply of machinery on a C.I.F. basis is the most

important, representing approximately ____ % of the total contract price, i.e. _____ million. Further, the Applicant is also to supply technical documentation, _____ training of the Buyer's personnel and technical services, related to the sale of machinery. The Buyer will be also reimburse the Applicant for the costs of the freight charges and the insurance fee in connection with the C.I.F. shipment. The total Contract price, equal to _____ million, will be paid by the Buyer to the Applicant in 36 semi-installments. As the Contract will benefit from seller's credit, the Applicant will also receive _____ million as interest income from the Buyer on the outstanding balance due from the Buyer to the Applicant during the term of the Contract.

According to Article 11 of the Income Tax Law of the PRC Concerning Foreign Enterprises a 20% withholding tax should be levied on income obtained from dividends, interest, rentals, fees for the use of propriatary technology and other sources in China by foreign companies, enterprises and other economic organizations which have no establishments in China. Thus, The Applicant may be subject to this 20% withholding tax on the technical service income and the interest income received pursuant to the Contract, since these two income items are generated with the People's Republic of China. However, we respectfully submit that, for the reasons stated in Section A and Section B, the Applicant should be exempted from this tax.

A.   Technical Service Income

Pursuant to the Contract, and at the Buyer's request, technical experts from the Applicant will come to China to provide the Buyer with technical services, as described in Article _____, and Appendix _____ of the Contract. These technical services comprise explaning the technical documentation, drawings and equipment performance and technical instruction in connection with the erection, mechanial tests, commissioning and performance guarantee test.

Since the technical service income is received in connection with technical instruction provided for installation and assembly of equipment, and it does not involve the transfer of any right to use proprietary technology, it should be exempted from the ____ % withholding tax in accordance with Article 4 of the document of the Ministry of Finance Regarding Questions of the Levy of Income Tax on Revenues from Patent Rights and Proprietary Technology (Document 82 CAISHUIZI No.109%) and Article 2 (d) of the Interim Provisions of the Ministry of Finance Concerning the Reduction of or Exemption from Income Tax on fees for the Use of Proprietary Technology (Document CAISHUIZI 82 No.326).

Further, in accordance with Article 2 (a) of the Interim Provisions of the Ministry of Finance Concerning the Levy of the Consolidated Industrial and Commercial Tax and Enterprise Income Tax on Foreign Businesses that Contract for Projects and Operations and Provide Labour Services (Document 83 CAISHUIZI No. 149 issued July 5, 1983), the technical service income should be exempted from tax, as the services are provided pursuant to the provisions of a trade contract for the sale of machinery and equipment, and only include services such as giving the Buyer guidance in the installation of the equipment and explaining and interpreting technical materials, while it does not involve the transfer of any right to use proprietary technology.

B. Interest income

Pursuant to the Contract, _____ % of the total Contract price will be financed by _____, and institution under the auspices of _____ Bank (the Central Bank of _____), through a Seller's credit. However, in addition to this, the financing arrangement will cover __ % of an amount corresponding to __ % of the total Contract price, representing a portion of the expenditure for the supply of goods from the PRC, which is to be supplied by the Buyer.

As a consequense of this arrangement _____ % of the total Contract price will reenter the PRC. This amount equals the down payment to the made by the Buyer to the Applicant pursuant to the Contract.

In accordance with Article 2 (c) of the Interim Provisions of the Ministry of Finance Concerning the Reduction of or Exemption from Income Tax on Interest Derived from China by Foreign Businesses (the interest provision, issued _____, _____), as extended by the Notice of the Ministry of Finance Concerning the Extension of the Reduction of or Exemption from Income Tax on Interest Derived from China by Foreign Businesses (Document 86 CAISHUIZI No. 1) the interest income received by the Applicant pursuant to the Contract should be exempted from income tax, since the interest rate on the Seller's credit provided under the Contract is _____ %, as stated in Article 3.2.3.2. of the Contract, while the interest rate charged on buyer's credits, at the date of signing of the Contract was _____ %.

C. Application for Exemption from Foreign Enterprise Income Tax

We respectfully submit that, (1) in view of the fact that the Contract is a trade contract, and in view of the reasons presented above, the Applicant should not be subject to any tax, under the Tax Law, on income received pursuant to the Contract (2) in view of the fact that an institution under the auspices of _____ Bank (the Central Bank of _____) is to provide a Seller's credit to the Buyer on preferential terms, the interest income received pursuant to the Contract should also be exempted from tax under the Interest Provisions, as extended by the Extension Notice.

We forward this to you along with a copy of the signed contract.

We sincerely hope that this application will receive your favourable consideration.

Respectfully yours,

The Applicant

(Signed & Sealed)

_____

Title

CHINESE AUTHORITY'S REPLY

Foreign Business of _____

Tax Bureau

    Code No.

To: The Applicant   Date:

        In reply to your firm's report on application
for exemption from tax

    Thank you for your firm's letter dated _____. In accordance with the stipulation of Article 4 of the document 82 CAISHUIZI No. 109 of the Ministry of the Finance of our country and the stipulation of Article 2 of the document 82 CAISHUIZI No. 143 of the Ministry of Finance, we agree that the provisional tax for technical document fee, training the personnel of the buying party fee and technical service fee collected from _____ _____ of China by your firm are to be exempt from taxation. In accordance with the stipulation of paragraph 3 of Article 2 of the document 83 CAISHUIZI No. 348 of the Ministry of Finance of our country, the interest derived from deferred payment of credit provided by your Party for the buying Party, if such interest is paid at a rate not higher than the selling Party's usual credit interest rate, provisional income tax can also be exempt from taxation on the ground that your firm can provide a certificate to show the interest rate of the bank granting the credit.
In accordance with the stipulation of the "Individual Income Tax Law of the PRC", the personnel sent to China by your firm under the Contract, shall declare to our Bureau for paying individual income tax.

    With best regards.

(No text is enclosed herewith)

                Sub-Tax Bureau Involving Foreign
                Business of _____ Municipal
                Tax Bureau

                Date _____

Duplicate sent to: _____ Branch Office of Bank of China, _____
Branch Offices of China National _____ Import & Export Corp., China
National _____ Import & Export Corp., _____.

(The total printed number: 8)

By the Individual Income Tax Section of the Sub-Tax
Bureau Involving Foreign Business
Issued on _____ , 19 _____

Offshore Joint Venture Contract General Reference

1. Usually, the contents of an Offshore Joint Venture Contract are related to laws of jurisdiction where the joint venture is situate. For this reason the influence of PRC laws is reduced to minimum.
2. Most Offshore Joint Venture Contract is drafted by the legal representative of foreign party. The Chinese party will usually request a copy of Chinese translation of the contract for reference.
3. Both parties should pay special attention to the financial arrangement and share distribution of the venture.
4. The Chinese parties will consult relevant Chinese Authority for approval of being a party to the venture.
5. At present, Offshore Joint Venture has become popular in China Trade.

Please refer to the following sample Offshore Joint Venture Contract which has special emphasis on financial and shares arrangements:

The Agreement
=========

Date:
Name of Both Parties:

Recital

A. Party A and Foreign Company are parties to a Joint Venture Agreement dated the _____ of _____ , 19 ____ ("the Original Joint Venture Agreement") which provides for the establishment of a joint venture _____ facility in _____ (to be called the Venture) to be conducted through a company to be known as Party C.
B. Foreign Company by Deed of Assignment date the _____ day of _____, 19 _____ assigned to Party B, with the consent of Party A all its right, title and obligations under the Original Joint Venture Agreement.
C. The parties having now established a _____ facility at _____ desire to resolve and clarify the various matters herein set forth for the mutual benefit of both parties and for the advancement of the Venture.

IT IS HEREBY AGREED AS FOLLOWS:
=======================

1. ORIGINAL JOINT VENTURE AGREEMENT:

Article 1: Each of the parties hereto acknowledge having received and

280

understood the provisions of the Original Joint Venture Agreement and agrees to ratify, adopt and become a party to or reaffirm the provisions thereof except to the extent that this addendum expressly provides otherwise. Accordingly each of the parties hereto shall ensure that he or it and all persons controlled by him or it will ensure full performance of the Venture in accordance with the Original Joint Venture Agreement.

2. NEW JOINT VENTURE COMPANY

Article 2: The parties have determined having regard to the laws of _____ that the Venture can more successfully be carried out through the use of the existing corporate structure of Party B. They therefore resolve that henceforth the Venture will be conducted by Party B but that Party B shall be renamed Joint Venture Company (or a name as close thereto as is permitted by the Registrar of Companies for _____). (Hereinafter referred to as JV.)

Article 3: That the existing company bearing the name JV being of no further use to the Venture shall be would up. Party B warrants to Party A that Party A shall have no liability whatsoever in respect of shares held by it in the existing company bearing the name JV and agrees to indemnify Party A accordingly.

3. CONSTITUTION AND PAYMENT OF SHARE CAPITAL

Article 4: As contemplated under the Original Joint Venture Agreement but subject to minor modification reflecting the introduction of Third Party the shareholding in A company shall remain on a _____ Chinese / _____ contribution basis (the existing Party B shareholders being the _____). Having regard to the existing capital structure of Party B (to be renamed as "A Company.") Party A shall immediately be allotted _____ (_____) ordinary _____ (____) "D" shares in the capital of A Company which shall be increased for this purpose to give a total issued capital structure of _____ (_____) shares allotted and subscribed for as follows:-

Shareholders	Number/Group of Shares
Company A	_____ "A" ordinary shares
Company B	_____ "A" ordinary shares
Company C	_____ "A" ordinary shares
Company D	_____ "B" ordinary shares
Company E	_____ "B" ordinary shares
(Third Party)	_____ "B" ordinary shares
(Third Party)	_____ "C" ordinary shares

Company G (Party A) _____ "D" ordinary shares

Article 5: Party A shall receive its allottment of capital in A company (representing _____) fully paid up in return for its contribution to the Venture comprising its commitment to supply technology and _____ to the _____ of _____ 19 _____. Notwithstanding the acknowledgement that Party A's contribution has paid up its allotted capital Party A acknowledges its ongoing obligation under the Original Joint Venture Agreement to supply prawns and technology and that fulfillment of that ongoing obligation shall not carry an entitlement to a further allotment of fully paid shares in A Company. A share certificate evidencing that the shares have been allotted fully paid shall be issued immediately upon allotment. All parties acknowledge that for reasons best suiting the existing shareholders of Party B the contributions actually made by Party A to the Venture to the above date have been made to Party B (and not in fact to the Original JV) and that the value thereof is at least equal to _____ ( ). Accordingly, the existing Party B shareholders shall procure full compliance with the Companies Act _____ having regard to the fact that the shares to be allotted to Party A are being fully paid up otherwise than in cash.

Article 6: The parties acknowledge that the only consequences of the four groups of shares shall be those expressed in Articles of Association of A Company which shall be restricted to:-

(a) Confirmation, that the holder or holders of the majority of the Group "A" shares shall control one member of the Board of Directors of A Company.

(b) Confirmation that the holder or holders of the majority of the Group "B" shares shall control two members of the Board of Directors of A Company.

(c) Confirmation that the holder or holders of a majority of the Group "D" shares shall control two members of the Board of Directors of A Company.

(d) Confirmation that there may be a further two Directors but that they shall be independent of all parties to this agreement and shall be appointed only in the event of a proposed listing of shares in A Company on the _____ Stock Exchange.

(e) Confirmation that the holders of Group "A", "B" and "C" shares shall have pre-emptive rights between themselves and that the holders of the Group "D" shares shall have secondary pre-emptive rights over Group "A", "B" or "C" shares.

282

(f) Confirmation that the holders of Group "A", "B" and "C" shares have pre-emptive rights over the Group "D" shares.

(g) Confirmation that the pre-emptive rights provisions shall become effective in the event of any change in effective control of any shareholder (directly or indirectly) other than a change of effective control in an ultimate parent being a publicly listed company.

4. PUBLIC FLOATATION OF THE VENTURE ON THE STOCK EXCHANGE:

Article 7: The parties to the Venture have determined that it will be advantageous to A Company for it to have its shares listed upon the _____ Stock Exchange. Each of the parties hereto accepts that any such listing would involve an invitation to members of the public of _____ to purchase shares in A Company and that in event the proportionate shareholdings of the existing Party B shareholders and of Party A will reduce.

Article 8: Notwithstanding Article 7 hereof, it is acknowledged that there shall not be any listing of A Company's shares on the _____ Stock Exchange or any other change in the capital structure of A Company unless:-

(a) The Board of A Company passes a resolution with the Party A nominees voting in favour that the Venture has successfully concluded its experimental stage.

(b) The Board of Directors of A Company passes a resolution with the Party A nominees voting in favour resolving to list or otherwise change the capital structure.

Article 9: The Technical Director shall supply monthly reports to the Board of Directors of A company advising as to the progress towards completion of the experimental stage.

Article 10: All parties hereto undertake that upon completion of the experimental stage and satisfaction of Article 8 they will do all things as may be necessary or desireable in order to enable the public floatation of A Company to proceed without delay. Nothing in this Article or elsewhere will oblige Party A to provide any Certificate or other document relating to any proposed prospectus.

5. ADMINISTRATION AND MANAGEMENT

Article 11: The parties agree that the administration and management of A Company shall be under the control of a General Manager (who shall report to the Board of Directors at least monthly) and an Assistant General Manager who shall report to the General Manager but be entitled to receive copies of all reports by the General Manager to the Board of Directors. Either the General Manager or the Assistant General Manager shall be a nominee from time to time of Party A although the appointment in each case shall be confirmed by the Board of A Company who shall also have the power to terminate any appointment.

(1) Party A accepts that the staff of A Company nominated by Party A will be under the jurisdiction of the Board of A Company and that it is the intention of the Board of A Company to establish, in conjunction with the General Manager, clear management responsibilities for all A Company staff. All Chinese staff will be advised of their responsibilities in writing (in English and Chinese) and it will be made clear that non-performance may result in termination of employment by the unanimous decision of the Board.

(2) A Company will take all action available to tit to endeavour to ensure that the _____ Government approval is for the appointment of such Chinese technical personel as the necessary for the Venture.

6. FINANCING AND CAPITAL RESTRUCTURING:

Article 12: It is acknowledged by all parties hereto that A Company requires additional funding in order to meet the balance of stage I capital costs and running costs for the Venture through to the time of the public floatation of A Company.

Article 13: Party A has advised that it may not wish to provide its pro rata contribution to this additional funding by way of cash payment but in that event it is prepared to allow A Company to introduce an outside shareholder which will have the effect of diluting the total percentage holdings of the then existing shareholders in A Company. Notwithstanding the aforesaid, it has been agreed that the perecentage shareholding of Party A in A Company shall at no time be diluted below __ % of the issued capital without the agreement of the Party A appointees to the Board of A Company.

Article 14: It has been agreed by the parties hereto that over the course of the period from the data of this agreement to the public floatation of A Company the Board of Directors may unanimously resolve to offer an interest in the Venture to a Financier from to time in return for provision of the funding required by the Venture and that subject to Article 13 the parties will dilute their total percentage holdings pro rata to the extent of the interest offered to the Financier.

Article 15: The parties have resolved that should the dilution of shareholdings contemplated in Articles 12 and 13 hereof occur and that as a result thereof the percentage shareholding of Party A in the Venture falls below a level of _____ % Party A shall hence forth be entitled to be reimbursed for the costs of the supply of Products the Venture in accordance with the following scale of charges:-

Party A % of the Total Capital on Issue			% of Cost of Products to be paid	
over	_____	%	nil	
_____	—	_____	_____	%
_____	—	_____	_____	%
_____	—	_____	_____	%
_____	—	_____	_____	%
_____	—	_____	_____	%
25%			100.0%	

It is agreed that "Cost of Products" means:
(a) In respect of adult products price of US$ ____ each for the five years from the date of the resolution referred to in Article 8A, and thereafter such price as the parties hereto shall agree.
(b) In respect of minor products a price of to be agreed between the parties hereto prior to shipment.

Article 16: It will be the responsibility of the Chinese Directors of A Company to provide a report to the Board of A Company before a prospectus is issued to the _____ public. This report will recommend a development program for the _____ which in the opinion of the Chinese Directors will allow full stocking from _____ sources if such development is viable and at the same time A Company will provide appropriate financial data in the light of the report. The Prospectus will therefore be able to carry as a material contract the obligation of A Company to pay for Products only for biological rejuvenation reasons which are expected, but not committed, to be of the order of _____ / _____ over any five year period.

Article 17: Nothwithstanding Article 15 hereof, Party A shall replace free of charge all of the Products supplied by it to A Company as follows:-
(a) On any consignments to the Venture of Products subsequent to this Agreement with regard to which Party A is entitled to charge at whatever specified rate in accordance with the table contained in Article 15 hereof Party A undertakes that it will replace free of charge all losses of products after reaching the _____ , unless such failure to survive results from transportation problems (excluding packing) after leaving the Chinese Airport of departure.

(b) Any serious losses of special products held by A Company where such losses are the result of technical fault by a Chinese Technician and such fault is acknowledged by the Party A nominees on the Board of A Company. Party A shall supply Chinese special product.

(1) It is acknowledged by Party A that it will hold in guarantine in the People's Republic of China all replacement products stocks supplied to A Company for such length of time as Party A shall consider necessary and the parties hereto acknowledge that A Company will further hold the aforesaid replacement Products stocks on their arrival in _____, separate and apart from the existing A Company Products stocks for such a period as Party A shall determine necessary to ensure that the aforesaid shipment is executed properly.

(2) In accordance with Article 3 of the Original Joint Venture Agreement party A shall be responsible for delivering Product required to ____ Airport or such other Airport as is agreed and A Company shall be responsible for all costs and expenses for transportation from Airport or such other Airport as is agreed to the site of the JV.

7. BOARD OF DIRECTORS

Article 18: Each Director shall have the right in accordance with the Articles of Association to nominate an alternate Director and to nominate an Observer and such nominations will take effect upon delivery of such Notices of Nomination to A Company.

Article 19: None of the Directors shall be subject to retirement by rotation but each shall hold office until removed by the party appointing him or until his office is vacated ipso facto in accordance with the Articles of Association.

Article 20: All matters requiring a Board resolution shall only be passed if approved by Directors representing at least _____ % of the capital with Appointees under Article 6D being deemed to represent the public shareholdings.

8. TRANSFER OF SHARES:

Article 21: The parties hereto resolve that A Company and the directors shall not register or approve the transfer of any shares in A Company otherwise than in accordance with the provisions herein setforth.

Article 22: Without the prior written consent of the holders of at least _____ % of the shares of A Company (in all cases which consent shall not be unreasonably withheld) no share may be transferred. Hereafter the provisions of the Articles of Association shall exclusively govern the transfer of shares.

Article 23: Notwithstanding the provisions of Article 22 the shareholders in A Company with notice to the Board of A Company may transfer their shares to wholly owned subsidiaries. It is specifically acknowledged that the _____ is in the process of establishing a _____ Trust to hold all or part of his shareholding and provided the shareholding will remain under his control A Company will approve such Transfer.

Article 24: Notwithstanding Article 22 hereof and the Articles of Association of A Company, the parties hereto acknowledge that those shares in the capital of A Company numbered _____ _____ (_____) to _____ _____ (_____) inclusive and presently held by the Company C shall transfer either to the _____ of _____, Company Director and Company D and Company E and the parties hereto specifically acknowledge that such transfers shall occur notwithstanding anything contained herein or in the Articles of Association of A Company. The parties hereto specifically acknowledge that such transfers shall be permitted to occur under the Articles of Association of the Company.

9.   SUPPLY OF PRODUCTS AND TECHNOLOGY

Article 25: It is acknowledged by the parties hereto that the obligation upon Party A to supply Products and technology as specified in the Original Joint Venture Agreement as modified by this Contract for the Establishment of a Joint Venture Product Company Dated _____ , 19 ____ extends for a ____ (____) year period from the ____ day of, ____, 19 _____ .

10. NO TRANSFER TO TECHNOLOGY

Article 26: It is acknowledged by all parties hereto that there will be transfer of technology without the unanimous consent of both the _____ and Chinese parties and in particular:
(1)   No Product or _____ will be permitted at any time to leave the _____ factility.
(2)   That the Product will not be available for inspection, photographing, scrutiny or otherwise, except by those _____ authorities having competent jurisdiction under the law.

11. DURATION AND TERMINATION:

Article 27: It is acknowledged by the parties hereto that Article _____ of the Original Joint Venture Agreement is hereby revoked and that the Company shall not be required automatically to cease operations after the _____ (_____) year period previously contemplated by Article ____. However all obligations upon Party A shall terminated as provided herein.

12. PRIOR OPERATIONS OF PARTY B

Article 28: It shall be an obsolute precondition of this agreement that Party A be satisfied with the affairs and status of Party B the intent being that Party B has not been involved in any matters other than those pertaining to the Venture and has no debts other than those pertaining to the Venture and that the existing Party B shareholders will prepare accounts satisfactory to Party A as at the date immediately prior to when Party A becomes a shareholder in Party B.

13. COSTS

Article 29: Each party to this Agreement shall bear its own legal, accountancy, stamp duty and other costs incurred by it in connection with this Agreement.

14. EXTENT OF AGREEMENT

Article 30: This Agreement shall be considered an amendment of the Original Joint Ventur Agreement pursuant to Article _____ and henceforth the Original Joint Venture Agreement shall be read as subject to this Agreement.

Article 31: To the extent of any inconsistency between the provisions of this Agreement and the provisions of the Original Joint Venture Agreement, the provisions of the Articles of Association or the Memorandum of Association of A Company the provisions of this Agreement shall prevail.

15. ENGLISH AND CHINESE VERSIONS:

Article 32: This agreement is executed in Chinese and English. Both texts shall have equal validity.

IN WITNESS WHEREOF these presents have been executed on the day and year hereinbefore set forth.

Party A   Party B

(Signed, Sealed)   (Signed, Sealed)

_____   _____

APPENDICES

Appendix 1
Sample Contract for Joint Venture Using
Chinese and Foreign Investment

Appendix 2
Sample Articles of Associations for Joint Venture
Using Chinese and Foreign Investment

Remarks

The Law and Regulations Bureau of the Ministry of Foreign Economic Relations and Trade of the People's Republic of China has distributed a set of Sample Contract and Sample Articles of Associations for Joint Ventures Using Chinese and Foreign Investment to all the enterprises in China. The purpose of which is to give some guidelines for their drafting of Joint Venture Agreement with foreign investors.

From these two samples, readers may have a rough idea of what Chinese Authority have in mind about the contents of a Joint Venture Agreement.

APPENDIX 1

SAMPLE CONTRACT FOR JOINT VENTURE USING CHINESE AND FOREIGN INVESTMENT

Chapter I : General Provisions

By reference to the "Law of the People's Republic of China on Joint Venture Using Chinese and Foreign Investment" and other related laws and regulations of China, _____(Name)_____ Company, and_____(Name)_____ Company, adhering to the principles of equality and mutual benefit as well as through friendly negotiations, have agreed to set up a joint venture enterprise with investment contributed by both parties. The joint venture shall be set up in _____(Address)_____ , the People's Republic of China. A contract for this purpose, is hereby, concluded.

Chapter II : Parties to the Joint Venture

Article 1: _____(Name of Company)_____ , China whose registered address is _____ , province, China (hereinafter to referred as "Party A") the particulars of its legal representative is:
Name　　　: _____
Title　　　　: _____
Nationality : _____

　　　　　　　　　　a n d

_____(Name of Company)_____ , whose registered address is _____ (hereinafter referred to as "Party B", the particulars of its legal representative is:
Name　　　: _____
Title　　　　: _____
Nationality : _____
(Should there be more than two investors, they can be named as Party C, D ... etc.)

Chapter III : Establishment of the Joint Venture Company

Article 2: By reference to the "Law of the People's Republic of China on Joint Venture Using Chinese and Foreign Investment" and other related laws and regulations of China, both parties agree to set up a joint venture with limited liability (hereinafter referred to as the joint venture company).

Article 3:   The name of the joint venture company is _____ Company Limited.
Company registered in China with limited liability.
The name in foreign language is _____ .
The registered address of the joint venture company is at _____ street _____ (city) _____ (province).

Article 4:   All activities of the joint venture company shall be governed by the laws, decrees and pertinent rules and regulations of the People's Republic of China.

Article 5:   The organization form of the joint venture company is a company with limited liability. Each party's liability is limited to the amount of capital it subscribed, thus the profits, risks and losses of the joint venture company shall be shared by the parties in proportion to their contributions of the registered capital.

Chapter IV :   The Purpose, Scope and Scale of Production and Business

The purpose of the parties to joint venture is in conformity with the object of enhancing the economic corporation and technical exchanges, to improve the product quality, develop new products, and gain competitive position in the world market in quality and price by adopting advanced and appropriate technology and scientific management method, so as to raise economic results and ensure satisfactory economic benefits for each investor.
(Notes: This article shall be written in conformity to the specific situations of the contract).

Article 7:   The production and business scope of the joint venture company are to produce _____ products; provide maintenance service after the sale of the products; study and develop new products.
(This article shall be written in comformity to the specific conditions of the contract).

Article 8:   The production scale of the joint venture company is as follows:
(1)   The production capacity after the joint venture company is put into operation is _____ .
(2)   The production scale may be increased up to _____ with the development of the production and operation. The product varieties may be developed into _____ .
(This article shall be written in comformity to the specific situation of the contract).

Chapter V :   Total Amount of Investment and the Registered Capital

Article 9:   The total amount of investment of the joint venture company is RMB _____ Yuan (or a foreign currency agreed upon by both parties).

Article 10: Investment contributed by the parties is RMB _____ Yuen, which will be the registered capital of the joint venture company.

Of which: Party A shall pay RMB _____ Yuen, accounts for _____ %; Party B shall pay RMB _____ Yuen, accounts for _____ %.

Article 11: Both Party A and Party B will contribute the followings as their investment:

Party A: cash RMB _____ Yuen

machines and equipments RMB _____ Yuen

premises RMB _____ Yuen

the right to the use of the site RMB _____ Yuen

industrial property RMB _____ Yuen

Other RMB _____ Yuen, RMB _____ Yuen in all.

Party B: cash RMB _____ Yuen

machines and equipments RMB _____ Yuen

industrial property RMB _____ Yuen

Other RMB _____ Yuen, RMB _____ Yuen in all.

(If contribution of capital goods or industrial property are used as investment, Party A and Party B shall conclude a separate contract which shall form an integral part of this contract.)

Article 12: The registered capital of the joint venture company shall be paid in _____ installments by Party A and Party B in accordance with their respective investment proportion.

Details of each installment are as follows:

_____

_____

_____

_____

(This article shall be written in conformity to the actual situations to the concrete conditions.)

Article 13: Should any part to the joint venture intend to assign all or part of his investment to a third party, consent shall be obtained from the other party to the joint venture, and approval from the examination and approval authority is required.

When one party to the joint venture assigns all or part of his investent, the other party shall have preemptive right.

Chapter VI : Responsibilities of Each Party to the Joint Venture

Article 14: Party A and Party B shall be respectively responsible for the following matters:

(A) Responsibilities of Party A:

(1) Handling of applications for approval, registration, business license and other matters concerning the establishment of the joint venture company from relevant departments of China;

294

(2) Processing for applying the right to the use of a site to the authority in charge of the land;

(3) Organizing the design and construction of the premises and other engineering facilities of the joint venture company;

(4) Providing cash, machinery and equipment and premises ... in accordance with the stipulations in Article 11;

(5) Assisting Party B for processing import customs declaration for the machinery and equipments contributed by Party B as investment and arranging the transportation within the Chinese territory;

(6) Assisting the joint venture company in purchasing or leasing equipments, materials, raw materials, articles for office use, means of transportation and communication facilities etc;

(7) Assisting the joint venture company in contacting and settling the fundamental facilities such as water, electricity, transportation etc;

(8) Assisting the joint venture in recruiting Chinese management peorsonnel, technical personnel, workers and other personnel needed;

(9) Assisting foreign workers and staff in applying for the entry visa, work license and processing their travelling matters;

(10) Responsible for handling other matters entrusted by the joint venture company.

(B)   Responsibilities of Party B:

(1) Providing cash, machinery and equipment, industrial property ... in accordance with the stipulations in Article 11, and responsible for shipping capital goods such as machinery and equipment etc. contributed as investment to a Chinese port;

(2) Handling the matters entrusted by the joint venture company, such as selecting and purchasing machinery and equipments outside China.

(3) Providing needed technical personnel for installing, testing and trial production of the equipment, as well as the technical personnel for production and inspecting;

(4) Training the technical personnel and workers of the joint venture company;

(5) In case the Party B is the licensor, he shall be responsible for the stable production of qualified products of

the joint venture company in the light of design capacity within the stipulated period;

(This article shall be written in conformity to the specific situation of the contract.)

Chapter VII : Transfer of Technology

Article 15: Party A and Party B agree that a technology transfer agreement shall be signed between the joint venture company and the Party B (or a third party) so as to obtain advanced production technology needed for realizing the production and operation purpose and the production scale stipulated in Chapter 4 in the contract, including products designing, technology of manufacturing, means of testing, materials perscriptioin, standard of quality and the training of personnel etc.

(This article shall be written in conformity to the actual situations.)

Article 16: Party B offers the following guarantees on the transfer of technology.

_____

_____

_____

_____

(This article applies only when Party B is responsible for transferring technology to the joint venture company.)

(1)   Party B guarantees that the overall technology such as the designing, technology of manufacturing, technological process, test and inspection of products *(Note: The name of the products shall be written)* provided to the joint venture company must be intergrated, precise and reliable. It is to meet the requirement of the joint venture's operation purpose, and be able to obtain the standard of production quality and production capacity stipulated in the contract;

(2)   Party B guarantees that the technology stipulated in this contract and the technology transfer agreement shall be fully transferred to the joint venture company, and pledges that the provided technology should be truly advanced among the same type of technology of Party B, the model, specification and quality of the equipment are excellent and it is to meet the requirement of technological operation and practical usage;

(3)   Party B shall work out detailed list of the provided technology and technological service at various stages as stipulated in the technology transfer agreement to be an appendix to the contract, and guarantee its performance;

(4) The drawings, technological conditions and other detailed information are part of the transferred technology and shall be offered on time;

(5) Within the validity period of the technology transfer agreement, Part B shall provide the joint venture company with the improvement of the technology and the improved information and technological materials in time, and shall not charge separate fees;

(6) Party B shall guarantee that the technological personnel and the workers in the joint venture company can master all the technology transferred within the period stipulated in the technology transfer agreement.

Article 17: Should Part B fail to provide equipment and technology in accordance with the stipulations in this contract and in the technology transfer agreement or in case any deceiving or concealing actions are found, Part B shall be responsible for compensating the fiscal losses to the joint venture company.

Article 18: The technology transfer fee shall be paid in royalties. The royalty rate shall be _____ % of the net sale value of the products turned out.
The term for royalty payment is the same as the term for technology transfer agreement stipulated in Article 19 of this contract.

Article 19: The term for the technology transfer agreement signed by joint venture company and Party B is _____ years. After the expiration of the technology transfer agreement, the joint venture company shall have the right to use, research and develop the imported technology continuously. *(The term for a technology transfer agreement is generally no longer than 10 years, and it shall be approved by the Ministry of Foreign Economic Relations and Trade or other examination and approval authorities entrusted by the Ministry of Foreign Economic Relations and Trade.)*

Chapter VIII : Selling of Products

Article 20: The products of joint venture company will be sold both on Chinese market and on overseas market, the export part accounts for _____ %, _____ % for domestic market. *(An annual percentage and amount for export and domestic consumption should be listed out in accordance with practical situations, under normal conditions, the amount for export shall at least meet the needs of foreign exchange expenses of the joint venture company.)*

Article 21: Products may be sold on overseas market through the following channels:

(1) The joint venture company may directly sell its products in the international market, the accounts of which will be _____ %.

(2) The joint venture company may sign sales contract with Chinese foreign trade companies, entrusting them to be the sales agencies or exclusive sales agencies, the accounts of which will be _____ %.

(3) The joint venture company may entrust Party B to sell its products, which accounts for _____ %.

Article 22: The joint venture's products to be sold in China may be handled by the Chinese materials and commercial departments by means of agency or exclusive sales, or may be sold by joint venture company directly.

Article 23: In order to provide maintenance service to the products sold both in China or abroad, the joint venture company may set up sales branches for maintenance service both in China or abroad subject to the approval of the relative Chinese department.

Article 24: The trade mark of the joint venture products is _____.

Chapter IX : The Board of Directors

Article 25: The date of registration of the joint venture company shall be the date of the establishment of the Board of Directors of the joint venture company.

Article 26: The Board of Directors are composed of _____ directors, of which _____ shall be appointed by Party A, _____ by Party B. The Chairman of the Board shall be appointed by Party A, and its Vice-Chairman by Party B. The term of office for the Director, Chairman and Vice-Chairman is four years, their term of office may be renewed if continuously appointed by the relevant party.

Article 27: The highest authority of the joint venture company shall be its Board of Directors. It shall decide all major issues.
(The main contents shall be listed by reference to Article 36 of the Regulations for the Implementation of the Joint Venture Law.)
Unanimous approval shall be required before any decisions are made concerning major issues of the joint venture company. As for other matters, approval by majority or a simple majority shall be require.
(Details of the clauses shall be explicitly stipulated.)

Article 28: The Chairman of the Board is the legal representative of the joint venture company. Should the Chairman be unable to exercise his responsibilities for some reasons, he shall authorize the Vice-Chairman or any other Directors to represent the joint venture company temporarily.

Article 29: The Board of Directors shall convene at least one meeting every year. The meeting shall be called and presided over by the Chairman of the board. The Chairman may convene an interim meeting based on a proposal made by more than one third of the total number of directors. Minutes of the meetings shall be placed on file.

Chapter X : Business Management Office

Article 30: The joint venture company shall establish a management office which shall be responsible for its daily management. The management office shall have a general manager, appointed by party _____; _____ deputy general managers, _____ by party _____; _____ by party _____. The general manager and deputy general managers shall be invited by the Board of Directors whose terms of office is _____ years.

Article 31: The responsibility of the general manager is to carry out the decisions of the Board Meeting and organise and conduct the daily management of the joint venture company. The deputy general managers shall assist the general manager in his work. Several department managers may be appointed by the management office, they shall be responsible for the works in various department respectively, handle the matters handed over by the general manager and deputy general managers and shall be responsible to them.

Article 32: In case of graft or serious dereliction of duty on the part of the general manager and deputy general managers, the Board of Directors shall have the power to dismiss them at any time.

Chapter XI : Purchase of Equipment

Article 33: In its purchase of required raw materials, fuel, parts means of transportation and articles for office use, the joint venture company shall give first priority to purchase in China where conditions are the same.

Article 34: In case the joint venture company entrusts Party B to purchase equipment on overseas market, persons appointed by Party A shall be invited to take part in the purchasing.

Article 35: During the period of preparation and construction, a preparation and construction office shall be set up under the Board of Directors. The preparation and construction office shall consist of _____ persons, among which _____ persons will be from Party A, _____ persons from Party B. The preparation and construction office shall have one manager recommended by Party _____, and one deputy manager by Party _____. The manager and deputy manager shall be appointed by the Board of Directors.

Article 36:   The preparation and construction and construction office is responsible for the following concrete works: examining the designs of the project, signing project construction contract, organizing the purchasing and inspecting of relative equipment, materials etc., working out the general schedule of project construction, compiling the expenditure plans, controlling project financial payments and final accounts of the project, drawing up managerial methods and keeping and filing documents, drawings, files and materials, during the construction period of the project.

Article 37:   A technical group with several technical personnel appointed by Party A and Party B shall be organized. The group, under leadership of the preparation and construction office, is in charge of the examination, supervision, inspection, testing, checking and accepting, and performance checking for the project design, the quality of project, the equipment and materials and the imported technology.

Article 38:   After approved upon by both parties, the establishment, remuneration and the expenses of the staff of the preparation and contruction office shall be covered in the project budget.

Article 39:   After having completed the project and finishing the turning over procedures, the preparation and construction office shall be dissolved upon the approval of the Board of Directors.

Chapter XIII :   Labour Management

Article 40:   Labour contract covering the recuritment, employment, dismissal and resignation, wages labor insurance, welfare, rewards, penalty and other matters concerning the staff and workers of the joint venture company shall be drawn up between the joint venture company and the Trade Union of the joint venture company as a whole of individual employees in accordance with the ''Regulations of the People's Republic of China on Labor Management in Joint Ventures Using Chinese and Foreign Investment and its Implementation Rules.''
The labor contracts shall, after being signed, be filed with the local labor management department.

Article 41:   The appointment of high-ranking administrative personnel recommended by both parties, their salaries, social insurance, welfare and the standard of travelling expenses etc. shall be decided by the meeting of the Board of Directors.

Chapter XIV :   Taxes, Finance and Audit

Article 42:   Joint venture company shall pay taxes in accordance with the stipulations of Chinese laws and other relative regulations.

Article 43:   Staff members and workers of the joint venture company shall pay individual income tax in accordance with the "Individual Income Tax Law of the People's Republic of China."

Article 44: Allocations for reserve funds, expansion funds of the joint venture company and welfare funds and bonuses for staff and workers shall be set aside in accordance with the stipulations in the "Law of the People's Republic of China on Joint Ventures Using Chinese and Foreign Investment". The annual proportion of allocations shall be decided by the Board of Directors according to business situations of the joint venture company.

Article 45: The fiscal year of the joint venture company shall be from January 1 to December 31. All vouchers, receipts, statistic statement and reports, account books shall be written in Chinese. *(A foreign language can be used concurrently with mutual consent.)*

Article 46: Financial checking and examination of the joint venture company shall be conducted by an auditor registered in China and reports shall be submitted to the Board of Directors and the general manager.

In case Party B considers it is necessary to employ a foreign auditor registered in other country to undertake annual financial checking and examination, Party A shall give its consent. All the expenses thereof shall be borne by Party B.

Article 47: In the first three months of each fiscal year, the manager shall prepare previous year's balance sheet, profit and loss statement and proposal regarding the disposal of profits, and submit them to the Board of Directors for examination and approval.

Chapter XV : Duration of the Joint Venture

Article 48: The duration of the joint venture company is _____ years. The establishment of the joint venture company shall start from the date on which the business license of the joint venture company is issued.

An application for the extension of duration, proposed by one party and unanimously approved by the Board of Directors, shall be submitted to the Ministry of Foreign Economic Relations and Trade (or the examination and approval authority entrusted by it) six months prior to the expiry date of the joint venture.

Chapter XVI : The Disposal of Assets After the Expiration of the Duration

Article 49: Upon the expiration of the duration or termination before the date of expiration of the joint venture, liquidation shall be carried out according to the relevant law. The liquidated assets shall be distributed in accordance with the proportion of investment contributed Party A and Party B.

Chapter XVII : Insurance

Article 50: Insurance policies of the joint venture company on various kinds of risks shall be underwritten with the People's Republic of China. Types, the value and duration of insurance shall be decided by the Board of Directors in accordance with the stipulations of the People's Insurance Company of China.

Chapter XVIII : The Amendment, Alternation and Discharge of the Contract

Article 51: The amendment of the contract or other appendices shall come into force only after the written agreement signed by Party A and Party B and approved by the original examination and approval authority.

Article 52: In case of inability to fulfil the contract or to continue operation due to heavy losses in successive years as a result of force majeure, the duration of the joint venture and the contract shall be terminated before the time of expiration after unanimously agreed upon by the Board of Directors and approved by the original examination and approval authority.

Article 53: Should the joint venture company be unable to continue its operations or achieve the business purpose stipulated in the contract due to the fact that one of contracting parties fails to fulfil the obligations prescribed by the contract and articles of association, or seriously violate the stipulations of the contract and articles of association, that party shall be deemed as unilaterally terminates the contract. The other party shall have the right to terminate the contract in accordance with the provisions of the contract after approved by the original examination and approval authority as well as to claim damages. In case Party A and Party B of the joint venture company agree to continue the operation, the party who fails to fulfil the obligations shall be liable to the economic losses thus caused to the joint venture company.

Chapter XIX : Liabilities for Breach of Contract

Article 54: Should either Party A and Party B fails to pay on schedule the contributions in accordance with the provisions defined in Chapter 5 of this contract, the breaching party shall pay to the other party _____ % of the contribution starting from the first month after exceeding the time limit. Should the breaching party fails to pay after 3 months, _____ % of the contribution shall be paid to the other party, who shall have the right to terminate the contract and to claim damages to the breaching party in accordance with the stipulations in Article 53 of the contract.

Article 55: Should all or part of the contract and its appendices be unable to be fulfilled owing to the fault of one party, the breaching party shall bear the responsibilities thus caused. Should it be the fault of both parties, they shall bear their respective responsibilities according to actual situation.

Article 56: In order to guarantee the performance of the contract and its appendices, both Party A and Party B shall provide each other the bank guarantees for the performance of the contract.

Chapter XX : Force Majeure

Article 57: Should either of the parties to the contract be prevented from executing the contract by force majeure, such as earthquake, typhoon, flood, fire and war and other unforeseen events, and their happening and consequences are unpreventable and unavoidable, the prevented party shall notify the other party by cable without any delay, and within 15 days thereafter provide the detailed information of the events and a valid document for evidence issued by the relevant public notary organization for explaining the reason of its inability to execute or delay the execution of all or part of the contract. Both parties shall, through consultations, decide whether to terminate the contract or to exempt the part of obligations for implementation of the contract or whether to delay the execution of the contract according to the effects of the events on the performance of the contract.

Chapter XXI : Applicable Law

Article 58: The formation of this contract, its validity, interpretation, execution and settlement of the disputes shall be governed by the related laws of the People's Republic of China.

Chapter XXII : Settlement of Disputes

Article 59: Any disputes arising from the execution of, or in connection with the contract shall be settled through friendly consultations between both parties. In case no settlement can be reached through consultations, this disputes shall be submitted to the Foreign Economic and Trade Arbitration Commission of the China Council for the Promotion of International Trade for arbitration in accordance with its rules of procedure. The arbitral award is final and binding upon both parties.

Or

Any disputes arising from the execution of, or in connection with the contract shall be settled through friendly consultations between both parties. In case no settlement can be reached through consultation, the disputes shall be submitted to _____ Arbitration Organization in _____ for arbitration in accordance with its rules of procedure. The arbitral award is final and binding upon both parties.

Or

Any disputes arising from the execution of , or in connection with the contract shall be settled through friendly consultations between both parties. In case no settlement can be settled through consultations, the disputes shall be submitted for arbitration.

Arbitration shall take place in the defendant's country.

If in China, arbitration shall be conducted by the Foreign Economic and Trade Arbitration Commission of the China Council for the Promotion of International Trade in accordance with its rules of procedure.

If in _____, the arbitration shall be conducted by _____ in accordance with its rules of procedure.

The arbitral award is final and binding on both parties.

(When formulating contracts, only one of the above-mentioned provisions can be used.)

Article 60: During the arbitration, the contract shall be executed continuously by both parties except for matters in disputes.

Chapter XXIII : Language

Article 61: The contract shall be written in Chinese and _____. Both languages are equally authentic. In the event of any discrepancy, the Chinese version shall prevail.

Chapter XXIV : Effectiveness of the Contract and Miscellaneous

Article 62: The appendices drawn up in accordance with the principles of this contract are integral part of this contract, including: the projects agreement, the technology transfer agreement, the sales agreement. (List out all the relevant documents).

Article 63: The contract and its appendices shall come into force beginning from the date of approval of the Ministry of Foreign Economic Relations and Trade of the People's Republic of China or its entrusted examination and approval authority.

Article 64: Should notices in connection with any party's right and obligations be sent by either Party A or Party B by telegram or telex or other means, the written letter notices shall be also required afterwards. The registered addresses of Party A and Party B listed in this contract shall be the postal addresses.

Article 65: The contract is signed in _____, of China by the authorized representatives of both parties on ____, 19____.

For Party A   For Party B

(Signature)   (Signature)

_____   _____

APPENDIX 2

SAMPLE ARTICLES OF ASSOCIATION FOR JOINT VENTURES USING CHINESE AND FOREIGN INVESTMENT

Chapter I : General Provision

Article 1: In accordance with the "Law of the People's Republic of China on Joint Venture Using Chinese and Foreign Investment" and the contract signed by __(Name)__ company (hereinafter referred to as Party A) and __(Name)__ company (hereinafter referred to as Party B), the Articles of Association is hereby formulated.

Article 2: The name of the joint venture company is (Name of Company) , a company registered in China with limited liability.
Its name in foreign language is _____.
The registered address of the joint venture company is situate at: _____ .

Article 3: The names and registered addresses of the parties to the joint venture are as follows:
Party A: _____ Company of _____.
Party B: _____ Company of _____.

Article 4: The joint venture company is a company with limited liability.

Article 5: The joint venture company has the status of a legal person and is subject to the jurisdiction and protection of Chinese laws. All its activities shall be governed by Chinese laws, decrees and other related rules and regulations.

Chapter II : Purpose and Scope of Business

Article 6: The purposes of the joint venture company is to produce and sell _____ products and to reach _____ level for obtaining satisfactory economic benefits for the parties to the joint venture company.
(Each joint venture company may set out its object clauses in accordance with its own conditions.)

Article 7: The business scope of the joint venture company is to design, manufacture and sell _____ products and provide after-sale services.

Article 8: The scale of production of the joint venture company is as follows:
Year _____ Quantity _____
Year _____ Quantity _____
Year _____ Quantity _____

Year _____ Quantity _____
Year _____ Quantity _____

Article 9: The joint venture company may sell its products in the domestic market as well as the international market, proportion of which is as follows:

_____ (year): _____ % for export;
_____ % for the domestic market.
_____ (year): _____ % for export;
_____ % for the domestic market.

(The means of marketing, method and obligations will be stipulated according to the actual conditions that the joint venture company encountered.)

Chapter III : The Total Amount of Investment and the Registered Capital

Article 10: The total amount of investment of the joint venture company is Rmb ____ yuan. Its registered capital is Rmb ____ yuan.

Article 11: The investment contributed by each party is as follows:
Party A: Investment subscribed is Rmb _____ yuan, accounts for ____ % of the registered capital, among which,
Cash _____,
Machinery and equipment _____,
Premises _____,
Land use _____,
Industrial property rights _____,
Others _____,
Party B: Investment subscribed is Rmb _____ yuan, accounts for ____ % of the registered capital, among which,
Cash _____,
Machinery and equipment _____,
Industrial property rights _____,
Others _____,

Article 12: The parties to the joint venture shall pay in all the investment subscribed according to the time limited stipulated in the contract.

Article 13: After the investment is paid by the parties to the joint venture, a recognised registered accountant practising in China will be invited by the joint venture company shall audit the statement of account it and issue a certificate of audit upon satisfaction. According to this certificate, the joint venture shall issue an investment certificate which includes the following items: name of the joint venture; date of the establishment of the joint venture; names of the parties and the investment contributed; date of the contribution of the investment, and the date of issuance of the investment certificate.

(Author's note: This may now be governed by the Accounting

307

Regulation of the People's Republic of China for Joint Ventures Using Chinese and Foreign Investment.)

Article 14: During the term of the joint venture, the joint venture company shall not reduce its registered capital.

Article 15: Should one party assign all or part of its investment subscribed, consent shall be obtained from the other party of the joint venture. When one party assigns its investment, the other party has preemptive right.

Article 16: Any increase, assignment of the registered capital of the joint venture company shall be approved by the Board of Directors and submitted to the original examination and approval authority for approval. The registration procedures for changes shall be dealt with at the original registration and administration office.

Chapter IV : The Board of Directors

Article 17: The joint venture shall establish the Board of Directors which is the highest authority fo the joint venture company.

Article 18: The Board of Directors shall decide all major issues concerning the joint venture company. Its functions and powers are as follows:

   (1)   deciding and approving the important reports submitted by the general manager (for instance: production plan, annual business report, funds, loans and related matters);

   (2)   approving annual financial reports, budget of receipts and expenditures, distribution plan of annual profits;

   (3)   adopting major rules and regulations of the company;

   (4)   deciding to set up branches;

   (5)   amending the Articles of Association of the company;

   (6)   discussing and deciding the termination of production, termination of the company or merging with another economic organization;

   (7)   deciding the engagement of high-rank officials such as the general manager, chief engineer, treasurer, auditor etc;

   (8)   being in charge of expiration of the company and the liquidation matters upon the expiration of the joint venture company;

   (9)   Other major issues which shall be decided by the Board of Directors.

Article 19: The Board of Directors shall consist _____ of directors, of which _____ shall be appointed by Party A and _____ by party B. The term of office for the Directors is four years and may be renewed.

Article 20: Chairman of the Board shall be appointed by Party A and Vice Chairman of the Board by Party B.

Article 21 : When appointing and replacing Directors, a written notice shall be submitted to the Board.

Article 22 : The Board of Directors shall convene _____ meeting(s) every year. An interim meeting of the Board of Directors may be held based on a proposal made by more than one third of the total number of Directors.

Article 23 : The Board Meeting will be held in principle at the location of the company.

Article 24 : The Board Meeting shall be called and presided by the Chairman. Should the Chairman be absent, the Vice Chairman shall call and preside the Board Meeting.

Article 25 : The Chairman shall give each Director a written notice 30 days before the date of the Board Meeting. The notice shall cover the agenda, time and place of the meeting.

Article 26 : Should the Directors be unable to attend the Board Meeting, he may present a proxy in written form to the Board. In case the Director neither attends nor entrusts others to attend the meeting, he will be regarded as abstention.

Article 27 : The Board Meeting requires a quorum of over two thirds of the total number of Directors. When the quorum is less than two thirds, the decisions adopted by the board meeting are invalid.

Article 28 : detailed written records shall be made for each Board Meeting and signed by all the attended directors or by the attended proxy. The record shall be made in Chinese and _____, and shall be filed with the company.

Article 29 : The following issues shall be unanimously agreed upon by the Board of Directors:
(This Article should be stipulated in accordance with each company's actual situations.)

Article 30 : The following issues shall be passed by over two thirds of the total number of Directors or by over half of the total number.
(This Article should be stipulated in accordance with each company's actual situations.)

Chapter V : Business Management Organization

Article 31 : The joint venture company shall establish a management organization. It consists of production, technology, marketing, finance and administration offices etc.
(This Article should be stipulated in accordance with each company's concrete situations.)

Article 32 : The joint venture company shall have one general manager and _____ deputy general manager(s) who are engaged by the Board of Directors. The first general manager shall be recommended by party _____, deputy general manager(s) by party.

Article 33 : The general manager is directly responsible to the Board of

Directors. He shall carry out the decisions of the Board of Directors, organize and conduct the daily production, technology and operation and management of the joint venture company. The deputy general managers shall assist the general manager in his work and act as the agent of the general manager during his absence and exercise the functions of the general manager.

Article 34: Decision on the major issues concerning the daily work of the joint venture company shall be signed jointly by the general manager and deputy general managers, then the decisions shall come into effect. Issues which need cosignatures shall be specifically stipulated by the Board of Directors.

Article 35: The term of office for the general manager and deputy general managers shall be _____ years, and may be renewed at the invitation of the Board of Directors.

Article 36: At the invitation of the Board of Directors, the Chairman, Vice Chairman or Directors of the Board may concurrently be the general manager, deputy general managers or other senior staff of the joint venture company.

Article 37: The general manager or deputy general managers shall not hold posts concurrently as general manager or deputy general managers of other economic organizations in commercial competition with their own joint venture company.

Article 38: The joint venture company shall have one chief engineer, one treasurer and one auditor directly employed by the Board of Directors.

Article 39: (1) The general engineer, treasurer and auditor shall report to the leadership of the general manager.

(2) The treasurer shall take in charge of in financial and accounting affairs, organize the joint venture company to carry out overall business accounting and implement the economic responsibility system.

(3) The auditor shall take in charge of the auditing work of the joint venture company, examine and check the financial receipts and expenditure and the accounts, and submit written reports to the general and the Board of Directors.

Article 40: The general manager, deputy general managers, chief engineer, treasurer, auditor and other senior staff who submit for resignation shall serve their resignation in writing to the Board of Directors in advance.

(Author's note: It is advisable to specify the number of days for such notice in the contract of employment.)

In case any one of the above-mentioned persons conduct graft or serious dereliction of duty, they may be dismissed at any time upon the decision of the Board. Those who violate the criminal law shall be under criminal sanction.

Chapter VI : Finance and Accounting

Article 41 : The finance and accounting of the joint venture company shall be handled in accordance with the "Stipulations of the Finance and Accounting System of the Joint Ventures Using Chinese and Foreign Investment" formulated by the Ministry of Finance of the People's Republic of China.

Article 42 : The fiscal year of the joint venture company shall coincide with calendar year, i.e. from January 1 to December 31 on the Gregorian calendar.

(Author's note: This is stipulated by the Joint Venture Law of PRC Using Chinese and Foreign Investment.)

Article 43 : All vouches, account books, statistic statements and reports of the joint venture company shall be written in Chinese.

Article 44 : The joint venture company adopts Rmb yuan as its accounts keeping unit. The conversion of Rmb yuan into other currency shall be in accordance with the exchange rate of the converting day published by the State Administration of Exchange Control of the People's Republic of China.

Article 45 : The joint venture company shall open accounts in Rmb Yuan and foreign currency with the Bank of China or other banks agreed by the Bank of China.

Article 46 : The accounting of the joint venture company shall adopt the internationally used accrual basis and debit and credit accounting system in their work.

Article 47 : Following items shall be covered in the financial accounts books :
(1) The amount of overall cash receipts and expense of the joint venture company ;
(2) All material purchasing and selling of the joint venture company ;
(3) The registered capital and debts situation of the joint venture company.
(4) The time of payment, increase and assignment of the registered capital of the joint venture company.

Article 48 : The joint venture company shall work out the statement of assests and liabilities and losses and gains accounts of the past year in the first three months of each fiscal year, and submit to the Board Meeting for approval after examined and signed by the auditor.

Article 49 : Parties to the joint venture have the right to invite an auditor to undertake annual financial check and examination at his own expense. The joint venture company shall assist in the convenience of such checking and examination work.

Article 50 : The depreciation period for the fixed assets of the joint venture company shall be decided by the Board of Directors in accordance with the "Rules for the Implementation of the Income Tax Law of the People's Republic of China Concerning Joint Ventures with Chinese and Foreign Investment".

Article 51: All matters concerning foreign exchange shall be handled in accordance with the "Provisional Regulations for Exchange Control of the People's Republic of China", and other pertaining regulations as well as the stipulations of the joint venture contract.

Chapter VII ; Profits Sharing

Article 52: The joint venture company shall draw reserve funds, expansion funds and bonus welfare funds for staff and workers after payment of taxes. The proportion of allocation is decided by the Board of Directors.

Article 53: After paying the taxes in accordance with law and drawing the various funds, the remaining profits will be distributed according to the proporation of each party's investment in the registered capital.

Article 54: The joint venture company shall distribute its profits. The profits distribution plan and the amount of profit distributed to each party shall be published within the first three months after the end of each fiscal year.

Article 55: The joint venture company shall not distribute profits unless the losses of previous fiscal year have been made up. Remaining profit from previous year can be distributed together with that of the current year.

Chapter VIII : Staff and Workers

Article 56: The employment, recruitment, dismissal and resignation of the staff and workers of the joint venture company and their salary, welfare benefits, labor insurance, labour protection, labor discipline and other matters shall be handled according to the "Regulations of the People's Republic of China on Labor Management in Joint Ventures Using Chinese and Foreign Investment" and its implementation rules.

Article 57: Staff and workers to be recruited by the joint venture company will be recommended by the local labor department or the joint venture will do so through public selection examination and employ those who are qualified with the consent of the labor department.

Article 58: The joint venture company has the right to take disciplinary actions, record a demerit and reduce salary against those staff and workers who violate the rules and regulations of the joint venture company and labor disciplines. Those with serious cases may be dismissed. Discharging of workers shall be filed with the labor and personnel department in the locality.

Article 59: The salary treatment of the staff and workers shall be set by the Board of Directors according to the specific situation of the joint venture, with reference to pertaining stipulation of China, and shall be specified in detail in the labor contract.

The salary of the staff and workers shall be increased correspondingly with the development of production and the raising of the ability and technology of the staff and workers.

Article 60: Matters concerning the welfare funds, bonus, labor protection and labor insurance etc. shall be stipulated respectively in various rules by the joint venture company, to ensure that the staff and workers go in for production and work under normal conditions.

Chapter IX : The Trade Union Organization

Article 61: The staff and workers of the joint venture company have the right to establish trade union organization and carry out activities in accordance with the stipulations of the "Trade Union Law of the People's Republic of China."

Article 62: The trade union in the joint venture company is representative of the interests of the staff and workers. The tasks of the trade union are: to protect the democratic rights and material interests of the staff and workers pursuant to the law; to assist the joint venture company to arrange and make rational use of welfare funds and bonuses; to organize political, professional, scientific and technical studies, carry out literary, art and sports activities; and to educate staff and workers to observe labor discipline and strive to fulfil the economic tasks of the joint venture company.

Article 63: The trade union of the joint venture company will sign labor contracts with the join venture company on behalf of the staff and workers, and supervise the implementation of the contracts.

Article 64: Persons in charge of the trade union of the joint venture company has the right to attend as nonvoting members and to report the opinions and demands of staff and workers to meetings of the Board of Directors held to discuss issues such as development plans, production and operational activities of the joint venture.

Article 65: The trade union shall take part in mediation of disputes arising between the staff and workers and the joint venture company.

Article 66: The joint venture company shall allot an amount of money totalling 2% of all the salaries of the staff and workers of the joint venture company as trade union's funds, which shall be used be the trade union in accordance the "Managerial Rules for the Trade Union Funds" formulated by the All China Federation of Trade Unions.

Chapter X :   Duration, Termination and Liquidation

Article 67:   The duration of the joint venture company shall be _____ years, beginning from the day when business license is issued.

Article 68:   An application for the extention of duration shall, proposed by both parties and approved at the Board Meeting, be submitted to the original examination and approval authority six months prior to the expiry date of the joint venture. Only upon the approval may the duration be extended, and the joint venture company shall go through registration formalities for the alteration at the original registration office.

Article 69:   The joint venture may be terminated before its expiration in case the parties to the joint venture agre unanimously that the termination of the joint venture is for the best interests of the parties.
To terminate the joint venture before the term expires shall be decided by the Board of Directors through a plenary meeting, and it shall be submitted to the original examination and approval authority for approval.

Article 70:   Either party shall have the right to terminate the joint venture in case one of the following situations occurs:
(It shall be stipulated according to each joint venture company's concrete situation.)

Article 71:   Upon the expiration or termination of the joint venture before its term ends, the Board of Directors shall work out procedures and principles for the liquidation, nominate candidates for the liquidation committee, and set up the liquidation committee for liquidating the joint venture company's assets.

Article 72:   The tasks of the liquidation committee are: to conduct through check of the property of the joint venture company, its claim and indebtedness; to work out the statement of assets and liabilities and list of property; to formulate a liquidation plan. All these shall be carries out upon the approval of the Board of Directors.

Article 73:   During the process of liquidation, the liquidation committee shall represent the company to sue and be sued.

Article 74:   The liquidation expenses and remuneration to the members of the liquidation committee shall be paid in priority from the existing assets of the joint venture company.

Article 75:   The remaining property after the clearance of debts of the joint venture company shall be distributed among the parties to the joint venture according to the proportion of each party's investment in the registered capital.

Article 76:   On completion of the liquidation, the joint venture company shall submit a liquidation report to the original examination and approval authority, go through the formalities for nullifying its registration in the original registration office and hand in its business license, at the same time, make an announcement to the public.

Article 77: After winding up of the joint venture company, its account books shall be left in the care of the Chinese participant.

Chapter XI : Rules and Regulations

Article 78: Following are the rules and regulations formulated by the Board of Directors of the joint venture company:

(1) Management regulations, including the powers and functions of the managerial branches and its working rules and procedures;

(2) Rules for the staff and workers;

(3) System of labor and salary;

(4) System of work attendance record, promotion and awards and penalty for the staff and workers;

(5) Detailed rules of staff and worker's welfare;

(6) Financial system;

(7) Liquidation procedures upon the dissolution of the joint venture company;

(8) Other necessary rules and regulations.

Chapter XII : Supplementary Articles

Article 79: The amendments to the Articles of Association shall be unanimously agreed and decided by the Board of Directors and submitted to the original examination and approval authority for approval.

Article 80: The Articles of Association is written in Chinese language and _____ language. Both languages shall be equally authentic. In the event of any discrepancy between the two above-mentioned versions, the Chinese version shall prevail.

Article 81: The Articles of Association shall come into effect upon the approval by the Ministry of Foreign Economic Relations and Trade of the People's Republic of China (or its entrusted examination and approval authority). The same applies in the event of amendments.

Article 82: The Articles of Association is signed in _____ of China by the authorized representatives of both parties on _____, 19____.

For Party A   For Party B

(Signed)   (Signed)

_____   _____